Peggy Iris Thomas and Matelot in their 'pup tent'.
Canada, 1951.

First Published:
USA & Canada 1953
UK 1954

This edition 2012

Copyright Rixon Groove 2012

Photographs originally printed by *The Motor Cycle*
magazine are reproduced with the permission
of the Mortons Archive, www.mortonsarchive.com

Paperback ISBN: 978-0-9561168-4-0
Hardback ISBN: 978-0-9561168-5-7

For additional copies, see:
www.gasolinegypsy.co.uk

For another BSA Bantam journey, see:
www.overlandtoegypt.co.uk

Rixon Groove
464 Stockport Road West
Bredbury
Greater Manchester
SK6 2EE
United Kingdom

About The Author

Born in 1925, Peggy Thomas was raised and educated in Ewell, Surrey. At the age of 17 she joined the WRNS and spent three and a half years during the Second World War working as a radio operator. At the end of the conflict, her wanderlust took her to Europe for two and a half years where she worked as an au pair, taught English in schools and with families, and studied languages in the French Alps, Switzerland and Madrid.

Peggy bought her first motorcycle, a 125cc BSA Bantam, in 1950 and, accompanied by a friend, soon took it on a six week tour of Scandinavia. At the end of the journey she wrote an article for *The Motor Cycle* magazine about her trip. In April 1951, accompanied by her Airedale pup, Matelot, Peggy and her BSA departed Liverpool for Halifax, Nova Scotia. The ensuing 18 month adventure is the basis of this book.

At the end of the ride, in early 1953, Peggy sailed from New York to Denmark, where she married her fiancé, Carl-Erik. However, the marriage was short lived and she returned to the UK in the late 1950s, settling first in the London suburb of Richmond before moving to Hampton Hill, Middlesex, in 1963.

A Ride in the Sun/Gasoline Gypsy was the only book Peggy wrote but friends remember that she retained her affection for motorcycles and certainly continued to ride. Her love of travel also prevailed and her further trips included visits to Europe and Africa. In 1955 she rode the prototype Douglas Dragonfly motorcycle from the Uk to Corsica and Sardinia, writing a two-piece feature for *The Motor Cycle* about her experiences. The article ended with Peggy dreaming of a motorcycle ride from Moscow to Vladivostok the following year, but no one remembers her actually undertaking this project.

However, it was her love of dogs that endured most. Peggy set up and ran a dog trimming and boarding business from her home and was accompanied by dogs wherever she went. Friends and neighbours remember her still riding around London on a motorcycle in the 1970s with an Airedale called Guinness in a box on the back.

In her later life, she bought a traditional cottage in Donegal, Ireland, and set about a lengthy restoration. It was while returning from a visit to the cottage in February 1982, driving her Ford station wagon full of dogs, that Peggy was killed in a traffic accident on the Isle of Anglesey.

In the words of Marjorie Marshall: "Peggy was such a brave, indomitable person, always brimming with enthusiasm, always the first out of the tent when we were camping! She had such a strong personality. When I heard she had died it was impossible to realise that she would never breeze into our house again, like a whirlwind!"

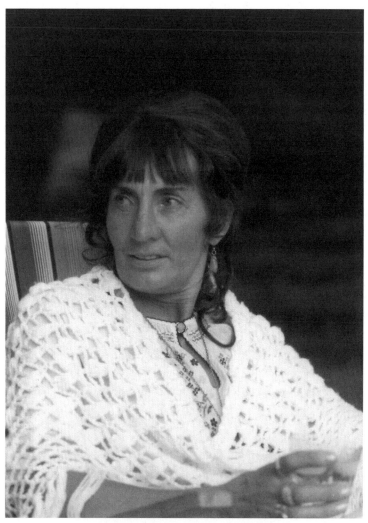

Peggy Iris Thomas, 1925 - 1982

A RIDE
IN THE SUN

by
PEGGY IRIS THOMAS

GASOLINE
GYPSY

Publisher's Note

The manuscript was first published in the United States and Canada as *Gasoline Gypsy* in 1953 by *Thomas Y Crowell*. Retitled *A Ride In The Sun*, it was released in the UK in 1954 by *Hodder & Stoughton* with just a few tweaks to Anglicise the language (which considering the author was English is probably how it was first written). It was finally translated into German and published under the heading, *Peggy braust durch Amerika* ('Peggy speeds through America') in 1955. To appeal to all English speaking readers without having to produce two separate but, to all intents and purposes, identical volumes, we have called this 2012 edition *A Ride in the Sun - Gasoline Gypsy*. The original UK manuscript has been used as the basis of the work.

It has been printed in paperback and as a limited edition, hardback volume of 1000 numbered copies, commissioned to celebrate 60 years since the completion of Peggy's journey.

None of the original editions contained any photographs from her travels. What happened to her own photographic collection is not known, although it would have been limited to the early part of the journey because she lost all her exposed film stock, along with her typewriter, into the waters of the Gulf of Mexico when departing Veracruz for New Orleans. However, during the course of her 18 month adventure, Peggy wrote a number of articles, accompanied by photographs, for *The Motor Cycle* magazine, which covered, in the main, the Canadian section of her trip. We have purchased the copyright for a selection of these images from the *Morton's Archive* as we believe they help bring to life the characters of Peggy, Oppy and Matelot.

Our sincere thanks must go to Peggy's sister, Pamela, for her permission to reprint this book. It is highly unlikely that it would ever have reached that point without the kind and enthusiastic assistance of Peggy's lifelong friend, Marjorie Marshall. Marjorie also provided the picture of Peggy (see page 4), which was taken shortly before her death.

Thanks also to Pete Snidal of Canada and Hilda Burgess of New Zealand for assistance in tracking down original copies of *Gasoline Gypsy* and Bryan Price of Sleaford, membership secretary of the *BSA Bantam Club* (www.bsabantamclub.org.uk) for the use of his original *A Ride in the Sun* dust cover. The help of artist Roy Barrett (www.art-of-motoring.co.uk), who brilliantly finished off the jacket image, is much appreciated. We would also like to acknowledge the contributions made by Derek Thom of Runcorn, Alan Graham of Horsham and Jane Gregory of Romiley, UK.

Gordon G. May

CONTENTS

A Ride in the Sun

14,000 miles Through Canada, The United States and Mexico on a 125 c.c. B.S.A.

PEGGY IRIS THOMAS

CHAPTER I *Two's Company*

IT was a beautiful June morning as I wended my way through the busy Vancouver traffic. After all the delays and last-minute fever of packing for my trip it was a wonderful feeling to be off once more, completely free to wander where and how I pleased. I had no routine or schedule to stick to, no planned route to follow and no hotel reservations to worry about. Before me stretched unending highways to adventure and new friends, and a hundred new camp sites for my little pup tent. The warm sun poured down on the hurrying city crowd. Watching this scurrying mass I thought to myself, "Well, there, but for my unceasing curiosity and love of the unknown, go I, part of the great army of citizens intent upon going about their work and daily routine." So as we sped down Fraser Street I felt as free as air.

But my contentment with life was shortlived. For suddenly clouds of smoke appeared from nowhere and flames leapt from beneath me! I braked fiercely and brought my motor-cycle to a sudden stop, threw it against the kerb and jumped clear. Matelot, anticipating the emergency, had already leapt gracefully to the pavement and was regarding the scene of havoc with nonchalant doggy stares. Was our trip over even before we had started?

The rucksack containing my waterproof clothing had slipped against the hot metal exhaust pipe and ignited. Flames curled round the side of the petrol tank, and the whole machine was fast disappearing behind a smoke screen. At any moment poor Oppy might explode, and something had to be done quickly. Two observant pedestrians had already raised the alarm—Fire! Almost at once a bucket of water appeared on the scene, into which we dropped the flaming rucksack. The motor-cycle had been saved, but the rucksack sat in the water hissing and smoking furiously. With some help, though, I did manage to salvage a few things—my green plastic mac, which now had a hole in rather a vital spot, also my rain goggles and Matelot's brush and comb. But my new rubbers and the

9

waterproof jacket for Matelot were a black, ruined heap. A little crowd was beginning to gather, so I threw the burnt garments into the gutter and hurriedly packed Matelot and the remaining things into the back-seat box.

The Canadian Pacific Railway docks were a hub of activity, and I am afraid we caused much head scratching and a few headaches among the officials. A girl riding a motor-cycle loaded like a pack mule with suit-cases and camping equipment causes enough stir. However, if she is accompanied by a sixty-pound airedale dog as well, things tend to get out of hand.

But actually since I first bought and trained Matelot to ride on Oppy, the motor-cycle, I have never let him be a problem. Wherever I go, he follows, except when I tell him to stay on guard beside the parked machine. So by the time we set out from Vancouver, Matelot was already an old hand at jumping on to lifts, escalators and buses, while the London Underground and the Atlantic Ocean had become as familiar to him as cattle ranges are to a Texan.

And now I was able to assure the Canadian Pacific Steamship Company that the easiest way to get my dog aboard was to let him sit on his own motor-cycle, and finally convinced the officials that he did not need a crate, a muzzle or a chain. Still sceptical, they checked my ticket, stuck a forty cent label on Matelot's collar, and then away we went down the ramp to the car deck. I found myself sandwiched between a green Buick from Hawaii and a large Cadillac from California. Smothered laughter greeted me on both sides as I tried to concentrate on the British Columbia licence plate in front of me. I knew we were an extraordinarily funny sight. The moving line of traffic cut short the avidly curious questioning of the young couple from Honolulu.

The face of the young officer collecting our tickets was a study of amazed amusement as Oppy bounced and jumped her way down the slipway and came to rest against the bulkhead. One of the crew chained her in a corner while I arranged Matelot on his blanket and gave him a drink of water. As I went up on deck I looked back at him lying there a little forlorn, but patient and trusting as always.

The sunshine was warm on my back as I leaned over the rail and watched the hurried, last-minute departures. On one side of me lay the busy docks, crowded with shipping from all over the world, and behind me rose the tall stone skyscrapers of this West Canadian port. Across the water to my left rose the green wooded slopes of the Coastal Range, and beyond the snowy peaks of the Lions. The ships' sirens blew their last blasts of warning, the s.s. *Princess Elizabeth* shuddered, and we slowly steamed away across the blue waters of Burrard Inlet. Under the shadow of the Lions Gate Bridge we passed, while above us towered the pine-laden slopes of Grouse Mountain. Here the trees come down to mingle with the blue waters and rocky shores.

The two-hour crossing over to Vancouver Island began a trip that I hoped would eventually end that autumn in New York City, and by way of such exciting places as California, Texas, Mexico and Florida. As I stood on the deck and watched the rugged coastline slip by, all kinds of thoughts flitted through my mind.

I remembered that the very start of my vagabonding had begun on another ship, but this one had tossed and bounced its way from Liverpool to Nova Scotia in the spring of 1951. It brought Oppy, Matelot and myself to Halifax to begin our long drive west from the Atlantic coast to the Pacific Ocean. Now, just over a year later, we were on the go once more.

Oppy, the motor-cycle, so christened because of her British registration plate, OPE 811, is like some Sahara camel train or a reindeer sledge in Lapland. She carried our bed, shelter and food—in fact, our every need. Strapped to her sides, resting on metal frames, were two outsize yellow canvas bags. These held a pocket stove, cooking pots, enough food for several days, my typewriter, sleeping bag, air mattress and warm clothes. A pup tent was stowed beneath the saddle, while the metal box welded to the carriage for Matelot has two brackets bolted to the back into which I slip spare oil and petrol cans.

Two more brackets on the sides of Matelot's box held small suitcases of more crushable clothes, such as seersucker sundresses for California and Mexico, shorts for Florida, and nylons and a skirt for New York. Beneath Matelot in the box were stored the overflows, such as tent poles, water bottles and tins of dog food. To complete this one-girl camel train, a large map case was tied to the petrol tank and a lunch box of tools was strapped to the frame of the machine.

A Ride in the Sun

Poor Oppy only weighs a hundred and twenty-five pounds, and as I had added a further weight of at least three hundred and fifty pounds, it was definitely a case of cruelty to dumb motor-cycles. Although she was born in the summer of 1950 with just one cylinder and only three horse-power, I think there must be something about the North American air that suits her constitution. Her constant good behaviour on my trans-Canada trip was certainly not due to my mechanical skill, which at that time was non-existent.

I shall never forget the day I decided to fulfil this long-repressed urge to see the North American continent on my newly acquired motor-cycle. There were cries of horror from all my English friends. "You can't possibly travel the all-Canadian route to the Pacific! The roads over the prairies are just loose dirt and the gradients in the Rockies far too steep." And "You've just no idea of the vast distances between towns in the States, and the bears, wolves and wild-cats you may meet camping," or, "A girl alone on a lightweight motor-cycle who has no mechanical knowledge and can't even change a tyre? Impossible!"

But I blithely ignored all these objections and spent more and more time poring over maps and planning a journey that I reckoned would take me about six thousand miles across Canada one summer and about the same distance through the United States and Mexico the following year. This proved to be a slight underestimation of about eight thousand miles; but for someone brought up in England, a country which has no point farther than about seventy miles from the sea, distances as vast as those of Texas and Saskatchewan are hard to understand.

One thing, however, was certain—from the time I landed my funds would be almost non-existent. So I planned to work at least two-thirds of the year in Canada.

Actually, six months before this, rather by mistake and more as a means of transport to Norway than anything else, I had bought this pale green, slim-framed B.S.A. Bantam. I had chosen her for colour, because her paint job happened to go nicely with my new corduroy jacket. She cost me about six months' savings, and I was left with only about twenty pounds for the trip my Australian girl friend and I had planned through Scand-inavia that summer. Well, that trip opened up quite a new interest in my

12

life. Earlier I had trained, hitch-hiked, walked and cycled my way through a great deal of Europe, but for sheer fun and care-free delight I found there was no more practical and economical means of transport than this little motor-cycle.

Of course a few readjustments had to be made. No one likes to sit huddled on a moving vehicle in the pouring rain, but when caught without my oilskins I would firmly tell myself that it was so good for the complexion. Unluckily I usually got wet in the wrong parts of my anatomy. But whether I was whirling along in shorts during a sudden Danish heat wave, or muffled to the eyes under a Yorkshire snow storm, it was always fun, and there were always new experiences and friends to be found round every corner.

So many people have dreams like mine. Dreams of satisfying that inner voice that says "Go on, quit that job, take the plunge and see if it really is greener on the other side of the hill. Meet those new friends and see those strange-sounding places—Medicine Hat, Moose Jaw, Mississippi." But if you feel this call of travel strongly enough, you just have to take the plunge. And if you want to travel in the true sense of the word, then it is worth leaving if necessary your job, your loved ones, and above all the security of your home land. I am, of course, only speaking of someone like myself who is single and has no responsibilities or ties that cannot be easily broken.

Now I wanted to expand the many friendships that I had made in Britain, during the war years, with the visiting Americans and Canadians; and the idea of driving every inch of the way through their countries, living completely outdoors, and taking jobs when my money ran out, seemed to me to be the only real way of saying "I am going to see the United States and Canada." I meant really *see* them.

Well, I possessed the first two essentials, a gypsy spirit and my means of transport which ran an economical hundred miles to the (U.S.) gallon. Moreover Oppy was small enough to manœuvre through a forest in search of the ideal camp site or in and out of congested city traffic, yet large enough to carry all my camping gear and clothes.

Still I lacked a companion for the long, lonely rides across prairie and desert and my solitary camps at night. With the warnings of my friends about grizzly bears and mountain lions still ringing in my ears, I began

A Ride in the Sun

to think how useful it would be to have a large dog along. I had done some camping in Europe, but never by myself, and now the idea of pitching my tent quite alone frankly terrified me.

After much searching I found my answer in a sturdy little six-weeks-old airedale pup. With liquid brown eyes he implored me to take him adventuring too. I named him Matelot, which was the French nickname given to British sailors when I was in the W.R.N.S.

Well, Matelot certainly lived up to his name as he sat up there behind me in his metal box, swaying with the machine as we turned corners, his ears and tail flying in the wind. Sometimes he would nestle up to me, his warm little head on my shoulder, then another time he would leap to all fours to challenge a mere pedestrian dog as we whirled by. Funniest were the times when he caught sight of another dog in a passing car; a furious battle of barking insults would ensue, with poor Oppy's rear doing a snake dance while I wondered whether Matelot was going to take a dive into the moving traffic or if the car dog would leap on to my machine.

However Matelot is a smart dog and only jumps down when I pull into the kerb or to a petrol station. Once, though, his excitement got the better of his judgment, and a police horse prancing under his very nose completely overbalanced him. Luckily his four paws landed on the pavement!

Dear, shaggy-coated Matelot, he solved so many problems. There was no danger of petty thieves with him lying patiently beside Oppy on the pavement, and my tent couldn't seem too dark and lonely with his warm, breathing form curled against my sleeping bag. Because of him reckless drivers slowed down and passed us with care, impatient policemen grew kind and smiling, and girl-chasing wolves became ardent dog lovers.

I thought of Matelot now, lying down there on the lower deck, probably wagging his tail at an admiring throng of sailors, and I wondered if his thoughts were turning like mine to that other voyage and that other ship that had brought us over the Atlantic Ocean.

CHAPTER II *Land of the Maple Leaf*

DURING the winter of 1950 I worked so hard in London saving up for my boat ticket, that, before I realized it, April had arrived and we were packed and on our way north to Liverpool.

For eight days and nights we tossed across the Atlantic, and poor Matelot could hardly wait to get his four paws on firm land once more. But landing in Halifax meant for me the end of the warmth and security of the s.s. *Nova Scotia*. Now, I realized, thousands of unknown miles, country and people lay ahead of me; and I must undertake all this on an initial stake of about sixty dollars.

Those first few days driving through Nova Scotia were just how I had imagined Canada would be. Deep pine forests intermingled with rolling green farmland set against the sweeping, windswept coastline. The days were crisp and sunny as we sped along under clear blue skies; on through neat villages of white-framed houses and steepled churches, sloping lawns, and the maple trees in their first spring bud. When I want to recapture those first days driving through the Canadian spring, I shut my eyes and remember first the smell of warm pine trees in the sun, and then the sudden sharp feel of snow in the air.

At night Matelot and I slept in little overnight cabins, because it was far too cold to camp out. In the morning we would start out early to capture the best of the day, when the first rays of the sun rose above the forests and the frost sparkled across the valleys. About ten o'clock we used to stop by the road to make a fire and cook bacon and eggs.

The sight of a girl cooking her breakfast along a highway naturally caused a lot of friendly waving and curious glances. Sometimes I would have to put on extra coffee water and get out my visitor's mug for some passing motorist who had stopped to be friendly.

Everything seemed so care-free and easy until we reached New Brunswick, with a change of weather and roads. The strong winds buffeted Oppy from one side of the highway to the other, and for two days we were blanketed in snow flurries. I was glad to reach the wide, calm St. Lawrence river, which we followed all the way to Quebec city. Then another day's driving brought us to Montreal, where I had planned to stay for the next six weeks and earn some money.

Matelot was kennelled out near Dorval airport. And Pamela Mack, an Englishwoman from Kent, said she would mother him until I was ready to move on westward. I had a room reserved for two nights at the Y.W.C.A., and my two suitcases of city clothes had arrived there safely from Halifax. Also I was lucky enough to run across, the first evening I was there, a tall dark Welsh girl. Marion Edger said if I was looking for a room for a few weeks she thought her mother would be glad to help me out.

So I found myself installed in a large comfortable room in the Edgers' apartment in the centre of the city. Mrs. Edger was a plump and kindly soul who welcomed me and gave me the run of her big kitchen to cook whatever and whenever I liked. Her husband was an enormous man with a mop of grey hair and a deep voice. He told me fascinating tales about his early days in the Welsh coal mines and about how he ran away to Canada and joined the Royal Canadian Mounted Police.

Now that I had a delightful place to stay, the next thing to think about was a job to earn enough money to take me the rest of the way across Canada that summer. In the newspaper I found an advertisement saying that the Canadian Pacific telegraph office was looking for typists on the night shift. Suddenly it occurred to me that if I could get a job at night I could work part-time during the day as well, and thus boost my savings considerably. I went round to the telegraph office, and after a short typing test I was told that I could start that evening at midnight.

Next I scanned the help-wanted columns for a part-time job, but there seemed to be nothing I could do. Then I noticed a firm advertising for a temporary stenographer, so I went round to find out if perhaps I could work there short hours. A high-powered business executive told me his secretary was ill and he needed somebody immediately who could work from eight-thirty in the morning until five in the afternoon. Before I realized it, I had agreed to start the following morning.

Back at the flat feeling rather bewildered, I sat in the warm kitchen and told Mrs. Edger that I had just landed two jobs, which meant that I was going to work sixteen and a half hours a day! She flung up her hands in horror and packed me right off to bed to get some sleep before my first night with the Canadian Pacific.

That evening I walked through the dark, deserted streets near the river until I came to a tall, lighted building. Above me I could hear the sound of the teleprinter machines working and through the wide swing doors a crowd of young girls and men were jostling one another on their way to work. My boss was a tall, handsome French Canadian who showed me where to sit, introduced me to the girl who would work with me the first night, and strolled off, telling me to ask about anything I didn't understand. The noise in the room from all the machines seemed deafening, and the atmosphere was hot and stuffy. I felt sure that there were a hundred things I didn't understand, but I didn't dare ask a single question.

Mary, a highly strung blonde with an efficient manner, rapidly showed me the proper way to type out the telegrams and then promptly left me to my own devices. The night passed very quickly, because I was too worried about my new work to feel sleepy. At eight o'clock in the morning I punched myself out on the time clock, and went to the ladies' room to brush my teeth and wash the sticky night atmosphere off my face. Then I dashed out into the fresh morning air to look for a café and a strong cup of coffee.

After breakfast I made tracks for my daytime job, and once again a new colleague showed me where to hang my coat and which desk was mine. Then, promptly at nine o'clock, boss No. 2 rang my telephone and told me to come in for dictation. I sat in front of his huge desk nearly falling asleep over my pad, and writing the weirdest of shorthand symbols which I was afraid I never could decipher.

By lunch-time I had got my second wind and didn't feel tired any more. But my poor boss wasn't very pleased with the work of his new secretary, because I had spent the whole morning rushing back to his office asking him what he had said in previous letters.

The office was quite near the Edgers' apartment, so I flew home during the lunch hour. If I ate very quickly there was just time enough to climb up on the flat roof and sun bathe for about half an hour in the early May sunshine. But I had to take an alarm clock with me or I should have slept all afternoon. On the way home from my daytime job I shopped for food, so that after I had supper it was usually about seven o'clock. When the alarm sounded four hours later I could hardly crawl out of bed. Then I took a quick bath, ironed and washed my clothes for the following day, and cut some sandwiches to eat during the night shift.

Everybody at the telegraph office suspected that I was leading too gay a life during the day, because I was constantly nodding to sleep over my machine. Once I woke up with a start to find a large note stuck in my typewriter and everybody in the office furiously ringing the bells on their machines. The note said, "Miss Peggy Thomas c/o C.P. Telegraphs —Please wake up.—The Boss." Monsieur Duval winked at me across the room, and I blushed and started pounding the typewriter keys like mad.

During our three fifteen-minute breaks through the night, I staggered downstairs to our rest room and went to sleep on a bed provided for first-aid cases. Usually one of the girls woke me up after ten minutes, but once poor Monsieur Duval missed me for over an hour, and finally sent out a search party. I returned to the office with a very red face, which became even redder after my boss had lectured me gently about getting more sleep when working on the night shift.

Luckily both these jobs were on a five-day-a-week basis, so early on Saturday morning I would jump on Oppy and fly out to Dorval to see Matelot. He would be playing around quite happily with the other dogs in the open run, but as soon as he heard Oppy coming he started acting like a mad dog, leaping and tearing at the wire fence and barking at the top of his voice. Until I arrived Matelot had been quite a model boarder. But now he and I would go to the café opposite, where I spoiled him with a large cup of ice cream; then I would make for the nearest field and park Oppy. And while Matelot romped in his new-found freedom, I would fall asleep in the sun and forget all about typewriters, telegram forms and shorthand pads.

After six weeks of this very full and busy life my savings account was beginning to grow, and when it reached one hundred and sixty dollars I gave in my notice on both jobs and started packing Oppy for the long trek west. Then, early one morning at the end of June, with Marion

Edger and her parents waving me good-bye on the balcony above, I set out once more for the open highway. And after stopping to pick Matelot up from the kennels, I pointed Oppy's nose due west.

CHAPTER III *West to Vancouver*

THAT first night driving along the highway to Ottawa I put off camping for as long as I dared, refusing to face the fact that I was too frightened to stop. By eleven o'clock it was almost too dark to find a suitable camp site. At last I saw a small clearing in the forest, so I slowed down and bumped Oppy across the springy turf.

A little nervously I spread my ground sheet and blew up the air mattress. I pulled out the tent and then I found that the poles were missing! They must have been left behind in Montreal! So I was obliged to climb into my sleeping bag and pray against rain. I lay there quite a long time looking up into the starry night sky; now that I was part of the dark forest and night stillness myself, I somehow didn't feel afraid. Matelot, warm and alive, slept at my side.

We journeyed on through Ontario and then into the prairie provinces, where camping became even more lonely. Because of this I often stopped at farms and asked permission to camp in their yards. Invariably I was welcomed with friendliness and shown the best place to pitch my tent, and even invited into the house for supper.

Once I arrived at a big farm quite late at night, in the middle of the haying season, and a plump, smiling farmer's wife showed me a grassy lawn where I could camp. Next morning a little girl with fair plaits hanging to her waist came out to ask me in to breakfast. Packed round the long wooden table in the big kitchen were a dozen sunburnt men in blue jeans eating a hearty farm breakfast. I didn't have to worry about being one more mouth to feed, because the table was literally groaning with food.

There were great bowls of cooked oatmeal and fresh cream, two eggs

A Ride in the Sun

and a thick slice of bacon apiece, and the coffee-pot was never empty. As each man left for work he picked up a lunch bag left on a side table; and when I thanked my hostess and prepared to leave, she pressed sandwiches on me too.

But the kindness of these prairie folk could sometimes be embarrassing. The Winnipeg press had written up our trip, stating that my funds were very limited, and told how I cooked my meals outdoors. This was of course true, but in print the account somehow took on a very exaggerated air. One morning, soon after the story appeared, I was driving down the hot, dusty highway, when I was stopped by a car full of friendly, curious people wanting to know if I was the girl driving to the Pacific coast. Then everybody jumped out of the car to get a closer look at Oppy and to fondle Matelot. As they were preparing to leave, there was a lot of whispering and jingling of coins, and to my astonishment one of the party tried to drop a pile of quarters, fifty cent pieces and dimes into my hand. I protested, but the man dumped the whole fistful of silver into Matelot's box, laughed and told me to buy some extra dog food for the dog. For days after that I found odd quarters and dimes in between the folds of Matelot's blanket.

Another time a car passed me sending a shower of fine dust all over us. I was so blinded that I didn't see that he had stopped just ahead, and I nearly ran into the back of his car. A car load of kids goggled out at us, while Father gave me a tin of ice-cold orange juice from his portable refrigerator. He asked me to follow him down the road, and at the next petrol station insisted on filling my petrol tank and oil bottle; and the whole family sent me on my way with shouts of good luck.

And so on across the burning, dusty prairies we journeyed until we reached the green foothills of Alberta and the towering distant peaks of the Rocky Mountains. It was a very thrilling moment when I realized that on the other side of that great snowy range lay the Pacific Ocean and my goal—Vancouver.

Very gradually we climbed higher and higher among those craggy peaks and eternal snow summits, where rushing green rivers wind through the pine forests and the air is strong and invigorating. I had planned to spend about a week in the Rockies, but it was nearly three weeks before I could tear myself away.

Gasoline Gypsy

In the park areas of the Rockies I was forced to use the official camping grounds. Here I met many more people, though amenities like taps, tables, hot showers and laundries struck me as being just a little too civilized for the great outdoors. Still, it was a lovely feeling waking in the early morning to watch the sun rise across the silent lake, its golden rays melting the mist across the valley. There would be a glorious smell of frying bacon and the sound of wood chopping, but the icy morning air made me snuggle back into my warm sleeping bag and snooze just five minutes more. However, one morning, camping at Moraine Lake, over six thousand feet high, I awoke to icicles on my tent roof, and then I knew that my camping days were drawing to a close.

By the time I reached the Okanagan Valley, the beautiful fruit-growing region of British Columbia, I was almost penniless. Actually I had twenty-five cents; and I also had a letter of introduction to some English people who owned a fruit ranch in Kelowna, a small city nestling beside the blue Okanagan Lake.

Driving up into the green hills above the town, we passed mile upon mile of apple-tree orchards with fruit about ready to be picked. Mrs. Butler, a tall charming woman, welcomed me into her house and told me that she and her husband had been expecting me to turn up asking for a job. We talked about her cousins in England who had bred Matelot and who had given me the letter of introduction. And then she told me I was just in time to join the gang of apple pickers. Meanwhile, Matelot had been making himself completely at home. He and Ajax, the Butlers' golden retriever, were tearing round the garden after each other like a couple of ninnies.

A few minutes later I found myself cosily installed in a small three-roomed cottage next to the ranch house, with the luxury of my own bathroom and a big old-fashioned range in the little kitchen. That evening I was introduced to the boss, a big, bluff man from Kent, England, who said he was starting to pick his first crop of McIntosh the following week, but meanwhile I could help finish picking the plums.

Next morning, clad in my oldest blue jeans and my thickest shoes, I went out to the orchard with the boss. He introduced me to the foreman, Bill, a tall, gangling young man with a shy smile, who lifted a twelve-foot ladder on his shoulder and told me to follow him. I struggled through the thick rough grass carrying the metal bucket for my fruit. Bill put the ladder against a tree hanging with thick, dark clusters of purple plums, showed me how to hook the bucket on to the branch while I was picking, and told me to be sure that the ladder had a good footing when I moved it.

At first I climbed up rather gingerly, because it was some years since I had done any fruit picking on a ladder. The branches scratched my bare arms and the leaves clung to my hair. But up there on the top step the view was glorious. I could see clear across the seventy-five acres of orchard to the valley below, where the blue lake was gleaming like a small pond. For the first hour or two I picked furiously, running up and down the ladder and filling the wooden baskets laid out on the ground under the tree, but as the morning wore on I settled down to a steadier pace. I ate less too now, but my hands were stained a deep purple and my hair was as sticky as honey with the aphid from the leaves.

I was standing on the top step reaching for a particularly high branch when my ladder slowly folded up beneath me, and I found myself gently floating through the air with time enough to decide where to fall. I decided on a sitting posture, as there seemed to be less bones to break in that region of my body. Actually I arrived on the ground only bruised and slightly shaken, and luckily my bucket of plums was still firmly hooked to the tree above. I was being paid by the number of baskets I picked, so I didn't want to lose a whole bucketful of labour.

That night in bed I ached in every bone, but it was the nice satisfying feeling that comes from unaccustomed physical labour, and I knew I was getting limbered up for the far heavier work of apple picking which would follow soon.

At seven o'clock on Monday morning I drove Oppy across the bumpy orchard grass to where the gang of pickers were gathering for their first day of work. From a distance they had looked like a motley crew. So now I sat down on an empty box and took a closer look at my fellow workers. There were two old men in work clothes and cloth caps talking together in German, and then I noticed a very respectable-looking young woman and her young daughter. They were dressed in neat blue jeans, check shirts and scarves over their heads. A large family of noisy young men and small children were shouting together excitedly in a language that sounded like Russian, while a very fat, very short little old man with a battered hat and fraying trousers was struggling to strap on his picking bag. These picking bags were made of stout canvas and hung at the waist, supported by adjustable straps on the shoulders and round the stomach. There were several other people gathering near the entrance of the hut, where Bill was passing out the picking bags and ladders. In all, we were a gang of about twenty pickers.

Everybody was eyeing the trees with a professional air, discussing the crop, and deciding which trees looked the best for picking. Soon the boss arrived with the book of tickets which we were supposed to leave in each box of apples we picked. Then everybody was given a row and told to get started. There was a mad rush as all the pickers, myself included, flung their ladders against the trees and scrambled up into the foliage. The first picker down with a full bag was a young fellow from the Russian-speaking Doukhobor family. He whooped triumphantly on his way to empty the heavy bag into the row of empty boxes waiting under the trees.

Each box took about forty pounds of apples and an overflowing bag held a like amount. So it was quite a heavy job climbing and stretching over the ladder with thirty pounds or more of dead weight around one's waist. I loathed going to the very top of the ladder for some of those almost unreachable branches, but Bill was very firm with us. If a picker tried to escape on to another tree while the last one picked still held even a very small bunch of apples, Bill would haul him back to finish the job properly. We were not allowed to shake a tree, but how I longed to, whenever I was balanced precariously with one foot on the top of the ladder vainly groping for one miserable apple. Some of the trees were old and high and we had to use fourteen-foot ladders which only the men could lift; so I found myself scrambling into the middle of the trees, my heavy bag swinging out from my waist and the safety of the ladder several feet away. I would come down afterwards, bruised, scratched and filthy, but completely triumphant, as I regarded my cleanly picked tree with not an apple in sight. Then on to the next tree I would stagger, with my heavy ladder dragging in the long grass, and my feet tripping in the irrigation ditches.

23

A Ride in the Sun

We were paid ten cents a box, and on some energetic days when I got up before dawn and was still picking by moonlight that evening, I managed to fill over one hundred boxes. The afternoons were desperately hot, and with the temperature rising into the nineties, I grew reluctant to drag around ladders and bags of apples, so I sometimes lay down under the trees in the cool, long grass and took a siesta. Then the young Doukhobor men, who were always full of high spirits, would pelt me with apples and jeer at my laziness. And Jack, the ex-soldier who had been stationed in Britain during the war, would pass by on his tractor and yell in a pseudo-British accent, "You ain't in St. James's Park now, ducks."

In the evenings it was lovely to get back to my cosy little cottage, tired and ravenously hungry. I would start a fire of peach wood, which gave off a delicious smell as it cooked my supper. Sometimes Mrs. Butler would come over and invite me to drive to town with her and see a film or visit some friends. Or Mary, Jack's rather homesick Scottish wife, would drop by for a chat about the Old Country. They were lovely care-free days full of fresh air, hard work and new people.

By the end of October the last of the apples had been picked, and my thoughts began to turn to the last leg of my journey to Vancouver. I wrote to Marion in Montreal and asked her to forward to Vancouver my two suitcases of city clothes which I had left with her. The last week before my departure I rested up from the hard work and bought warm clothing for the long, cold three-hundred-mile ride ahead of us over the mountains to the coast.

Then one morning at the beginning of November I said good-bye to the kind Butlers, Mary and Jack, and all the rest of the fruit-ranch people; Matelot barked a last farewell to his pal Ajax, and Oppy turned westward once more. Winter had almost come, and a freezing wind blew across the highway from the lake shore. The leaves were turning their glorious autumn shades of golden and scarlet against the background of blue lake and green mountain.

As I climbed into the Selkirks it began to snow heavily and presently I was stopped by a car with two Mounties, who refused me a motor-cycle passage over the now deeply snow-covered Allison Pass. So I had to hitch-hike, and this I managed to do very successfully in a small truck, motor-cycle, dog, girl and all!

24

When at last we reached Vancouver I had practically forgotten how to drive in a large city, and even travel-hardened Matelot glanced nervously at the roaring buses and swaying trams. And once again the sight of a woman motor-cyclist with dog pillion rider was so overwhelming that speeding taxis fell back and overtaking motorists gave us a wide berth. Up Kingsway we drove and on through the centre of the city until we reached the Lions Gate Bridge which connects West Vancouver lying across the blue waters of Burrard Inlet. Then I stopped and caught my breath—there out of the water rose the snow-laden Coastal Range, dominating the entire harbour and city. I felt like shouting, "Well, we've finally made it!"

But really my troubles were just beginning. A letter at the post office informed me that a railway fire had destroyed my two suitcases of clothes, and as they were not insured the express company regretted that they could not allow me compensation. I was sorry too, because all I had to wear was some very well-travelled dirty motor-cycle clothes, and winter was just around the corner. And now I needed to find a good, steady job!

At the motor-cycle shop I met a kind young motor cyclist who sized up my difficulties in a few moments, made a quick telephone call, and then told me his English parents had invited me to stay for the weekend. Mrs. Hull welcomed Matelot and me like a mother, pushed me into the bathroom and threw my clothes into the washing machine. And an hour later we all sat down to a big supper of roast beef. During the weekend I went room hunting, which proved difficult because nobody wanted to take Matelot. After about the twentieth refusal, when it was dark and pouring with rain, I knocked on the door of a small brown house and swore it would be the last one that day.

A big woman with a mass of white hair and horn-rimmed spectacles glared out at me where I stood dripping my oilskins on her front step. I explained I was looking for a room and she all but flung her arms around me, as she pulled me into the warm, lighted hallway. Then she led me downstairs to the basement and showed me a big, homelike room with pale green walls, a lot of old-fashioned furniture and a large black range. With my own entrance through the cellar it seemed an ideal place to keep Matelot, so I tactfully broached the subject of my dog. Mrs. MacMillan beamed all over her plump face and said in her thick Ukrainian accent, "Why, sure you can have the dog here; why didn't you bring him in with you?"

She insisted that I stay for supper and found a juicy bone for Matelot too. Her husband was a tall, thin, very dour Scot, who was deaf. They spent the whole meal shouting at each other and he kept on insisting that he didn't want another damn woman about the place! But beneath his rough manner and pretended contempt for women he hid a kind heart, as I discovered during that winter. And even this first meal ended in a cheery note, because after all he was pleased that he had someone new to listen to his early manhood adventures. Mr. MacMillan had been up in the far north of Canada in the North-West Mounted Police, and had many a wild tale of his lonely and often dangerous duties there.

Now I started to look for a job. Working in an office was out of the question because of my rough and inadequate clothing, so I got on Oppy and drove down to the Fraser River to a large lumber mill, and asked to see the personnel manager. Within five minutes I had been hired as an unskilled employee to make plywood on the graveyard shift starting the following midnight.

The work was hard and at times I felt sure my poor muscles would quit on me as I lifted those enormous sheets of veneer off a moving belt, and then pushed the great loads across the mill. I liked the job, but at first I could not get used to the deafening noise of the whining power saws, the steady roar of the huge drying machines, the smell of sawdust and the terrific cold that crept through the enormous plant at night. Bundled up in a thick mackinaw jacket, I looked like a northern backwoodsman, and by flexing every muscle in my body I soon learned how to keep warm.

My work consisted of standing in front of a steadily growing pile of thin veneer sheeting, and I was responsible for removing a certain graded width of this wood. At whatever pace it came rushing down the endless moving belt, I somehow had to grab it and throw it into place on its proper pile. My eyes buzzed with watching the moving belt and I couldn't read the Chinese-like symbols denoting the grades of sheeting. My sheeting would go hurtling past me to the bottom of the chain with everybody yelling at me, but before I had retrieved half of it, there would be *more* rushing by. In sheer desperation I would throw everything to the floor and hope to find time later to sort out the hopeless mix-up. Somehow the foreman always happened to be standing just behind me whenever this happened. And once after I ripped a perfect piece of seventy-eight-inch sheeting clean in half, I almost knocked his hat off!

The first month on this job I lost about fifteen pounds in weight with all this running and lifting, but gradually I became an Old Hand and learned that no running and little lifting were necessary. A flick of the wrist and a steady eye did the trick. Only when my piles reached shoulder level did I feel strained, and then there was always the first-aid room in case of a ruptured blood vessel. This happened to me one evening when a splinter drove itself into my wrist, piercing first my thick work gloves and then my tender flesh. My blood on the sawdust-covered floor would have made a Mexican bullfighter feel at home!

Another night the seat of my blue jeans came into violent contact with a seventy-eight incher and the nurse removed from my posterior a decidedly outsize toothpick. Anyone who works in a plywood plant can easily spend all his leisure extracting splinters from every crack and cranny of his body.

My co-workers were a cheery, noisy bunch, and twice during the night we would all stop work. Then, while a relief gang took over our jobs, we poured out into the warm, lighted canteen. Hot bowls of soup or coffee made us fighting fit to return to duty, until with the grey light of dawn the eight o'clock whistle shrilled above the din of the plant, and another night's work would be over.

Soon after I came to live in Vancouver, I met Bernice Ramesay; rosy-complexioned with a thick, fair plait round her head, she was as great a motor-cycle enthusiast as myself.

One evening in Bernice's poorly lit basement she and I studied the insides of a B.S.A. motor-cycle engine. Poor Oppy had been losing a lot of her power and I thought that a good cleaning out of her "innards" would do her good. Minus her tank and saddle she looked pathetically naked; while removal of four nuts and a piece of metal called a cylinder head left bare the top of a very black and disgusting-looking piston. If this was the "thing" that drove her, then I thought we ought to go a stage further. When the whole cylinder came off, matters really began to get

27

complicated, because the piston was wobbling around on something loose. We hurriedly consulted an enormous volume entitled *Simplified Motor-cycle Mechanics,* which we had borrowed from the local library. It was anything but simple, and a first glance at it showed weird and awful little diagrams which we couldn't possibly connect with Oppy.

Eventually Bernice and I found that this seemingly unnatural wobble was termed "normal play in the big end." This sounded rather *risqué,* so we turned to other matters. Hard, black carbon was stuck like limpets all over the cylinder walls and piston, and there was hardly a finger-nail left between us when we had finished this revolting scraping task.

Finally I managed to feel around well enough in the semi-darkness to slip some new rings round the piston, and then came the big assembly job. All the bolts and nuts had been laid out in strict rotation on the floor, but inevitably some were moved and mislaid, and there were many cries and wails, sore fingers and muffled swearing, before Oppy looked back to normal. My hands were black and my face smudged, but I was completely triumphant as I kicked the engine over and the machine burst into life.

"Well," Bernice and I said to each other, "what a lot of money we've wasted on mechanics! From now on let's be our own."

But the next day Oppy practically refused to budge. So with great humiliation I pushed her up to Frank's motor-cycle shop. I was still determined to learn mechanics the hard way, but now admitted that a little expert guidance at crucial moments might help. The whole grue-some business of removing Oppy's head had to be done all over again. By the light of day I soon found that I had fitted the rings wrongly, so, with the minimum of bad temper and the maximum of black grease, the job was once more completed. Frank's only praise was grudgingly bestowed.

"At least, nobody can say you don't try."

With any of the repairs I have since attempted I have run into endless difficulties, because I am certainly not mechanically minded, but I do think half the fun of owning a machine is to mess around with it and try to do your own repairs. There is one thing girls should remember, though, if they want to buy and service their own motor-cycles; their lily-white hands and moon-shaped nails will be things of the past.

Gasoline Gypsy

That winter and the spring that followed were the busiest and happiest I had known. When I wasn't throwing plywood around at the plant, I was exploring Vancouver on Oppy or ski-ing on Grouse Mountain with Bernice. Now I was writing more and more frequently to a young Danish civil engineer, whom I had got to know through motor-cycling in Scandinavia the year before. But he was not content with only writing to me; one day I received a package containing a tape-recorded message from him. I flew down to the local radio station and begged them to play it for me, but I had rather an embarrassing few minutes trying to ignore the two engineers who had to listen to Carl-Erik's message too! One day in May, soon after this, he wrote asking me to come back to Denmark and marry him as soon as my summer trip was over. There were no doubts in my feelings for him now, but nevertheless it seemed strange to be engaged to someone seven thousand miles away, and I was thrown into a state of confusion about my trip, but finally decided to do what he suggested and return to Europe just as soon after the trip as I could scrape together the boat fare.

Before I knew it, June had arrived. I left my job at the plywood plant and for three days my room was a sea of half-packed luggage and road maps. Mrs. MacMillan kept popping down to the basement to find out how I was getting on, worrying about my safety that summer, and bringing me bowls of soup to fortify me, and pots of home-made jam to slip into my pack. Mr. MacMillan grunted and said I ought to have a gun, and it was my own damn fault if I had my throat slit down in Mexico. Meanwhile Operation-Pack continued.

This time I was far better equipped in every way for the second half of my North American wanderings. My purse seemed to be overflowing with travellers' cheques, my sleeping bag was re-stuffed with goose feathers, and my clothes were new and more suitable for hot climates. But somehow I was a little scared, and then my thoughts came back to the present; as I watched the rugged coastline of Vancouver Island approaching, I was sincerely longing for the security of that little room in Vancouver. Mexico City seemed awfully far away and New York another world.

CHAPTER IV *California, Here We Come!*

TWO hours after we had left Vancouver, the s.s. *Princess Elizabeth* docked in Nanaimo on the north-east shore of Vancouver Island. Our road lay ahead of us down Vancouver Island to Victoria, and then by boat again over to Port Angeles, Washington. This was the route that I had chosen to enter the United States, rather than the more obvious way across the border south of Vancouver and straight down to Seattle.

We were the first off the ship, and as Oppy wound her way slowly up the steep hill from the dock, I glanced at my speedometer, which read 19,123 miles. Then I set Oppy's nose due south, pulled back the throttle and yelled with care-free abandon, "California, here we come!" while poor Matelot got the fright of his life and nearly fell out of his box.

The road that winds down Vancouver Island cuts through green hills and sweet-smelling pine forests, giving one from time to time a magnificent view of seascape and mountains. As I sat on top of a hill eating my first roadside meal, I looked out across the blue water, small isles and snow-capped mountains in the distance; it might almost have been some view on the western fjord coast of Norway.

A few hours later we arrived in Victoria, and after passing the Canadian customs we boarded the ship that was to take us to the United States. The magnificent Olympic Range stretched into the sky to south, and was a lovely introduction to the new country ahead of us. Above, the gulls wheeled across the wake of our ship and then past the Stars and Stripes fluttering in the wind. Technically we were already on American soil.

The face of the United States Customs officer at Port Angeles didn't move a muscle as he surveyed the bursting figure of Oppy and the dignified appearance of Matelot perched aloft.

"Anything to declare?" he grunted.

30

"Well, apart from a typewriter, I only have a sleeping bag, cooking pots—"

"O.K., O.K. How about the dog, does he go in shows?"

"What, Matelot?" I laughed. "Goodness, no, he's just my navigator and co-pilot."

But customs and emigration is a serious business. Our bulging bags were dismissed with a distasteful glance, but my passport, motor licence and Matelot's veterinary certificate were carefully studied.

Behind us a string of returning tourists laughed and shouted greetings. "Good luck and have fun in the States." Then, as we swayed up the main street, someone remarked, "Say, that really looks like rugged travelling."

I hoped that I didn't look too rugged a figure myself, because I had taken the pains to put on my nicest scarlet shirt with socks to match, to honour this first day in the States.

At the top of the hill I found a signpost pointing to Seattle, so I slipped into high gear and away we flew down the straight Washington highway. To say we flew is really an exaggeration, because Oppy hadn't yet settled down to her excessive load, so I let her roll along at a comfortable thirty miles an hour. This is a nice speed at which to view the passing country-side. At high speeds I find I see nothing and I can't even smell the hedge-rows or hear the birds singing. As a matter of fact, I don't care to drive at more than forty-five miles an hour at any time, because my hair gets too blown around and my eyes begin to stream.

But now I found that if I kept Oppy well over on the right-hand side we didn't obstruct the traffic which was roaring and hurtling past our slow-moving vehicle. Presently I stopped by the roadside to study the map. This took quite a long time, because I was kept busy waving and smiling at the hooting trucks and cars which passed us in both directions. This was summer holiday time and I was an obvious member of that recognized sorority, traveller and tourist. Returning Canadians, their cars a mass of stickers from California to Florida, slowed down to say "Hi!" while one Washingtonian made me laugh when he stopped and asked "Are you real?"

I chose a route to Seattle across the Hood Canal which entailed two ferry-boat rides. Driving on board the first little boat, I realized that it was our third trip over water in one day. An elderly gentleman stepped out of a large Cadillac, gave Oppy the once over and asked "Where y'bound for, sis?"

"New York, via Mexico City, bud!" I replied, and everybody round us laughed.

After that ferry ride it was quite a rest to get back on the road driving, because the number of questions shot at me by the motorists that crowded round us was quite overwhelming.

There were twelve miles between the two ferries with only twenty minutes between sailings, so I really had to coax poor little Oppy along. As I rounded the corner and saw the boat still lying in the harbour, my watch showed I had taken twenty-five minutes, so I hurried on across the wooden bridge. A crowd was hanging over the top railings, sailors were standing by, and the ticket collector winked and said, "Well, so you finally made it, eh?"

Only then did I realize that I had kept the whole ferry waiting, because news of our impending arrival had been spread by the other passengers. I felt like Royalty at least, as I drove aboard to a slight cheer from the deck above!

It was very late as we scuttled through the lighted streets of Seattle and up over Magnolia Boulevard. Behind us lay the city, like a million stars twinkling across the water and up the hillsides, while the warm glow from the lighted houses beckoned to us. Oppy wound down the narrow little lane leading to the houses that overlook Puget Sound. Matelot jumped off and ran ahead down the steps—he knew the way to the Feringers' house from our previous visit to them in the spring.

I had first met Jo-Anne and Dick in the summer of 1950 in a Norwegian youth hostel. Jo-Anne had been in the bunk next to me in the dormitory, and we had hit off from the first moment we started talking. She was such a gay, humorous person in spite of her serious appearance. I liked her tall, ex-Navy husband equally well, with his cheery grin and teasing manner. And back there in Norway Jo-Anne had given me, half jokingly, their home address in Seattle, and written underneath—Come Any Time!

I found Jo-Anne and Dick enjoying a midnight feast of ice cream and strawberries, and I didn't need a second invitation to join them. Outside

Matelot had chased Rama, the Siamese cat, up a tree, but we ignored all the scuffling and barking as we talked about the possibility of meeting again in Europe.

"It's just no good," said Dick, "We'll have to go for another trip on our bicycles over there. You unsettle us so much that my feet feel permanently itched."

It was at least two in the morning before I pulled out my sleeping bag and rolled up on the couch. I always try to discourage my hostesses from furnishing such unnecessary items as sheets, when I have my own bag to hop into.

Next morning found Jo-Anne and me waiting outside Dick's office of nautical instrument makers, while he braved the boss for that day of freedom owing to him. There was a lot of shouting back and forth, but finally Dick reappeared with a smiling face to say that he was all set for our trip to Mount Ranier.

As we wanted to spend as much of the day as possible in the mountains, we didn't stop for lunch but ate our sandwiches en route. I was at a slight disadvantage because two hands are better than one for driving a motor-cycle. Dick managed to make his station wagon crawl at our pace, while Jo-Anne handed me a series of sandwiches. When they contained cheese, Matelot breathed greedily down my neck and a very cold, wet black nose caressed my cheek. Two wild furry paws were flung round my neck, and just when I thought I was going to lose control of Oppy, Jo-Anne threw Matelot a decoy. Oppy lurched madly as Matelot chased round in his box pursuing the lump of cheese.

I had just reached out for another sandwich, when there was a roar from behind and a loud voice said, "Now, come on there, folks, break it up. What d'y think this is, feeding time at the zoo?" I turned and gave my most winning motor-cycle comrade smile to a tough-looking patrol cop on an enormous machine. Of course that was the last I saw of Dick's little station wagon until we reached Tacoma, and those sandwiches were so darn good, too!

Because we feared that Oppy could not make the grade up Mount Ranier with all her luggage, I parked her in a friendly petrol station and joined Jo-Anne and Dick in their station wagon. Poor Matelot missed his fresh-air motor-cycle seat and kept trying to get head and shoulders out of the window. He is used to leaning his head on my shoulder when driving, but Dick didn't enjoy this trick at all. As for me, the smooth movement of the car soon sent me fast asleep.

When I awoke, there was Mount Ranier, a towering pyramid of ice and snow rising out of the soft, green hills against a background of clear blue sky. Majestically she stood alone with no other peaks to rival her beauty; sheer walls of ice and deep glaciers shone green-blue in the sunshine. Higher and higher we climbed through the pine woods until we reached the snow line.

On that first day in July we hiked and romped our way across the great unmelted snow fields, and when we found a little patch of melted forest we lay down and ate a second lunch. The world was a mass of snow, ice, sunshine and scented pines; the air was that special sort that one only breathes in high mountains, and at that moment I thought life was very good.

That evening I said good-bye to Jo-Anne and Dick on the highway, with their little Nash pointed north to Seattle and Oppy looking southwards, and I think we were all feeling very reluctant to part. The blue station wagon honked its horn, two hands hung out of the window waving to us, and then away it sped towards Seattle.

It was growing dusk as I left Tacoma and headed into the pinky glow of the sunset. I felt rather as I did that first night looking for a camping spot in Canada. Once again I had lost the old courage and habit of sleeping outdoors. Then, too, Oppy's power was beginning to decrease, and this was so noticeable on hills that several times I made Matelot run alongside to ease the weight on the machine.

Now it was almost dark and I could see no likely spot to pitch the tent. Then suddenly, high above the pine trees, the moon rose, bright and golden. The road stretched before us like an illuminated ribbon, and in the beauty of the night my troubles vanished. At last, travelling at an average speed of twenty miles an hour, we reached Olympia, the state capital of Washington.

Southwards, our way lay up a steep hill, and I thought for a moment Oppy wouldn't be able to make it as she coughed and spluttered her way to the top. I really didn't believe she would last much further and I had no idea what sort of country lay ahead, so I stopped and consulted a map.

A state park camping ground was marked about three miles off the main highway. This might make a nice first camp for us. The road leading to the park was lonely and dark and wound beneath thickly overhanging trees, until even the bright moon was obscured and my trail took on an eerie atmosphere.

If only Oppy could have been coaxed to go faster—but she was losing speed every minute, and I was feeling pretty nervous. We drove for what seemed hours and then the hard surface gave way to loose, washboard gravel. Apparently we must have missed the turning into the park, so when I saw a lighted farmhouse I drove into the yard. Approaching the lighted barn, I was shocked to see a young calf hanging from the rafters, its head dripping blood into a bucket.

The way I felt at that moment I wouldn't have been surprised if I had come across a human murder. When I found my voice I saw two gnarled old farmers regarding me suspiciously. Finally they grunted that I was six miles out of my way.

The return journey to the camp ground was less eerie because I picked up two New Yorkers in a car, who were just as lost as I. Together we bumped and fumbled our way down the dark road, until at last the entrance of the park came into sight. The camp ground was set in a huge silent forest of tall, straight pine trees; so tall I could barely see the sky above. Too exhausted to pitch the tent, I pulled out my sleeping bag and lay down in all my clothes on the leafy ground and slept like a log.

Next morning I awoke to a chorus of bird songs, a damp cold dew settling over my sleeping bag, and a row of silent tents all about us. The discovery of such a civilized thing as a wash-house with running water was completely wasted on me, because a few minutes later I had Oppy's carburettor in several pieces and once more my face and hands resembled those of a Pennsylvania coalminer. Finally, when I traced the trouble to a perforated float in the carburettor, I knew we'd have to return to Olympia and look for a motor-cycle mechanic.

Oppy really shamed me on that return journey, which was completed at a top speed of about ten miles per hour. An enormous double trailer truck was so furious at our slow and wobbling figure that he took to the shoulder of the road, passing on our right in a roaring cloud of dust and shouting curses at us. Our humiliation was complete when a slow-moving farm tractor pulling some farm equipment overtook us with much sniggering from the driver.

To make matters worse the White Elephant insisted upon slipping its strap and trailing in the dust every few yards. The White Elephant was a large, bulky ex-G.I. duffle bag into which was stuffed my enormous mackinaw and sheepskin jacket. The only uncovered space on Oppy was a few inches between the bottom of Matelot's box and the top of one of the side bags, and the wretched thing had squeezed itself in there.

For about the tenth time that morning I pushed the bulging monster back into place, while hooting motorists missed our rear by an inch and shed us glances that clearly said "Women Drivers!" It had taken a good hour and a half to cover the few miles back to Olympia, the sun was pouring down like a furnace and my temper was getting shorter every minute. It was sheer heaven as we coasted down the hill into the city at a good twenty miles per hour. Then I heard a sudden yell—"Hey, lady, you dropped something." The White Elephant—Oh, damn!

All the searching on my part and the helpful suggestions from pedestrians only revealed that my now very loved and indispensable warm jacket had rolled out of sight. There was only one thing to do.

I leaned Oppy against the post marked No Parking—Police Department, and entered their building opposite. Two burly blue figures surveyed me with amusement.

"Young lady," one of them finally said, "could you take things one at a time? First, you've lost a coat; second, you want us to supply you with a motor-cycle mechanic; and third," he glanced out of the window, "you are about to get a ticket."

"Please," I begged, "our English Bobbies are so kind when one is in trouble, and I am sure you American cops are just the same."

"Joe," said the sergeant, "get on your machine and go look for the lady's jacket, and tell Frank to come in."

Poor Frank, he didn't look very happy escorting me slowly through the centre of the city on his enormous machine, to the Specialized Services workshop.

Here I was lucky enough to find Burt, a carburettor expert and a motor-cyclist enthusiast into the bargain. In no time at all the damaged float had been repaired and Oppy spluttered into life again. Burt said

36

that he had a good idea for helping me find my lost jacket, and as it was his lunch hour, suggested he drive me down to the local radio station.

A few minutes later, the face of a young radio announcer was beaming at us. "Yes, we'd be glad to put it on the midday news. It'll make a nice story. Where did you say you came from?" When I had given all the details that were needed for this news flash, Burt suggested we go and have a bite to eat.

As we sat munching hamburgers in his car outside the drive-in restaurant, I was amused to hear the voice over the radio saying—"An attractive English brunette [I was a horrible sight of black grease, dirty jeans and no lipstick] is on her way through our fair country . . . . I hope therefore that some honest Olympian will return this young lady's jacket to the Police Department." At one o'clock Burt had to go back to work, and I went off on Oppy to look for something to do until my jacket was found.

The temperature was mounting into the nineties when I found the city park and stretched out under a tree. I was awakened from my siesta by an anxious-faced youth standing over me and dangling a bulging bag. He explained that he had found the White Elephant lying under his parked truck, and later on, hearing the radio flash of my loss, he had set out to look for me. I thanked him warmly for his trouble and then hopped on Oppy to return to the police station. Joe, Frank and their sergeant all looked very happy when I told them what had happened, and one of them said they were glad that I would now have a good memory of their city. Well, I couldn't leave until I had told the good news to Burt too. He protested when I tried to thank him and said that all he would like was a postcard from me at the end of the trip.

The next morning we sped along through the green countryside. The snowy peaks of Mount Ranier and Mount Hood rose high in the sky to the east of us, and I found it difficult to keep my eyes on the road straight ahead. It was the Fourth of July week-end and the traffic was thick and hell-bent in both directions—that is, until they saw us. Then brakes were applied, windows rolled down and heads, hands and cine-cameras appeared on all sides.

All that day we flew southwards down the straight Washington highway, until just before sunset I started to feel hungry and the sign

"Sorensen's Groceries" caught my eye. I stopped and bought a loaf of bread, a tin of beans and some sausages, and the girl who served me asked if I was going to camp opposite. I seemed doomed for wash-houses, running water and all the usual mod. con., so as it was nearing dusk, I decided to camp in the Lewis and Clark State Park.

I drove down the beautiful forest pathway, avoided the notice stating —"Stop and pay seventy-five cents overnight fee," and picked my spot beneath a towering pine. My next-door tent neighbour strolled over and stared at Oppy's licence plates. He was a slight, blond young man in an old golf jacket and grey flannel trousers, and he smiled as he said, "Please let me introduce myself, my name is Gunnar Åsvärn and I come from Stockholm." As if to prove his statement he bowed slightly with Swedish dignity.

"Who's that?" I asked pointing to two large hairy legs protruding from a small and ancient tent.

"May I present you to my friend Sven Stalin," he said in a loud voice. The silence was broken by vigorous snores.

"Manners aren't what they used to be in ancient Scandinavia," apologized Gunnar.

"Well, here's your chance to resurrect the past," I said, throwing him my deflated air mattress.

When he finally came up for air, I had my tent pitched and the cooking pans unpacked. Then Gunnar and I hunted around for dry wood and soon had a fire roaring away, sending bright flames and blue smoke high into the air. I put on some coffee water and in no time it was bubbling away merrily.

"If we can smoke Uncle Joe out of the Kremlin," I said, "how about some sausages?" Then I modestly looked the other way while the ancient tent heaved and groaned and torments of furious Swedish flooded the peaceful night air. A few minutes later a tall, sleepy-looking Swede, in a pair of old shorts and sandals, was bowing over my hand.

We pulled some logs round the fire to sit on, and while the boys got busy with the sausages staked on the end of long sticks, I made the coffee. Silence was golden as we all bit into the first sizzling sausage. Over mugs of steaming coffee, Gunnar confessed that he was an exchange student and his allowance had given out in the spring, but he liked the States so much that he had set about making some money for this trip. In Chicago he had acted as a night janitor in a large apartment house. He had tended the huge furnace, emptied the garbage, and a beautiful blonde vamp on the third floor had kept him busy running up and down stairs with new lamp bulbs! Then early in June he had purchased a 1936 Chevrolet, complete with radio and heater, for one hundred and twenty-five dollars. She was named "Perlemor," mother-of-pearl in Swedish, and called Perle for short. He and "Uncle Joe" had started out with about three hundred dollars between them and a lot of faith.

They had just completed about four thousand miles through the midwest and over the mountains and up through California, and all without any mechanical trouble from Perle. Poor thing, she lay under layers of dust and mud gathered along the highways from Illinois to Colorado. But the boys explained that her shabby appearance kept them from being overcharged. Like me, they had a strict budget, and had slept in some strange places. One night they pitched their tent in the middle of a city park between a noisy ball game on one side of them and an enthusiastic prayer meeting on the other. Once a friendly cop let them sleep in the city jail and took them home to breakfast.

"If you receive half the kindness we did you'll be lucky," they both concluded.

Next morning I watched Perle rattle off down the road. The poor boys were on a strict one-meal-a-day plan, with their funds now dwindled to twelve dollars. And as I left the park the warden hailed me, "Hope you had a good night's rest, and say, I didn't bother you about that seventy-five cents; I reckoned you were short of dough just like those other two young foreigners."

CHAPTER V *Wandering Southwards*

I DROVE slowly that morning because it was such a beautiful, golden day. Portland would still be there in a couple of hours, so why hurry? On the wide green banks of the Columbus river I stopped for lunch.

39

This was the same green, rushing waterway which I had followed for so many miles through Canada last summer. Lettuce, tinned beans, peanut-butter sandwiches and cold coffee made an adequate lunch. Matelot devoured his tin of meat in one fell swoop, and stretched out under a shady tree.

The sun beat down strongly; drowsy and full of lunch, I too stretched out on the grass and dozed. My face felt warm and I was glad that I had remembered to pack my suntan make-up. The cars and trucks sped past unheeding my sun bath, except for an occasional hoot or shout of greeting.

Suddenly there was an extra loud woosh, a screech of brakes, and on to the scene appeared Wolf No. 1 of the trip. This one wasn't dressed in sheep's clothing, but in the guise of a fellow motor-cyclist, so I sat up smiling and prepared to brag of Oppy's sterling qualities. Matelot regarded the intruder with solemn eyes. And then, after a brief conversation which had very little to do with motor-cycling, this would-be Casanova of the road asked the fatal question—"Would your dog bite me?"

When men ask questions like that I start getting wary. A girl who travels alone should expect trouble, and then it usually doesn't come along. Actually Matelot has never so much as shown his teeth at a human being and usually he flings welcoming paws all over strangers. But sometimes it is useful to make believe that he is a regular Rin-Tin-Tin, so now I replied, "He's a killer when he gets mad."

The last I saw of that particular Casanova was the rear view of a motor-cycle going at eighty miles an hour. I was still laughing when we reached Portland.

On down Highway 99 we sped. If we hurried we would be in time to camp with the sunset over the Pacific. Suddenly I noticed a signpost on the corner of a road leading off to the east; it said "Dallas." That name sounded familiar, who did I know in this part of Oregon? I stopped and got out the map and then I remembered. Through one of my articles in a motor-cycling magazine, I had received an invitation from a dealer and his wife to visit them in Dallas, Oregon, on my way south. After replying I had lost the address, but now the name came back to me and the signpost beckoned.

The clock on the Court House pointed to ten o'clock when we reached a small, brightly lit town. At my first inquiry I found that the motor-cycle shop was just across the street, and a light was still burning in the back of the building. So, after parking Oppy, I pushed open the door and Matelot bounded through the unlit shop to the kitchen beyond. A tall figure rose and framed the door.

"Well," said a thickly accented voice, "you don't have to tell us who *you* are! Come in, Peggy, and meet the wife."

In a few moments I felt as though I had known the Proals for years. We sat there in the little kitchen drinking Tony's special home-made wine, and I watched Pearl fuss around making me a huge supper. Matelot wasn't forgotten either. He lay in a corner chewing a large ham bone. Soon the conversation turned to motor-cycles, and as always when enthusiasts get together, the hour drew late. At last Tony shut up shop and we all climbed on our machines and went home.

The Proals' house was very simple and comfortable and a home in the true sense of the word. My ablutions were scant, because only a very thin curtain divided the bathroom from the main living room. But after that I sank between clean sheets with a feeling that only a true camper can appreciate.

There was no departing next morning until Pearl had filled me so full of breakfast I could hardly move, and Tony had nearly killed himself in a cherry tree collecting a large bucket of fruit for me to take on the road. That morning I had an escort of three motor-cycles to see us safely on our way to the coast. And as I thanked Pearl and Tony for their hospitality, they told me a bed would be waiting for me in their home, any time I liked.

My first sight of the Pacific Ocean was certainly unforgettable. As I turned the corner of the road, the wind was tearing at my hair and buffeting the machine. Then I saw it! The white-capped aquamarine water swept in over the golden beach in an unbroken line, almost to where the pine trees and bright flowers mingled with the rocky cliffs. The air was a mixture of salty breeze, warm pine trees and sunshine. I felt as though I had stepped into one of Hollywood's Glorious Technicolor Epics. The wind drove strong from behind and helped us up the steep road which lay twisting and winding over the cliff tops.

Driving it had seemed cold for July, but as soon as I stopped the sun rays burnt through my thin shirt and the blue waters looked cool and inviting for swimming. Even Matelot was impressed with the view. He stood up behind me on all fours, his ears flying in the wind, and surveying the magnificent scene.

When I saw a break in the cliff, I parked Oppy, and Matelot and I scrambled down to the beach. But the hot sand under my feet only made the cold water seem icier. Now I understand why we had seen no swimmers anywhere along the coast. Still, I had been brought up by the North Sea, so I flung off my clothes on the deserted beach, and then gasped as the first icy wave nearly swept me off my feet. It was impossible to swim in those towering and crashing waves, but as I struggled in the foaming spray I thrilled to my first dip in the Pacific Ocean.

Matelot, sensible dog, stayed at a safe distance, and not so much as a paw touched the water. But as I raced along the sands to dry off, with the deafening roar of the breakers in my ears, the stinging wind against my skin, and Matelot galloping beside me nearly wild with the freedom and the soft sand beneath his paws, I told myself, "This is really living."

Now, for the first time since leaving Vancouver, I was wearing a sweater and windbreaker against the strong cold winds. Pitching my tent that night was a feat of sheer human endurance, and the whole kit and caboodle nearly took off into the greatest ocean in the world! For a long time I lay there listening to the wind tearing at the light canvas tent, and the sound of the thundering roar of the breakers crashing over the beach below.

Next morning our road left the coast and wound inland for about sixty miles, and here the change in temperature was incredible. Without the ocean wind the terrific heat was so intense that I could hardly stand the feel of my tight jeans and sticky shirt. Remembering that I had been bundled up in a ski jacket and cap the day before, I realized what a land of contrasts this was. Soon I stopped driving and did a quick change behind some trees, feeling sorry for poor Matelot, who couldn't shed his thick curly coat. And then, as I set off again on Oppy in my shorts and halter, I was amused at the horrified glances I received from sweet old ladies in plush, gleaming sedans.

Paused at the top of the hill on one of those maddeningly correct "viewpoints," I took in the scenery for about the hundredth time that day, and reached for my camera. Those maddening little notices of warning meet the eye at regular intervals all along this breath-taking road. "Viewpoint 500 yards." Then round the next corner one sees a second one saying, "Viewpoint 200 yards," until finally the biggest arrow of all times points to "VIEWPOINT."

Undoubtedly the road engineers are right, but I prefer to discover natural beauty without so much help from know-it-all experts.

I first noticed "Viewpointers" on that spectacular and beautiful Banff-Jasper Highway in the Canadian Rockies. A packed car would come tearing round the corner, having missed all the previous warning signs. Then someone would yell, "Honey! Look! Viewpoint!" Brakes would screech and out would pile an assortment of family, cameras and binoculars. "Stupendous, magnificent, out of this world!" Click—click—click, and everyone would return hurriedly to the thermostatically controlled Cadillac or de luxe Chrysler. "Sure must keep a check on those warning signs," says Dad, and away they would tear to the next viewpoint, amid a cloud of enveloping dust and gathering speed.

Yes, I'm sure the engineers are right, but personally I like to give some of that in-between scenery a break too.

That evening, dwarfed by towering cliffs and within hearing of the ocean, I found Humbug Mountain camping ground. High above from— yes, a viewpoint, I had looked down on a lush, green field dotted with friendly little tents, and well sheltered from the wind. But I very nearly missed the entrance altogether, because I was concentrating so hard on ignoring a wolf-whistling Plymouth that insisted upon racing alongside us down the long steep hill. Still, somehow I managed a neat U-turn, just avoided a huge logging truck hurtling round the corner, and bumped my way across the uneven grass.

The whole camp stopped operations to watch me pitch my pathetic little tent. On one side of us towered a monster aluminium trailer; on the other stood a tent which looked as though it could sleep the House of Representatives at least.

My tenting neighbour was finally overcome by curiosity and asked, "You don't mean to say you *really* sleep in *that*?" He waved a hand at my veteran pup tent.

A Ride in the Sun

I pushed aside the mosquito netting to show him the neat arrangement of sleeping bag on one side and Matelot's rug, overnight bag and typewriter on the other. "See," I said, "a two-sleeper tent, and three if you're a sardine."

"Really rugged," he marvelled, "but you can't possibly carry everything you need on that little machine."

Then he disappeared into his tent and came staggering back to my encampment under a load of folding table and chair, storm lantern and portable gas cooker. After this kind gesture I hadn't the heart to say that I really preferred sitting on the ground, writing by firelight and even relished my smoky cooking.

Camping makes everyone brothers. And a moment later another Good Samaritan came by in the form of a polite young twelve-year-old.

"I'm a scout, you know," he said, giving my tent a professional glance. "Has it ever fallen down on you?" he went on, testing one of the guy ropes.

Thinking of last night's windy cliff top, I stifled a smile and began, "Well—"

"I thought so," he interrupted, "it's quite a trick, this tent pitching. But we learn all about it in scouts. Darn it, I wish my parents hadn't bought a trailer," he added wistfully.

Well, I had to admit my tent had never before stood so straight as it did when my little scout finished his tweaking and pulling.

"Anything else?" he asked.

"How are you on air?" I said pointing to my air mattress.

"Oh! we American kids are full of it," he laughed.

And certainly he made a quicker job of the air mattress than Gunnar had.

After the nice little scout had disappeared inside his family's trailer, I decided to wash my hair, and went to look for some driftwood to make a good hot fire. When I reached the beach, the sunset had just reached its climax of glorious colour. Scattered across the sand I found some wonderful and weirdly shaped pieces of wood. Impounded and rubbed smooth by the sea, they had taken on the appearances of wild animals or even human faces. Gathering as many as I could carry, I staggered back to camp and soon had a roaring log fire ablaze.

Operation Hair Wash became the camp's most interesting event of the evening. Suddenly across the comparative gloom of my little encampment swept a bright searchlight. My tenting brother evidently kept a storm lantern in reserve, and his whole family was peering in my direction. By this time all my available pots and pans, including Matelot's dinner plate, were bubbling away madly in the leaping flames, so in spite of my total lack of privacy I could delay no longer. Kneeling in the firelight, I scrubbed and sloshed shampoo and water over my entangled locks, like a baby hippo taking a bath. The whole camp certainly got their money's worth in free entertainment, and when I had finished I quite expected someone to rush over with a portable electric hair dryer.

But actually I was reduced to a much more primitive method. Lying on my back, I leaned my head on two logs over the blazing embers, and gazing heavenwards I did a little star watching until my hair was dry.

In the morning there was a horrible damp feeling over the tent and beads of moisture were gathered on the roof. Something else, too, was up there on the roof, and not caring that I stood exposed to the whole camp in my red pyjamas and with my hair in pins, I leapt from the tent and yelled for my scout. He came running across the damp, misty field as fast as his little legs would carry him.

"Remove it, for heaven's sake," I quaked.

And presently the youngster crawled out of my tent carrying a large, repulsive daddy-long-legs, a horror from my early childhood. No amount of camping will ever harden me to the creepy-crawly bugs one is likely to meet outdoors.

"What are you going to do in Arizona with all those snakes and scorpions?" asked the scout scornfully. "I've heard they crawl right into sleeping bags for warmth."

That was one bridge I hoped I would never have to cross.

But now in the early morning the mist was rolling in from the ocean like a thick white blanket and the surrounding mountains denied us the merest glimmer of sunlight. Pulling on every available sweater and jacket, I set off up the steep and twisting highway. So this is where Hollywood comes to film those London fog pictures, I thought. As we climbed through the enveloping humid mist with our headlights blazing, we seemed to be clinging to the very edge of the precipice itself. And every now and again I would catch sight of swirling seas and jagged rocks far below.

To add to this hazard we soon met an army of logging trucks; they swung round blind corners in both directions, always meeting us at the most crucial and dangerous moments. One would come snarling and roaring up behind us until, completely unnerved by the sound of its hissing brakes, I would pull over to the right with one of Oppy's wheels practically hanging in mid-air. Then I would frantically wave it on. The driver's hoot of appreciation nearly sent Matelot bounding down to meet the Pacific pounding the beaches below us.

Then, round the next corner, another great monster would come hurtling towards us, the second driver perched up on the end trailer in an open seat high above the great tree trunk. He would wave us a greeting as he was swept out at a sharp right angle perilously close to sending us flying to our death below. And this nerve-shattering driving lasted for almost three days!

As we approached California I was sure that the cold mist would be cut as if by some invisible knife and the sun would pour down from a cloudless blue sky. The name California had always conjured up pictures of beautiful starlets sunbathing on surf-swept beaches, outsize grapefruit, and above all, hot blazing sunshine. Instead, as I approached the State line, the heavens opened up with a little patter of gentle rain, which back home might have been called Scotch mist. California in July and no sunshine! Even the fruit control inspector looked a little ashamed.

But if there was no sunshine, there were plenty of grapefruit, as well as oranges, cherries and ripe tomatoes. They rolled out of the searched cars like peas out of a pod, and although all I could offer now were a couple of onions and a few potatoes which I swore weren't carrying any disease from Oregon, the mad search went on. No lemon was left unturned, and the last sordid detail of my packing was exposed for all the world to see.

That afternoon we came to the first of the redwood forests. Before preservation of these great beautiful trees became general practice, the forests were logged almost clean, and evidence of this ugly destruction lay all along our way. Huge tree stumps large as banqueting tables were scattered on either side of the road; some served as novelty advertisements for cafés and stores, while others in backyards were covered with climbing vines and flowers.

Then gradually the forest about us thickened, and we were in the midst of the famous Californian redwoods that I had heard so much about. I was glad when the sun shone and cleared away the last of the mist, and a little warmth filtered down through the thick green foliage. It was like being in a cathedral, that drive along the redwood highway. The branches overhead met in great arches, and the sunlight shining through them fell in long shafts across the road.

My camp site that night was in a little grassy glade a couple of yards from the highway. It was nice to be away from the civilization of camp ground life. That evening my only companions were the blue jays and squirrels darting through the big trees surrounding our tent, but in place of the noise of blaring radios I had the steady roar of the traffic hurtling past on the highway. And because we were a mere two yards from the road, I was forced to wait until there was a good break in the traffic in order to slip into my pyjamas. Unluckily just at the crucial moment a particularly silent convertible glided into view. I stood stock still, hoping my red pyjamas might be mistaken for a redwood tree, and as nobody gave me a second glance perhaps the occupants of the car were deceived. Certainly at a distance Matelot might easily be taken for a bear cub, while the little green tent blended in perfectly with its leafy background.

Breakfast was a scant affair, because I had no fire permit enabling me to light a fire in the forest, and my small pocket stove had refused to work from the first day of purchase. Then I discovered that I had used my last drop of water brushing my teeth. Luckily Matelot had left a little drinking water for my coffee, and although it contained a few overnight visitors of ants, twigs and cobwebs, they didn't seem to make the slightest difference to the taste. The first coffee of the day is *always* delectable.

After my meal I dangled my legs over the mighty redwood stump against which Oppy was leaning, and headed my diary "Somewhere in the Redwoods, Calif." At least I knew which State I was in, but the precise name of the place and the exact time or day of the week meant nothing to me now. My watch had stopped and I saw no reason for having it fixed, because I got up with the sun, went to sleep with the birds, and ate when I felt hungry. A more ideal way of spending part of one's life I can't imagine.

Well, if that enchanting forest was an answer to a camper's dream, the next spot was a nightmare. I was very late finding anywhere to sleep the following evening, and it was quite dark when I bumped Oppy across a field and pitched the tent under some tall trees. There was a row of lights a few hundred yards away; a dog barked and Matelot gave an answering growl. The night was warm, and I sat on the grass awhile looking at the stars and thinking what a lovely free feeling it was to be rolling on southwards. But something always happens when I start getting smug about life.

Wham! a small object hit my cheek; then again something small and hard hit me on the face. The night was very still, then again, wham! My heart stopped beating for a moment. My hands felt clammy, but not from the heat. Wham! there it was again, and this time it stung a little. Someone who knew I had arrived alone and was going to stay all night. Now I sat very tense in the dark listening, and trying not to be melodramatic or to remember how I'd been warned of the dangers of camping alone. Even Matelot had deserted me; he was fast asleep on his rug! The very idea of anybody creeping up in the dark to throw stones at me was ludicrous, but, wham! there was *another* one.

Now I simply flew into my little tent, pulled the sleeping bag over my head and lay there trembling for an hour at least. Except for a muffled roar from the traffic on the highway beyond, the silence was ominous. Finally sleep caught up with me.

CHAPTER VI *So that was an Earthquake!*

I AWOKE to a hot sun streaming through my canvas roof. I poked my head out of the tent flaps and saw I was in a large field level with a small dirt road, up and down which several big fruit trucks rumbled. At the sight of my tousled but obviously feminine head there was a great deal of brake grinding and several whistles. I noticed too that there was a large packing house standing where I'd seen the lights the evening before, so I guessed that I had been pelted with some hard plums for a joke. Men! Odious men!

Then I crashed around inside my three-by-six-foot dressing room, trying to wriggle into my clothes in the low and narrow pup tent. Five minutes later I made what I hoped was a dignified appearance, turned my back on the audience of trucks and proceeded to cook my frugal breakfast. My rear view must have looked mighty unfriendly, because at last, amid a cloud of dust, a roar of engines and a final bravado of whistles, my tormentors bounced off down the road.

Wham! Suddenly something hit my head, then something else fell in my coffee. I looked above me into the laden branches of a eucalyptus tree and then out of my mug I fished a small hard fruit. Was my face red! The truckers were nice fellows after all!

As we headed south the scenery began to change now and take on a more tropical appearance. The earth was a rich dark red, while the hills above were burnt a golden-brown hue. We passed mile upon mile of vineyards and olive trees, until the green forests and cool breezes had completely given way to the warm California I had read about. The sun was really hot and poured down over the fields of flowers and fruit orchards, and glinted across the dazzling white Spanish architecture. As I listened to the Mexican store-keepers I felt as if I were already south of the border. Practising my rusty Spanish on the petrol station attendants often had a disastrous effect, such as an overflowing tank or low pressure in my tyres.

I began to feel so warm that I decided to discard my blue jeans and brogues until I reached the Atlantic coast. I pulled in at the next petrol station and used their rest room for a change of clothes. It was a relief to get out of my tight jeans and hot socks, and I felt much more comfortable and cool in sandals and a cotton sun dress. I had made this costume myself especially for motor-cycling, with an extra full skirt designed to drape decorously over Oppy's tank and billow gracefully down toward my gear shift. San Francisco was only a few miles away, and we hadn't been in the big city for a whole ten days, so I applied a little more lipstick, powdered my terra-cotta face and wished the whole effect wasn't so ruined by a peeling nose.

Now that we were so near to San Francisco I wanted to hurry for the first time since starting out. This was the first city where I had arranged to pick up my mail from home and from my fiancé in Denmark.

As the great structure of the Golden Gate Bridge loomed up I felt very thrilled, and thought that even if I had a complete breakdown and never finished the trip I could at least say that I had driven over the Golden Gate Bridge to San Francisco. But, contrary to all warnings, I parked Oppy halfway across the bridge and leapt around taking photos of her and Matelot posed against a background of Alcatraz and the massive steel girders; living proof for the folks back home.

At the toll station I was asked for forty cents and found myself in the embarrassing position of having exactly one cent in change. The policeman looked at me as though I really were trying to do the city of San Francisco out of that thirty-nine cents, so I hastily pulled over and cashed a travellers' cheque.

I had been told to avoid Market Street, especially during the evening rush hour, but while hunting for the post office I suddenly found myself caught up in this seething mass of traffic which even made Matelot sit up and take notice. Odd as it may seem, I like to drive in cities, but the first few minutes until I get the feel of a strange place are rather nerve-wracking.

San Francisco had a completely different traffic-light system from any I had seen up to then, and I nearly lost my mind as the great flow of traffic milled and jostled all around us. Oppy seemed dwarfed, hemmed in as she was on all sides by trams and buses, and my poor legs felt so vulnerable with nothing but a couple of inches between their tender skin and hard metal bumpers. Every time I put my feet down to balance, I wondered if some truck would run over them and mash my toes to a pulp.

Enormous skyscrapers towered above us (I hadn't seen New York City then) and innumerable tough-looking traffic cops blew whistles here, there and everywhere. I wondered if they were doing the slightest bit of good, because the traffic still flowed on obliviously. If one of them had whistled at me I shouldn't have known for a minute which one had done so or why.

On we crawled; but every yard or so we came to a stop, and then I had to exercise all my driving skill and concentration. Slowly we footed and wobbled our way along with an enormous bus on one side of us and a tram clanging a deafening warning from behind. I was in the right of way, but I couldn't possibly get out of the lane of traffic. And all the passengers were enjoying my predicament immensely, as they hung out of the windows and shouted advice. Every traffic-light proved an embarrassment as the crowds surged across the street in front of us, and I tried to ignore the shrieks of laughter and remarks that greeted us. Even Matelot bent his ears in shame.

Somehow I managed to squeeze my way through some madly dashing taxis and eventually found the post office. I couldn't see any legal parking space, however, so I just leaned Oppy against the kerb right opposite the entrance and left Matelot with strict instructions to bite any cop who came near him with a ticket. When I came back, staggering under a huge pile of mail, a dense crowd had gathered round Oppy, including two policemen. Matelot was busy guzzling biscuits furnished by a kind-hearted store-keeper and the two cops were scratching their heads and laughing. But I was so dying to read my mail that I excused myself from the enthusiastic crowd as quickly as possible and found my way to a nearby park.

The sun beat down on my back deliciously hot, and I sat and looked at the pile of blue air letters on my knee; six letters and a small package from Carl-Erik in Denmark and two letters from Mummy in England.

I tore open the little package and for a moment all I could see was a strip of cardboard, then I looked closer, something gleamed gold in the sunlight. I pulled at a little flap in the cardboard and out tumbled a ring—an engagement ring! It was a thrilling moment looking down at that gold band set with sapphires, which had travelled over seven thousand miles from Denmark. With it Carl-Erik had written a little note—"To remember me by when you are deep in the heart of Texas." After I had put it on my grease-stained hands I felt like rushing to the nearest beauty parlour for a manicure. Then I turned to the other six letters, preparing to enjoy myself for the next hour or so, but I was sadly mistaken.

For some time I had ignored the disturbance in the background, and the voices saying "Yes, that's her over there in blue." But the next thing

51

A Ride in the Sun

I knew a suave-looking young man came up to me, raised his immaculate trilby hat and said "Pardon me, is that your motor-cycle and dog?"

I realized my peace was at an end; still, it's always wise to co-operate with the Press, and so we all co-operated now, Oppy, Matelot and I. We did so even to the extent of practically being mown down and killed in the middle of the street for the sake of photography. And in a few minutes I was on the verge of arrest for making an illegal U turn, but the magic word "press" saved the day.

I shall always remember San Francisco as a medley of skyscrapers and waterfront, traffic cops and trams, steep hills and cable cars; sunlight streaming through the wrought ironwork of the Spanish patios and the glimpse of blue water against a cloudless sky. But most of all I think I shall remember it for the Bay Bridge.

At the entrance to the bridge there are many warnings telling you that if you run out of petrol on the bridge you will be charged five dollars for a gallon. Now, because Oppy runs around a hundred miles on a gallon, she is apt to become careless about little details like buying petrol. So that first evening in the city I was wobbling my way along through the streaming mass of cars, with the bridge in front of me swaying in the strong wind like a thistle in the breeze when Oppy suddenly stopped.

There was a shriek of brakes while I waited for the crash; none came, only black looks and muffled curses. Frantically I jumped off and whipped out my little can of spare petrol, then just as I kicked Oppy into life a wrecker came wending its way through the traffic. Now, as I shifted into first gear, I had the great satisfaction of waving my hand and saying "Too late, bud!"

Soon I was on my way south again anxious to reach the famous seventeen-mile-drive that skirts the Monterey peninsula. And I didn't regret a cent of the fifty that I gave for the privilege of using this private road. The entrance gate in old Spanish Mission style was surrounded by a mass of exquisite flower beds, and the road wound down along a rugged coastline. The water that swept over the pure white sandy beaches and dashed over the craggy finger-like rocks was blue, now green, then a swirling mass of white foam. The dark cyprus trees outlined against the sky looked like sentinels keeping guard over all this beauty. In little sandy bays lay great rocks black with birds, seals and sea lions; their noisy chorus could be heard plainly above the roar of the ocean.

After leaving the peninsula the road ahead lay for over a hundred miles of wild coastal scenery with a mere scattering of petrol stations along the way. I had been fiercely warned off this road because of its narrow hair-pin bends, steep hills and dangerous precipices. However, everyone forgot to tell me that it is probably one of the most beautiful roads in the whole of the States. I have never seen anything that appealed to me more than this spectacular highway that winds from Monterey to San Luis Obispo.

Hairpin bends are difficult to negotiate at any time, but with the distraction of the magnificent scenery our lives began to take on a suicidal edge. I wondered why it was we could drive along a rare stretch of open road without seeing another vehicle and yet on the first blind corner, there, almost as if it had been waiting for us, would appear a large and impatient Greyhound bus. It would hurl itself past our little equipage with such a snorting that the back draught nearly sent us rolling down over those fields of flowers below us. Really I can't think of a better place to end one's days, but after all Mexico beckoned and New York was just around the corner. So, in spite of the logging truckers and now the Greyhound bus drivers who wanted to hurry our days to a close, we very regretfully came to civilization once more in the form of Santa Barbara.

The last rays of the sun were just disappearing in the west, when I saw the signpost pointing to the city centre. I am afraid I thought "Well, so what? Just another town." I hope the city of Santa Barbara will forgive me. I started to bypass it, I don't know why, but something suddenly made me make a left turn and start slowly driving through the side streets.

Some places one just likes for no special reason, and that is how I felt about Santa Barbara. Perhaps it was the warm, lazy southern feel about the place, perhaps it was the Spanish-styled houses that reminded me of Seville, or the riot of flowers tumbling like weeds over the pavements, but all these things made me want to see more. And so I spent quite a long time poking around the colourful streets, when I should have been thinking about pitching my tent.

Next morning the sun poured down out of the cloudless Californian sky. My head nodded and bounced up again, while Oppy temporarily left the road and skidded along the shoulder. The combination of a large breakfast and driving in the hot sun made me drowsy, so I slowed down and leaned Oppy against a tree. By bitter experience I had learned never to keep on driving when I feel sleepy. One hot day, driving down a straight Saskatchewan road, I had felt my eyes closing and the next time I opened them I was sitting in a wheat field with Oppy on top of me.

So now I sank down on a carpet of golden flowers and closed my eyes, and Matelot went off to chase butterflies. When I woke up my face felt as though it had taken part in a sausage roast and the flowers were starting to give me violent hay fever. Matelot looked at me with reproachful eyes; it was long past lunch time and the sun showed me that the supper hour was approaching. I unstrapped the food bag and staggered down to the beach. My pocket stove still refused to work, so I shoved it to the bottom of the bag; from now on I was relying solely on the supplies of Mother Nature. A beach is always a wonderful place for an open fire because there is so much driftwood handy and no danger of forest fire. As I jumped and gasped among the huge, dashing breakers, I could see the smoke from my beach kitchen curling into the sky, the flames mingling with the heat haze across the bay. No corn on the cob ever tasted so good as those ears I ate sitting in my swim suit, letting the curling edges of the Pacific caress my toes.

Invariably I seem to arrive in cities when darkness is falling; this is very bad management for an old tent-pitcher like me. My entrance to Los Angeles was equally ill-timed, but once I had crossed the city limits I had to keep on driving across that vast city. For I have a very special complex about never turning round and retracing my steps. I won't do it for a passed camp site and even when the way ahead looks thoroughly un-inviting.

But when I found myself driving up Wiltshire Boulevard with its dazzlingly lit hotels and night clubs all practical thoughts vanished in the excitement of seeing such famous places as the Brown Derby and Ciro's. However, after I had gaped into a few fabulous-looking hotel foyers complete with swimming pools and waving palms, and goggled at a dozen exotically dressed women sweeping into equally exotic-looking restaurants, I began to get sleepy.

This really didn't look like tent-pitching country, so I just drove on aimlessly, not knowing at all where I was going. Clocks pointed to eleven o'clock, then twelve; I began to get quite depressed at the sight of endless suburbs of houses and shopping centres.

Finally I discovered a small, dark vacant stretch stuck between a large car-wash building and a tourist home. I found myself in what had once been an orange grove; the trees grew close together and they were over-grown with weeds now, but an abundance of ripe oranges hung from their stems. I only had to stretch a hand out of my tent to pick a juicy, sweet-tasting fruit. It was lovely lying there sucking oranges in my sleeping bag, while the downtown Los Angeles traffic roared past my ear. How surprised some of the pedestrians on the pavement would have been, if they had known a girl was sleeping in a tent only a few yards from where they were walking.

The car-wash next door was very noisy and woke me up long before the sun hit the roof of my tent. There seemed to be such a lot of water and soap noises coming from inside that I ventured in with my towel and toothbrush and asked for a little of each. Instead of a house and bucket, which would have been quite adequate, I was ushered into the most palatial and shining rest room, which soon made a new woman of me. As there was a lull in custom, two of the attendants got permission to take time off and insisted upon buying me breakfast. At the lunch counter across the street I munched waffles and syrup while I told Bill and Joe about our wanderings.

"Gee," said Bill, "if we'd only known you were sleeping out there, on that crumby old lot, the wife would have been tickled pink to have you over at our place."

Before I broke camp I stuffed all the spare spaces in my luggage with oranges, because I wasn't sure when I'd be getting so much free orange juice again.

The three days driving in San Francisco had hardened me to the dense city traffic, so that we spun around the centre of Los Angeles, dodging taxis and suicidal motorists without a care in the world.

A Ride in the Sun

First I had to go to the British Consul to have my passport endorsed for Mexico. Quite forgetting the slightly more reserved manners of my fellow countrymen, I poked my head round the door and said "Hi!" My reception was slightly frigid, but perhaps I was a rather sorry-looking subject of Her Majesty, with my sunburned face and windswept hair.

Now the week-end stretched before me, because I couldn't pick up my visa for Mexico until Monday. I was wandering along that evening wondering whether I should go back to my city site, or head out for some attractive place like Malibu Beach, when a maroon Ford drew up alongside us. A dark face with shining teeth and intelligent eyes smiled out at me.

"I wish you would pull over a minute," said the young Negro who addressed me. "You know," he went on as I came to a stop by the kerb, "my wife and I have been feeling quite guilty sitting here in the comfort of our car, and watching you blow along the dusty highway on that little bike. Isn't it awfully uncomfortable and difficult to drive?"

"Well, sometimes," I admitted, "but I wouldn't change it for a hundred cars."

It wasn't long before Bernice and Pat had found out that I was looking for a camping spot, and they chorused an invitation for Matelot and me to stay with them for the weekend.

"Matelot can keep Curly, our spaniel, company, while we take you to a concert at the Hollywood Bowl tonight," smiled Bernice.

I followed Pat's car until we came to a suburb of Hollywood, and presently the Ford drew up outside a pretty brick bungalow surrounded by a wide green lawn.

After I had changed into a clean dress and nylons, we had supper and then hurried into the car and drove to the famous outdoor amphitheatre.

Climbing up the path to our seats amid the first strains of a Rossini overture, I felt transported to another world. The music drifted up to us from the symphony orchestra seated far below us on the platform built into a half bowl shape, which was lit by soft blue lighting. And later a lovely Brahms symphony mingled with the warm night air and the stars in the dark sky above us.

Soon after the concert I tumbled in between cool green sheets with the lovely evening's music still sounding in my ears. However, a different sound woke me in the middle of the night. There was a faint rumbling noise and my bed seemed to be rocking.

"Shut up, Matelot," I hissed, thinking he was scratching himself against the bed.

Matelot got up from the centre of the carpet and regarded me inquiringly. Now other things in the room began moving; the light in the centre of the ceiling was swaying dangerously over my head. A couple of pictures slipped crooked, the house shuddered faintly. Vaguely I wondered if they were testing atom bombs out on the desert, but then as the whole foundations of the house seemed to tremble again, I realized what it really was.

"Guess I've been in an earthquake," I said to myself; "I mustn't forget to ask Bernice about it in the morning."

CHAPTER VII *Last Days by the Pacific*

EARLY next morning we were all gathered outside on the pavement discussing the earthquake damage. Our next-door neighbours had a slight crack in one of their ceilings, while our sitting-room chandelier seemed to be permanently crooked. When I saw some of the splits in the concrete pavement I was very glad that I hadn't been sleeping on the ground. Camping with the ground beneath me rumbling and trembling might have proved rather too terrifying.

Bernice was still suffering from the after effects of the rather alarming experiences of the night, so Pat took over in the kitchen. He donned an enormous white apron and proved himself to be an excellent cook. And in no time at all we were sitting down to a hearty breakfast of bacon and golden-brown pancakes. Then we spent most of the day lazing around in the comfortable living room, with everybody doing exactly as he liked. Pat played me a lot of his records and then sang a couple of songs, which he told me he used when singing professionally. But for his everyday bread-and-butter he admitted he was a music teacher in one of the Los Angeles public schools. Bernice was also a teacher and we found many interests in common.

But I am afraid that from the moment I discovered Pat's tape recording machine, I became the rudest of house guests. Earlier I had written a long letter to Carl-Erik, and now Pat suggested I put it on tape. I didn't need a second invitation; here was an opportunity to return a similar voice message to that I had received from Denmark in the spring. Finally, four hours later, I staggered out of the bedroom having satisfactorily recorded one hour of my voice, and vowing that I would never go through the ordeal again.

After that I felt like some fresh air and decided to see a little more of the city. I set out late in the afternoon having agreed to be back later on in the evening. I quite forgot how widely Los Angeles is scattered, and it was a long time before I bothered to stop and ask the way back to where I was staying. Then, from a population of over two million inhabitants, I had to pick a complete idiot who directed me to the east side of the city instead of the west. Unknowingly I drove on and on, right through the centre, until the hour drew late and the streets began to take on a very shabby and sinister appearance.

When I stopped to ask the way again, I realized what a rough-looking neighbourhood I was in; several drunks shufflled by and a tramp crouched in a dark doorway opposite. A car pulled up behind me, so I hopped off Oppy and went around to the driver's window. Before I could open my mouth he said,

"I was just about to stop you to find out what you're doing down here. I've been following you for the last ten blocks." The speaker proved to be a serious young city cop.

"I guess I'm lost, I'm trying to get back to my friends who live on the west side."

"I'll say you're lost! Don't you realize you're in the middle of Skid Row?"

"But I always feel safe enough so long as I have my motor ticking away under me and Matelot here breathing down my neck," I insisted.

"You've got more nerve than I, but if you'd seen some of the things that happen down here you might change your mind. Right now, though, I'll tell you how to get to your friends' place, and I'll follow you for a few blocks to see that you don't get lost again." Then he handed me a small card. On one side of it was printed "Los Angeles Police Department" and underneath—"Presented by Sgt. A. L. Erickson." I turned the card over and found detailed directions to Pat and Bernice's house, and a small plan of Los Angeles!

When I finally reached that quiet Hollywood suburb, I had to stand up to a great deal of teasing. "We never thought a girl who had found her way across fifteen thousand miles of this continent would ever get lost right here in Los Angeles," laughed Bernice.

Next morning the Ford accompanied me across the city and out on to the ocean highway, and then once again I was saying goodbye to two wonderfully kind people. Soon we were spinning along by the Pacific again; the wind was with us and the sun poured down across my bare back, deliciously hot. This was the last stretch of our trip beside the ocean. After this we would turn east into the burning heat of the southern California desert. So now, wanting to make the most of these lovely, tempestuous waters that I had grown to love, I drove slowly and lingeringly along the coastline.

The lovely blue Pacific! She had been my bathroom when I was dirty, my swimming pool when I was hot; her shores had been my kitchen and on her cliffs I'd laid my head. Now, as I drove along, her cooling waters beckoned to me a dozen times. After swimming, I lay on the golden beach until my skin turned a copper shade beneath the blazing sun and salt winds. It was a perfect, lazy day and so I only drove about seventy-five miles, which brought us just north of a small town called Oceanside. San Diego was only a few miles away, but I felt my mail would have to wait one more day.

I found a rather narrow strip of cliff space for the tent. It was very near the edge of the highway. Still, the view was so wonderful that I took a chance on a truck skidding into our encampment from the shoulder of the road. I was struggling to raise my tent in the strong wind, when an old man, carrying two enormous long fishing rods, passed me on his way to the beach. He was wearing a pair of ancient blue jeans rolled above his ankles, a moth-eaten T-shirt and battered cap.

"Want to come fishing?" he asked.

This sounded like great fun, because I had never fished in my life, and I had nothing special to eat for supper. So I dropped everything and followed him down to the beach. I was surprised to learn that he spent practically the whole night standing on the shore, casting his line into the ocean.

"Generally the wife comes too," he explained, "but tonight she's got a bad back."

Well, I'm sure that if I were almost seventy-five years old and spent the best part of every night standing on the beach holding a long fishing rod, I should have worse than a bad back! Anyway, I took off my sandals, hitched up my skirts and waded into the warm, lapping surf, beside the fisherman.

He gave a mighty sweep with his arm, then away went the bait and line into the swirling waters. "Here you are," he said handing me the rod.

I took it rather gingerly wondering what on earth I should do if something like a man-eating shark started biting. I had seen people madly winding a little wheel on the edge of the rod, their two feet firmly planted on the ground, and gradually reeling in a mighty prize towards them. However, I was certain that if this happened to me I should be swept off my feet and carried out to sea, line, rod and all. Evidently my companion had full faith in me, because he was busy baiting his second rod. He looked rather like a picture I had seen of Babe Ruth batting, as he swung around with far more grace and energy than seventy-five years usually permits.

Apparently I lacked both the expert touch and beginner's luck, because I just stood there in the water holding my lifeless rod until my arms ached and I became thoroughly bored with the idea of fishing for my supper.

The sun sank behind the horizon, bathing the beach in pink and orange light; and the sky turned from blue to pink, and pink to deep purple. The light faded and the stars began to peep through above us. I was surprised to find that the beach was now full of other enthusiastic fishermen, who apparently carried on this sport far into the early hours of the morning. Below us someone had lighted a fire on the beach, and the bright flames shot up into the darkness, disclosing a happy supper party. My line was quite dead, but suddenly there was an excited whoop from my old friend.

He was dancing around like a two-year-old, pulling in his line and yelling hysterically, "Come on, baby, come on!"

I was completely useless, I could only stand and stare until "baby" finally came to rest on the shore, gasping her last fishy breath.

"There you are, young lady, go get your supper," said a very breathless but triumphant old man.

Happily I built a fire of driftwood and went to fetch my frying pan. No fish tastes so wonderful as when it is transferred from ocean to frying pan all within five minutes, and eaten beneath a warm, starry sky round an open fire. Even the Waldorf Astoria could not have provided a better supper than this. I was alone with my delicacy, because the fish were still biting fast and furiously and because my fisherman said he only liked to catch them.

"Can't stand the taste of fish," he explained. Finally I left him there still standing in the dark waters swinging his rod with the grace of a ballet dancer.

My camping ground was hard and dry and covered with large rocks. I removed enough of these for my tent space and then started to struggle in the dark with the flapping, unruly canvas. I got the two tent poles in position, but when it came to securing the canvas walls, no amount of pounding would drive the pegs into the hard rocky ground. And after the horrible thing had fallen down for about the tenth time I just gave up.

Pushing a grunting Matelot further to the edge of his ground sheet, I unrolled my sleeping bag. It was really too warm for any covering, my bag merely served as a protection against exposure to the roaring night traffic in my pyjamas. It was marvellous lying there under the stars, the wind tearing at my hair and the ocean crashing on the dark shore below.

A Ride in the Sun

The first light of the dawn woke me up and once again I found myself in the embarrassing situation of being so near to the edge of the road that getting into my clothes was going to be almost an impossibility. Luckily a lull in traffic allowed me to wriggle around in my bag like a caterpillar in a cocoon. If I had thought it was difficult to dress in my little tent, the sleeping-bag ordeal was a hundred times worse! Just as I pulled my dress over my head, a fast truck appeared on the road. I pulled bag and everything else within reach over my head and tried to look like a sleeping male. In such situations Oppy's presence always helps, because nobody ever connects a motor-cycle with a girl. And now a cloud of dust from the shoulder of the road covered my prostrate form, and the truck passed on its way with a mighty roar.

That morning I didn't feel like getting soot black all over again from a wood fire, so I decided to cook breakfast on the new stove Pat had given me in Los Angeles. I am usually terrified of petrol stoves, because I'm afraid they'll blow up in my face. However, this type was supposed to be safe. It had been tested by G.I.s who had tossed it from fox-hole to fox-hole, with no explosions and no threat of fire even when it overturned.

Still, I followed the directions very carefully now, pumping in air to the right pressure, and then holding my breath as I struck a match near the wick. Orange flames leapt into the air, and so did Matelot; we seemed to be in for a grass fire. But presently the orange flames subsided and a steady blue one settled down to a steady hissing.

My water boiled so quickly that I decided to heat up some more for my face and make myself really respectable for San Diego. I was in the middle of scrubbing my teeth and spitting vigorously into a nearby bush, when I caught the fascinated gaze of two young hitch hikers on the road opposite. At that point it was much too late to think about modesty, so I went ahead with my full morning's toilet. In Oppy's rear-view mirror I cleaned away the dust which had been flung on my face all night, while the two youths let car after car pass them by without so much as raising a thumb. By the time I had reached the lipstick and comb stage, I think they were trying to decide whether they dared cross the road to get a better view.

Then as I cleaned my shoes I began to feel directly responsible for their probable late arrival in Los Angeles, or wherever they were going. But the repacking of Oppy is always quite a long job, even with all the practice I had had then, so when I looked up next my interested pair had finally disappeared on their way.

I had been given a great deal of advice about driving across the desert lands of California and Arizona, and I had sifted it into three categories; exaggerated, helpful and obvious.

"Exaggerated" were the statements that I wouldn't find petrol stations or water for two hundred miles at a stretch, that my little engine and tyres would never stand the heat, and that I would collapse physically, and in all probability mentally too, from the hot sun rays of July.

"Helpful" was the suggestion to wear something on my head and not have Matelot clipped, because his coat would help insulate him against the heat.

"Obvious" was the advice to drive at night if the heat became too unbearable.

I decided now to leave the coast and head into the desert in the early evening, thus missing the hottest time of the day. And after collecting my mail in San Diego I headed for Mission Bay to spend my last day by the Pacific.

There I enjoyed a delightfully lazy afternoon and about five thirty I called to Matelot that we were going. When we got back to Oppy I found several firemen in uniform standing around her in an admiring circle. A young man with a shock of fair hair addressed me just as I started hunting around for my towel.

"Say, I suppose you wouldn't like to come in and have supper with us," he waved a hand at the fire station across the road, and added, "We've asked the chief, it's O.K. with him; and we'd sure love to have you."

"I'm not exactly dressed for visiting," I laughed, looking down at my dripping swim suit.

"Well, bring your things over and you can change in our shower room," suggested another fireman.

Jack, the fair-haired boy, had just shown me the way to the shower, when a bell rang suddenly, someone yelled, "This is it, boys," there was a mad scramble, and then away raced the fire engine, with all the firemen hanging aboard and the siren screeching and whining its warning.

After I had finished changing into my prettiest skirt and blouse in honour of my dinner date, I took advantage of the endless hot water supply to wash out a few dirty clothes. I wondered what a visiting fire chief would have said at the sight of these feminine garments hanging in the backyard of an all-male fire house!

A delicious smell was coming from the kitchen, and I hoped that the cook hadn't answered the fire call too. However, the kitchen proved to be deserted, so I poked my head into the oven of the stove to see how things were coming along. Fortunately everything was under control.

The next minute there was a roar, a screech of brakes and all the boys reappeared. Soon the kitchen was filled with a noisy bunch of firemen all eager to play the perfect hosts. I sat with the chief on my right and Jack on the left, and the other four men grouped themselves round the table. We had a sizzling hot roast with baked potatoes, peas and my favourite, corn-on-the-cob. I found this a rather hot menu with the temperature in the nineties, but like a camel I often eat with a view to the future, so I gladly accepted "seconds."

The best meals on my trip seem to have been cooked by men, and the firemen's corn bread certainly put to shame my tin-opener cooking, although really my steady diet of Boston baked beans was an economy measure.

Just as the boys and I were about to start on a cooling dessert of ice cream and home-made cake, the bell went again.

"Put the ice cream in the frig, honey," they cried as they grabbed their fire-proof coats and scrambled aboard the engine once more. More sounds of shrieking sirens and skidding tyres, and again I was left in the silent kitchen. I busied myself packing away the ice cream, and then cleared up all the dirty dishes. I was just wiping the last plate, when all the gang came trooping back.

"Guess we'll have to invite a gal to supper every night so we'll get our dishes done," laughed the chief.

We sat over coffee a long time and I listened to many of their funny and tragic stories of fires. They made my hair stand on end with some of their tales of blazing buildings and daring rescues.

After I had completed a tour of inspection of the whole fire house and admired the shining red monster of an engine with all its brass and chrome, the hour was far too late to start out across the desert. Jack said that he knew just the place for my tent, and told me how to get there. So after I had packed away my freshly laundered clothes, and thanked everybody for such a lovely evening, I left amid a wave of goodbyes from my six gallant hosts.

Following Jack's directions, I found myself in a beautiful park with soft green lawns which sloped down to the edge of a lake. Across the water shone the twinkling lights of San Diego, and the night was warm and friendly. The spot was so perfect that before I found a notice saying "No Camping Allowed" I hurriedly threw up the tent and hopped inside. Next morning I awoke to a very liquid pattering on my tent. It seemed hardly possible that it would rain at that time of year in San Diego, but the gentle sound persisted. When I finally looked out I found a large garden spray playing merrily over the tent, while poor Oppy seemed positively drowned. A Mexican gardener, in a large straw sombrero, was looking daggers at me, hoping to force me to evacuate. I obliged him by breakfasting on the lake shore so he could water the last little spot on his precious lawn.

It was unbearably hot as I wended my way through San Diego's main street. Oppy was pulling a very heavy load, since I had just stocked up on food after one of my much too enthusiastic shopping sprees. When my rear wheel first started to wobble, I thought this was due to the extra weight, but finally my knowledge of Oppy's peculiarities warned me that this was something quite new. The sun was beating down on my bare back unmercifully, and beads of sweat covered my face, as I knelt in the gutter and tried to peer underneath all the luggage to see what was wrong.

The back wheel seemed to be out of line, but axle nuts holding it in position were absolutely tight, so I guessed that a bearing must have worn. Thanking my lucky stars that this had happened then, and not in the middle of the desert, I wobbled my way along to the motor-cycle shop. The whole wheel proved to be in a poor shape, and if I had been in my right mind I would have bought a new complete one then and there. For after all Oppy was pulling a load three times her own weight, and all the wear was centred on this one area.

A new bearing and a few new spokes were fitted, and I vowed to buy a new wheel when I got to Mexico City, and didn't mind spending the time waiting for the repair to be done. Up to then I had never liked cola drinks, but that day in San Diego, sitting in the breathless heat of the motor-cycle shop, I drank bottle after bottle of this gassy beverage. I never quenched my thirst and the sweat poured off me in a most uncomfortable fashion. Next door was a butcher's shop, and Matelot fared much better than I. He lay in the shadow of an awning and gnawed bones to his heart's delight.

By the time we were ready for the road again the sun was high in the sky and the heat was at its height. I deposited a sticky, sweaty letter to Carl-Erik at the post office, and it was here that I met David mailing a huge stack of envelopes.

A slight man in his late thirties, he introduced himself and Miriam, his pretty dark-haired wife, and their many kids who were hanging out the windows chuckling at Matelot and Oppy.

"I don't know how you can stand being out in this heat without a hat! You do look so warm. Why don't you come back to the house and take a cold shower?" asked Miriam.

I accepted gladly and once more I found myself following a car of unknown but hospitable folk.

I could hardly bear to turn off the taps and stop the lovely spray of cooling water seeping over me, but the cry "Supper's ready" brought an end to my shower. The meal was delicious, particularly the dessert of chocolate layer cake, baked jointly by Miriam and David. I even packed a large hunk of it to take along with me. It's fun to eat on a motor-cycle, and I thought chocolate cake and a cooling night breeze would go very well together. At least, I hoped there would be a cooling breeze, because there was no escaping the desert now.

CHAPTER VIII *The Desert*

FOR the first time Oppy was heading due east, and ahead of us lay over a thousand miles of desert and the vast Texan ranges, until once more we would turn south and into Mexico.

At least I hoped we would, but after the verdict on Oppy's slightly sick wheel, I was beginning to wonder whether we would even see Mexico City! Turning my back on San Diego meant we wouldn't find another motor-cycle dealer carrying B.S.A. parts until we reached El Paso, Texas, more than six hundred miles away.

However, I am an eternal optimist, so I gave it only a passing thought and concentrated on enjoying the night about me. I felt as though I were already in the tropics, the air was so warm, and the sky was quite light and carpeted with stars.

It was the first time the weather had been warm enough after dark for me to drive in my sun dress. As the road sloped gently upwards, I looked back at the lights of San Diego, knowing that this was my last view of the Pacific Ocean.

Presently I passed an open-air film show and from pure curiosity bumped Oppy down a side lane and across a field nearby to have a look. Without paying a cent I sat down on the grass and watched the antics of Danny Kaye, and even toyed with the idea of pitching my tent right there and enjoying a free show for the rest of the evening.

The field, however, was rather a long way from the highway, and somehow it gave me the creeps. Occasionally, for no reason at all, I get a strange feeling about places and then I would prefer to drive all night rather than stop and camp. But now I was dead tired from the heat of the day and I didn't dare drive much farther for fear of going to sleep.

I had just got back on the highway and was calling Matelot to hurry up, when a motor-cycle cop stopped and asked if I was in trouble. In turn I asked him if he knew of any likely camping site. He expressed the usual disapproval of a woman camping alone, then after his little lecture he strongly advised me to go to a small civic park about ten miles up the road.

Twice I passed the entrance to this park, but finally with the help of a petrol station attendant, I found a small wooded area surrounding a dark, unlit house. There were several picnic tables and seats scattered beneath the trees; otherwise I would have mistaken it for somebody's private backyard.

Straightway I slung up the tent, inflated my air mattress and lay down on top of it, using my sleeping bag as a pillow. Now that I was stationary the night felt breathlessly hot and I could hardly sleep. The tent flaps were open, but only a hot stifling breeze came through the mosquito netting. However, nothing ever troubles Matelot's rest. As soon as the tent was half up he crawled in and arranged himself on his side of the canvas floor. Long before I was in my pyjamas he was curled up and sleeping peacefully.

After a time a dazzling light shone in my face and I opened my eyes with a start. I had no idea how clearly the inside of my tent could be seen, so I tucked my head down lower and kept quiet. The headlights of a car played over the tent and then a rough male voice said, "Look here, young fellows, camping is forbidden in this park. I'm the caretaker, and what the devil do you think you're doing here?" I unbuttoned the mosquito netting, Matelot stuck out a hairy paw, and I followed him with my sleepy face. "I'm terribly sorry," I stammered piteously, "but I have to sleep somewhere and we'll be away at the crack of dawn, really we will."

There was a stifled exclamation and the rough voice became gentle. "Say, lady, I sure am sorry I disturbed you, just you stay there as long as you like. Gee whiz! a girl in a tent . . ." his voice trailed off.

"Dad, did you see that big dog and the motor-cycle? Jeepers!" said a small voice obviously that of a child.

"Ssh! son, let the gal get some rest."

The headlights were switched off and the car backed quietly away. Once more we slept.

I thought I was up early next morning, but I was beaten to it by a small freckle-faced boy who bombarded me with a torrent of questions. While

I broke camp I recounted the life history of Oppy, Matelot and myself, until the small face in front of me shone with excitement.

"Jeepers!" he said, "you ought to be in the funnies, you're almost as brave as Hopalong Cassidy." I thought that was quite the nicest and most genuine compliment that any American male has ever paid me.

Matelot and I were just ready to hit the road when Dad appeared. He was a tall, red-haired, large edition of Tommy, but much more nervous of this strange girl to whom he had been so rude.

"Coffee is just perking," he said. "It sure would be a pleasure if you'd come in and have breakfast with us."

I told him I would love to, and we entered a small, neat kitchen and sat down at the wide table neatly set with three places.

"Afraid it won't be very fancy," my host apologized. "There's just the boy and me."

Then, for the benefit of Dad and the delight of Tommy, I had to repeat our adventures all over again.

"You sure do make our life seem dull," said Dad, then turning to his son he added, "How about you and me, Tommy, buying us a motor-cycle and heading back east? Wouldn't that be something!"

"Jeepers! Oh, Dad, Jeepers!" was all that round-eyed little Tommy could say.

After breakfast I waved goodbye to the tall figure of Dad and the smaller one at his side, and set off up the road. It began to climb slowly but steadily away from the farm land and grassy hillsides, and the scenery began to take on a harder, rougher appearance. I looked out across rugged hills of loose boulder and rock, and presently those hills turned into low mountains and the road became steeper. Down in the valley we had endured a temperature of nearly a hundred degrees, and now as we climbed steadily the air became slightly cooler, until it was quite bearable to stop without first looking for some shade.

The perfect spot for lunch proved to be on the crest of a long steep hill. I looked out across a wide, deep valley, away beyond to range after range of humped-back mountains; mountains which form the natural frontier between the United States and Mexico. They looked dry and arid and not a bit like the cool, majestic peaks of Washington. The change in scenery was so exciting that I didn't miss the ocean as much as I expected.

Both our water bottles were empty now, and to guard against thirst in the middle of the desert, and against having our bones picked dry by vultures, I started driving up the road to where a notice said "Drinking Fountain—100 yards." Matelot led the way, refusing to be caught and made to ride on Oppy. He needed good daily exercise, so if the poor fool wanted to run a hundred yards uphill in the heat, I thought I might as well let him do so. We pulled in beside the little mountain spring that was gushing down the steep rockface, and I was just filling my first water bottle, when a loud and disagreeable voice said, "You'd better get the hell out of here before I call the cops."

Looking round to see who had spoken, I saw a fat, elderly man with wild eyes and a dirty torn undershirt leaning out of an ancient model T Ford.

"I beg your pardon, but are you talking to me?" I asked in my best hoity-toity English manner.

"You heard me. Get going and run that poor animal some more in the heat until he drops—I'll have the cops after you, don't worry."

By this time two car loads of tourists were goggling out of their windows, open-mouthed.

"My home is about seven thousand miles away! Do you really think a dog could run that far, including a swim across the Atlantic Ocean?" I laughed, and went on filling my water bottles.

Matelot, however, decided to speak for himself; he wasn't going to let his mistress be insulted. To the rescue he flew, and the obvious victim of his attack was a snarling, yappy terrier, equally as bad-tempered as his master.

For the first time in his life Matelot had a fight, and I let him go right ahead and enjoy it. His thick curly coat was almost impregnable from attack and his sharp, white teeth snapped in the air trying to find a hunk of yapping terrier.

But when my fellow dog lover picked up a large rock and started to aim it at Matelot, I thought it was time to intervene. Diving into the seething, snarling mass of fangs, paws and fur, I seized Matelot by the base of his strong, stocky tail and yanked him clear. The white terrier still hung on, his jaws firmly locked in Matelot's curly coat; and only when the rock came flying past, just missing his thin white ear, did he relinquish his grip.

Then I dumped Matelot on to Oppy, turned my back and hurriedly shoved the water bottles in place, all the time expecting a rock to come flying at my head. The air was still blue with profanity, and the two sets of tourists let in their clutches and drove away.

I never looked back, but I think there were a few drops of scattered blood on the ground, and it certainly wasn't Matelot's blood.

We soon reached the town of Jacumba, which wasn't only Mexican in name but full of border atmosphere and colour as well. Mexico itself was only a few miles to the south, although there was no actual road leading across the frontier at this point. The streets of the town were crowded with real Mexican types—dark and fierce of face and wearing enormous straw sombreros. They squatted in the shade along the pavements. Why this painful-looking position didn't cut off their blood circulation after a couple of hours of crouching I have no idea, but I suppose they learn the habit young. Anyway they squatted contentedly on their haunches, buried beneath their outsize hats and gay-coloured blankets and looking for all the world like extras from a Hollywood Mexican melodrama.

Now we entered a great arid plain with a view of mile upon mile of scrub land and dry earth. If this is the desert, I thought, where on earth was the unending sea of sand that I'd been told about? I was quite disappointed not to be burning to a crisp and pulling at my water bottle every half mile. Having prepared myself for the worst, I felt let down. Again we started to climb and all around us towered loose rocky cliffs and gigantic boulders.

A car passed us and stopped just ahead; three heads poked out of the windows. Herb, a greying man in his early forties, introduced himself, as well as the couple in the back of the car.

"Follow me," he said, "I'm going to show you something real beautiful," and started off down the road. After a few miles we turned into what had been part of the old highway, and an additional hundred yards brought us to a café built in low, rambling Spanish style. "Welcome to Desert View Café," said Herb, and after showing me where to leave Oppy he urged me to follow him.

We picked our way over the boulders and large rocks to where a high tower, built of rough stones, was standing. All at once I looked to the east and the scene that caught my eyes was an overwhelming surprise. As far as the eye could see was a rolling landscape of golden desert. Before us it stretched, like an unending ocean of sand, and banked by a craggy range of mountains to the north.

"You haven't seen anything yet," promised Herb.

The last of the tourists were just leaving the tower, but the caretaker was Herb's friend, so he let us sneak up. We climbed the narrow stone stairs which brought us out into a large circular room.

"Now," said Herb, "what do you think of that?" and he waved his hand toward one of the windows cut out of the stone wall.

The view was really magnificent. The sun had already disappeared behind the mountains to the west of us, and the great sea of desert that stretched in front of us—as far as time, it seemed—was bathed in exquisite shades of pink blue and purple.

There was this same unending vista of desert to the east, while to the north lay a great mountain range tinted to the pale rose hue of evening. Directly below us lay the highway, winding and twisting its way through the rocky canyon, away down to where the desert began. The scene before us was an ever-changing kaleidoscope of colours, and I began to think that perhaps sunset over the desert was almost more beautiful than the sight of the sun sinking across the ocean.

As the last shadow faded I could distinguish, very faintly, the twinkling lights of El Centro, a small city situated in the middle of the desert to the east. It lay surrounded on all sides by flat, dry desert and had a reputation of being one of the hottest spots in the United States.

When we came down from the tower the caretaker was waiting to ask me if I would like to see his house, which he said was rather unusual. This proved to be an understatement, for it certainly was a fascinating place and very practical for the hot climate. Built right against the entrance to a large cave, the kitchen ceiling, walls and floor were entirely of solid rock. And surprisingly enough a power lead ran from the café, making possible such conveniences as an electric stove and lighting. A refrigerator was hardly necessary, because the temperature was kept beautifully cool by the natural rock face. Bright saucepans hung from the walls and gay Indian rugs covered the floor. The living room and bedroom were built only part against the rock, the outer wall consisting of man-made flagstones. The furniture was delicately carved from white pine, and the caretaker admitted to me that building and carving were his hobbies. The lovely paintings of desert scenes hanging on the walls were his wife's work. It was really the most intriguing three-roomed house that I have ever seen.

Then as Herb and I picked our way back over the boulders to the café he said, "I hope you like Italian food?"

It seems that he had recently bought this restaurant and, deciding to have a little fling before opening it to the public, had invited several friends and their children, up from San Diego for a visit. We were a merry party sitting on the porch in the warm night air and sipping delectable Italian white wine. Herb would allow no woman in his kitchen, and even his spaghetti sauce recipe was a jealously guarded secret. When we finally sat round the big table to eat, I could well understand Herb's pride in his cooking; it really was a magnificent meal. And I hadn't tasted such choice wine since I lived in France; but perhaps everything was extra delicious because we were such a gay and happy party.

It seemed so strange that one minute I was bowling down the hot, dusty highway alone, and then all at once I was here laughing and talking with people who acted like old friends.

"No, we're not going to let you go tonight," protested everybody, when I mentioned that I must be on my way. And finally, after considerable discussion, it was arranged that I should set off just before dawn next morning, which would give me about three hours driving before the intense heat of the day.

Then a terrific argument started as to where I should sleep, everybody was shuffling everybody else's children and husbands around, to try and find some bed space for me. This time I held firm, and insisted on sleeping outdoors on my air mattress.

So, after saying my thanks to Herb and wishing goodnight and goodbye to his friends, I pulled my air mattress to the edge of the rocky canyon, where I could look out over the dark desert at the lights of El Centro. Then I took off my sandals and lay down in my cotton dress. The stars above shone like bright sequins in the midnight sky; far away I heard the cry of a coyote, and Matelot stirred at my feet.

The night was hot and the sky too clear and light for restful sleep. I dozed fitfully until I saw the first pale light of dawn stealing over the horizon. Then, washing my face under a garden hose, I packed Oppy as quickly as possible.

The pale glow of the coming sun was just creeping across the sky as I pushed off quietly on to the desert highway. Hopping aboard, I slipped into first gear and let out my clutch gently. The engine picked up, and then away we went down the steep winding hill. Round and round we sailed through the rocky canyon, the cliffs and great boulders enclosing us on either side.

The downward slope seemed unending, so I shut off the motor and glided along silently. A delicious warm wind wafted through my thin dress, and it felt like heaven after the hot night.

Losing height steadily, we covered over ten miles through this rough and rugged country; the half light gave the boulders and rocks weird and wonderful shapes, and I felt as though I were dreaming all this. Then on to the desert we rode; the loose rocks and steep cliffs were left behind, and all around us was flat sandy ground scattered with barren scrub. It was like riding into a rainbow; all across the desert were reflected the gorgeous colours of the rising sun.

Then suddenly the sun burst across the horizon, almost blinding me with its light, as it shone directly into my eyes. The road was straight and monotonous for mile after mile, until all at once the dry, arid desert land stopped abruptly and on either side of the road lay miles of green, fertile fields. A great deal of this desert land had been reclaimed by irrigation and turned into fertile soil. All the year round it grows rich, thriving crops and is actually called the Salad Bowl of the United States.

El Centro was asleep when Matelot and I rode through its deserted streets and out on to the dry desert once more. By this time I was beginning to get terribly sleepy with the sun shining in my face and from lack of sleep, so when I saw a small wayside café I pulled in for coffee. It was only seven o'clock as I came out into the bright sunshine again, but already the sun was scorching my face, and my nose had started to peel again. So I covered all my exposed skin with cream, pulled the brim of my cap further down over my eyes and set off once more. The sun beat down like a furnace, but as long as I kept moving it was bearable. Soon the stunted scrubs disappeared and all I could see on every side of me was an unending vista of sand; dry, fine yellow sand. It lay in small hillocks, its surface rippled like ocean waves; clouds of it drifted over the road, and I was sometimes blinded for seconds at a time. The sand clung to my sticky face, scratched against my sun glasses and covered poor Matelot until he put a protesting paw up to his sore eyes. I stopped and hunted around until I found his goggles, for which he was most grateful.

The day before the temperature had been at a hundred and thirty degrees in El Centro and that's exactly how hot I felt as I approached a tiny oasis, consisting of a few waving date palms and a spring of water. The feel of the shade from the trees was wonderful and the water tasted like vintage champagne. Matelot just lay down right in the middle of the overflow puddle and drank every drop in sight.

Then we were negotiating a particularly unpleasant bit of road, with drifting sand in both directions, when it happened—we stopped dead. Oppy was out of petrol! A worse place for this to happen I can't imgaine. The sun was pouring down and I could hardly bear to stand still under its burning rays. Then I remembered having passed a deserted-looking petrol station about five miles back. I didn't dare take the chance of going on any further, but decided to go back and see if this place was possibly open. My emergency tin of petrol was good for about fifteen miles, so we reached the station in safety.

The small wooden building was falling apart and all the windows were barred. I hallooed but got no reply. Then I tried the door and found it was locked. Inspection of the petrol pump proved much more hopeful; there was a definite and cheerful aroma of petrol. So I investigated a little further and reached up for the hose.

At that moment the door of the building flew open and the most amazing character shuffled out. Buried beneath an enormous tattered hat was the gnarled brown face of an old Indian woman. She wore a pair of outsize baggy trousers from which protruded dusty bare feet. Silently she filled my tank, giving me suspicious dark glances as she did so. I counted the money into her outstretched hand and I really expected her to spit on it to see if it was counterfeit.

Soon after this we crossed the Colorado river and passed an enormous notice saying "Welcome to Arizona." The State line fruit control inspectors here were much more trusting than the Californian ones.

When I swore that I was carrying no blighted oranges from the San Fernando valley they nonchalantly waved me on my way.

Almost every second house in Yuma was advertising "Quick, cheap but binding marriages." Bold and eye-catching lettering assured me that I could be married in English or Spanish, while another sign promised me changing rooms and refined music. A less romantic wedding atmosphere I cannot imagine! The whole place looked like the fair ground of a cheap carnival show.

By this time I was beginning to feel quite limp from the heat and I knew that I couldn't drive another mile. I decided to find some shade and wait for the cool of the day to arrive. In a small park I lay down under a tree in the shade. Poor Matelot dug himself a large hole and lay panting, until I thought his heart would give out. His long pink tongue hung from his jaw, dripping, and his eyes gazed at me as much as to say, "Why did you bring us into this hell hole?" I longed to sleep myself, but it was impossible to do anything but lie and sweat and pray for the cool of the evening.

As I shifted around to get away from the penetrating sun rays, I tried to think of cool things like ski-ing in the Canadian mountains, driving through the rain, and plates of ice cream. Actually the ice cream was close at hand, but I didn't have energy enough to move. The time was only about eleven in the morning and it would still be awfully hot for at least another six hours. I wondered whether boredom wouldn't force me to take to the road again, heat or no heat. Apparently I had dozed off, when a frightful racket woke me up. Four very noisy, brightly painted motor-cycles were gathered round Oppy, and four young men were searching for her owner. I put my head down and tried to sleep again. But four pairs of boots on the grass close by made it impossible for me to ignore my motor-cycle compatriots any longer, so I sat up and said "Hi!"

A tall young fellow with a crew cut, tight western jeans and high-topped boots addressed me, "We were looking around everywhere for a fellow, but when we saw your purse hung on the handlebars of the machine we realized the owner must be a girl."

Then they told me that they were in the Air Force and because of the heat didn't work long during the day. We sat and talked motor-cycles for several hours, which helped me to forget the sweltering heat. Lee, a good-looking young sergeant from Chicago, depressed me by saying that the very peak of the heat would be about five in the evening, so my idea of starting off about that time seemed impossible.

After a while the three other boys drifted away, but Lee stayed and asked me if I'd like to go and get something cool to drink. When we entered the air-conditioned restaurant the difference in temperature was shocking. With my dress soaked in perspiration and beads of sweat rolling down my face, I felt almost chilled now.

By the time I had gulped down my second iced coffee I felt more normal again, and cursed myself for not having thought of spending the whole day in an air-conditioned café or cinema. However, I would have felt rather guilty, because this would have left poor Matelot to suffer all by himself.

After we had finished our coffee, Lee said he would like to ride a few miles up the road with us, so at seven o'clock, with the thermometer outside the café still registering a hundred and twenty degrees, we set off across the desert.

The road to the east lay straight and unending across the sandy wastes which were scattered with scrubs and stunted cactus growth. I led the way, setting a modest pace, and Lee followed on his larger, powerful machine. He had difficulty driving so slowly, for his engine tended to overheat in low gear, and the hot air around us made it even worse. The atmosphere seemed to rise off the desert in great waves, as if the whole heat of the day was concentrated in one unbearable hour. And even as the sun sank out of sight the heat stayed with us. My thin dress and sandals stuck to me, and the air that seeped up from the motor beneath me was so burning hot that I took my feet off the foot rests and hung them over the crash bars in front of the machine. With the last fading light of the sunset, the night dropped around us like a black cloak; there wasn't a star in sight. My lights became dimmer and dimmer and I would have seen nothing of the road ahead if it hadn't been for Lee's strong headlight just behind me.

A few flashes of lightning showed far away to our left, but as we drove on down the straight black road the flashes increased, until with every streak of electricity the sky and road were lit up for several blinding seconds. It was a queer combination, this almost tortuous heat, the complete darkness and then the terrifying and ever-increasing forked lightning. But it wasn't until we heard a loud clap of thunder that Matelot took any notice of the gathering storm.

He and I are a sorry pair, because I am terrified of lightning, while thunder turns him into a cowering little puppy. The great flashes of light seemed to be directly overhead and yet I kept driving ahead expecting to be struck to the ground at any moment. Presently the wind came up; it swept across our path fast and furiously until I could hardly steer Oppy. She was swaying now all over the dark road. We crawled through the inky darkness at a snail's pace, and Lee had to drop into low gear to avoid passing us. As the sand started swirling across my face and covering the road in fine drifts, I blessed his strong headlights. On several occasions I was completely blinded, and then suddenly we were in the midst of a wild and enveloping sand storm.

There was a line of halted cars ahead of us, so I pulled over to the side of the road and tried to protect my eyes from the sand. I managed to pull out my goggles and also threw a scarf over my head, and while I crouched low over the tank with my head bent, the sand whirled around me, stinging my bare legs and arms. Matelot had curled up completely in his box, his nose buried under his tail and a layer of sand covering his quivering body.

I had tried to tuck his ground sheet across the box for shelter, but the strong wind whipped it loose and it rose up now like a yacht in full sail. Too blinded to look for Lee, I hoped that the motorists approaching us from behind would see his red tail light and not run us both down.

But, mingled with the discomfort and pain of the merciless sand storm, I experienced a feeling of excitement and almost pleasure. After all, I had started out with the idea of adventure, and coming such a short time after the earthquake, a sand storm seemed a thrilling experience.

After a bit the whirling sand subsided, but a relentless tropical rain took its place. Enormous drops fell on us, hitting me in the face with tremendous force and soaking me to the skin in a matter of seconds. I couldn't get at my rain clothes because Matelot was firmly settled on them and refused to budge an inch. He had crouched low to avoid first the sand storm and now the driving rain.

Then Lee drew up alongside me, his head bent for shelter against the storm, "Come on," he said, "let's make a dash for it. Gila Bend can't be far now."

So I wrapped the scarf tightly around my head and followed Lee's tiny red tail light up the rain-swept road. The rain felt agonizing as we gathered speed under the raging wind, and it cut across my body from all sides. One of my hands was constantly brushing my goggles free of raindrops, though most of the time I was driving half-blind. Then at last I caught sight of a faint glimmer of lights through the storm and this gave me fresh courage. However, my optimistic feelings soon disappeared, because as we battled on against the head wind those glimmering lights came no nearer.

I began to think they were some frightful mirage and that I was living a nightmare—the sort of nightmare which is unending. I imagined myself driving for ever down the dark, wind-torn highway, and always those lights would be just a little way beyond my reach, enticingly visible and encouraging enough to keep me going *on* and *on* through the miserable night. If only there had been pitch darkness I might have lain down on the edge of the desert and given myself up completely to the dominating elements.

However, human endurance can be stretched, and besides I didn't want to appear a sissy before a fellow motor-cyclist, so I tried to think of pleasant thoughts. First I made believe I was back in that park in Yuma, with its dry stifling heat; but later I longed for my beloved Pacific Ocean, and gradually my sanity began to return. Still those bright lights gleamed ahead of our straight road; we never seemed to get any nearer! But at last we were driving through the lighted streets of Gila Bend, a small desert town which stands at the head of a junction where the highway divided for Phoenix and Tucson, Arizona.

The first visible bit of shelter was a large petrol station, and we pulled in there quickly and leaned our dripping machines against a wall. With true western friendliness, the garage-men treated us like long-lost friends. Our machines were wheeled inside out of the weather and several rags were produced for us to wipe them off. The thunder was crashing over the roof-tops now and driving poor Matelot crazy. The garage was just closing, so grabbing my typewriter, overnight bag and Matelot's chain, I followed Lee across the street to a brightly lighted café.

I was really too exhausted, hungry and soaking wet to care much about my personal appearance, but I was conscious of looks of startled horror from the lunch counter attendants. Then a friendly old character in an enormous stetson hat pulled a cigar from his mouth and said in the most enchanting western drawl. "Honey, you look kinda wet. Come on and sit down; I bet you could use a cuppa coffee." Seeing Lee, he added "Oh! You've got your young man with you! Well, I'll buy you two cups of coffee!"

I sat down in my sopping dress; the hem was dripping on to the floor and sending little rivers of water running in all directions. My sandals flopped like boats, while my hair hung in lank rats' tails; a more horrible sight, I am sure, had never adorned that café.

Lee didn't look particularly happy either, in his soaking blue jeans and T-shirt and boots that squelched at every step. Besides, he still had the hundred-mile return journey to his air base to complete before morning. Well, nobody was very optimistic with their weather predictions.

"Hard to tell, it might stop raining in five minutes, and then again it might keep up all week," said one old boy cheerfully. "These desert storms are mighty queer things."

So now it looked as if I'd have to buy myself a bed for the first time on the trip, but the mere thought of clean white sheets and a spring mattress was heaven at that moment. Lee too had decided to stop over, and kept saying that it would be just too bad if he was late getting back on duty.

When Lee, Matelot and I entered the small, shabby hotel lobby, I saw the clock pointed to midnight. A couple of men were sprawled on an ancient horsehair settee reading newspapers, and an elderly stout man in shirt-sleeves sat behind the door. He glanced at us non-commitally and granted his permission for Matelot to stay in my room. I asked for the cheapest single room and paid his price of $1.50. The clerk reached up for two large keys hanging on the hook above and beckoned us to follow him up the dark stairway.

Down a long, ill-lit passage Matelot and I followed him, until, after some fumbling with a lock, he threw open a door and switched on the light. At a glance I took in the dusty table, peeling wallpaper and cracked basin, but noted that the two essentials, clean bed linen and a bolt on the door, were there. Matelot flopped wearily on a tattered rug and was dead to the world in a matter of seconds.

On closer inspection my room proved to be even more ghastly than I first realized. The ageing wallpaper was actually peeling off the yellow walls in ribbons, and chunks of plaster from the cracked ceiling lay in mounds on the floor. The only window opened on to a narrow space between the next building, and not a breath of fresh air penetrated the room. The filth of ages lay under the bed and across the window ledges. The air smelt musty and disagreeable and a dirty shirt was still hanging across the chair, left there by the last occupant. Fortunately the sheets were really clean, even if several bed springs seemed to be sagging.

I was just struggling to take off my oozing sandals when Lee yelled through the door, "I paid for a room with shower. Come on over and use it if you like."

Gathering up my pyjamas, soap and towel, and leaving Matelot gnawing some biscuits under the bed, I fairly flew across the passage. A shower was essential to get the sand out of my ears, toes and hair. Now, some people think I am brave to pitch my tent alone along the highway, but as I knocked on Lee's door I felt far more reckless at that moment, when I was about to take a shower in a third-class hotel room occupied by a strange young man.

CHAPTER IX *Cactus Country*

I MUST have left enough sand in the shower to fill a suitcase, and I don't believe I got rid of every grain for a good week later. Still, after washing out most of my things under the hot spray I felt so refreshed with clean clothes that I decided to sit up part of the night and type out the evening's adventure.

Lee jumped up to open the door as I came out of the shower, my arms full of wet clothes and a damp towel. For a moment he barred my way. "You know, you look just like a girl I used to go around with back home," he said.

"I'm always being told I look like somebody's sister or favourite cousin. I must be a definite type."

"Well," I went on hastily as I started for the door, "it's been nice meeting another motor-cyclist. Thanks a million for the help with your headlights. I don't think I would ever have made it otherwise. Have a good trip back to Yuma." Then I edged a bit closer to the door.

"I guess I'll have to go in the morning before you get up," Lee said. "Anyway, lots of luck on your trip." He opened the door and I managed to extract a wet hand to shake his in farewell.

It was not only fresh air that was unable to penetrate my room, neither did the light of day or the bright sunshine. For after a fair night's rest, I left the hotel and went across to the garage to find that it was already after eight o'clock and the sun was already rising high into the cloudless hot sky. Before I could get near to Oppy I had to dust off a small plague of grasshoppers that covered her from stem to stern, and had crawled into every crack in the luggage. They infuriated Matelot, who gave chase to half a dozen of them as they hopped over the dry, dusty ground.

That morning on my way to Tucson I drove through the most lovely country. The flat sand dunes had disappeared and the land around us was covered with brightly flowering cactus plants. It was still very hot, although not the stifling heat of Yuma, and driving became quite bearable now even in the middle of the day. On the outskirts of Tucson I passed several fabulous hotels with blue swimming pools set in sunken rock gardens surrounded by exotic desert flowers.

Arriving in Tucson I left Matelot to guard Oppy and went to the post office to ask for my mail. When I got back, Matelot was nowhere to be seen. A white-coated man from a nearby café came over to tell me that if I was looking for an airedale, he was inside his store. I found Matelot surrounded by an admiring circle of customers in the centre of the store, drinking water from an enormous aluminium bucket. He seemed to be well satisfying his thirst, so I sat down at the lunch counter and ordered an iced coffee for myself. As I was enjoying it a lovely looking dark-haired girl on my right started talking to me, and soon I was telling her all about the trip. She suggested that I come and visit her during the heat of the day and wait until evening before continuing my journey. She introduced herself as June Caldwell, the wife of Erskine Caldwell, and giving me her address she told me how to get there.

I found her home set in a rambling garden alive with buck rabbits, which Matelot immediately chased as fast as his four paws would carry him. The flat-roofed yellow house was built in Indian style. My hostess welcomed me into a large high-ceilinged room with a picture window giving the most perfect view out to the distant mountains. The room was graceful and charming; full of books, lovely paintings and flowers. All evening we sat in the comfortable deep armchairs getting acquainted, and talked about everything under the sun. June apologized because her husband was away on a trip, and having read many of his books I was sorry to have missed him. After supper another sudden desert storm started to blow up. The lightning flashed above the mountain tops and the rain lashed against the window panes. It looked as if we were in for a bad night. So June kindly offered to put me up and I accepted with alacrity.

Next morning the streets were still wet from the storm as Matelot and I drove along under the first light of the dawn. The surrounding mountains were tinted pink with the morning light, and soon the scrub land became less arid, great cattle ranges swept from both sides of the highway to a point where the mountains towered into the sky.

I was having lunch under a cactus tree when the longest train of all times chugged slowly into sight. I heard it down in the valley well before it crept up the slight incline into view. The driver and fireman waved to me as they chugged slowly past with the huge black-smoking engine pulling its cargo of countless freight cars. It was like a giant snake wriggling across that desert valley.

A few hours later I came to a large notice on the side of the road which said "Welcome to New Mexico." All that afternoon I drove across the wide rolling ranges. Shaggy-headed cattle with long horns and lovely cream-coloured faces peered at us over the rough wire fences, sending Matelot wild with desire to jump off and chase them. And a few minutes later Oppy lurched precariously when my dog caught sight of the wild horses that galloped off across the turf at our approach. The mountains were closing in a little and our endless vista of grasslands stretched gradually up into the green foothills.

All along the highway to El Paso there were numerous scattered Indian trading posts. They weren't as fascinating as their names imply. No full-blooded Indian warrior in his feather and war paint came out to greet us from a tepee hung with hand-sewn moccasins or woven rugs. All we saw was shack after shack selling cheap eye-catching souvenirs together with car stickers, postcards and hot dogs.

At El Paso I crossed into Texas; here the road dipped down into the centre of the city and the hard rocky mountains closed in even nearer. This busy border city was bristling with tourists on their way in and out of Mexico. However, I had decided to drive through southern Texas and cross the border at Laredo to shorten the trip to Mexico City by a few hundred miles. I also wanted to see something of Texas and enjoy more of its wide open spaces.

Now, it is almost an unwritten law among motor-cyclists who are on a trip that they must stop at the dealers in the different cities who carry their make of machine. So in El Paso I searched for the B.S.A. dealer. Oppy had been behaving beautifully since the new hub bearing had been fitted in San Diego, and I didn't even need any oil, but nevertheless I thumbed through the yellow pages in the telephone book and finally located Raymond Rathbone.

I found him and his teen-age son in the back of the shop busy working on an old racing machine. They dropped everything to come and admire Oppy, and agreed that she must have been the star model of her assembly line to stand up so well to her tremendous load. We spent a pleasant hour or so in motor-cycle gossip, and then later that evening Raymond and his wife took me to supper. And then as dusk fell we had a small escort of motor-cyclists, who rode with us to the edge of the city limits and saw me off on the road south.

As the weather became a bit more bearable Matelot perked up noticeably. In the cool of the evening he loved to stretch his legs, and would go bounding off at about thirty miles an hour, his back paws hardly touching the ground. When I was driving through a town I could make

him pause at the traffic lights if I shouted "Stop" in a loud and command-
ing voice.

This would bring him with perhaps one impatient paw in the gutter,
pushing and nosing his way to the front of the crowd of pedestrians
waiting to cross the street. The second the light changed to green and I
said "Come on," Matelot would dash off again oblivious of the frightened
glances and retreating feet of the people he rushed past. He was always
anxious not to lose sight of Oppy. Sometimes for fun I sneaked round a
corner to hide from him, then he would come tearing down the street,
ears and tail flying and a look of desperation on his face. One toot of the
horn would bring a panting and relieved dog jumping up at my lap and
scratching poor Oppy's paintwork.

Actually he liked best to run along the open highway so as to keep us
well in view. And his speed would gradually diminish as the miles clocked
away on my speedometer. Running beside a motor-cycle is wonderful
exercise for a dog of Matelot's size.

I was cruising gently along through the main street of the small town
of Alpine, Texas, debating whether I'd open the tin of pineapple to eat
with peanut-butter sandwiches, or the tin of beans with a cheese and onion
salad, when a man shouted at me, "Say, ma'am, your rear tyre sure looks
low."

I stopped and bent my head beneath all the luggage to have a look.
Low! Oppy's rear tyre was as flat as a pancake, and at that moment the
last bit of air wheezed out of the tube. Luckily we were just in front of a
large Texaco station, so I pushed the machine over to the air pump.

Then a tall young attendant in faded blue jeans and a bright check
shirt took one look at Oppy and said, "You sure got a nice little flat
there, ma'am. Don't reckon there's anyone in town knows how to
fix one on a motor-cycle."

With the realization that I was about three hundred miles from a
motor-cycle shop, I began to rack my brains trying to remember what
I could about the complicated process of removing Oppy's wheel.
Whenever I had had a flat before this I had always seemed to be in the
centre of a city with a motor-cycle shop just around the corner. This time,
however, I was truly deep in the heart of Texas.

After I had taken off all the luggage, I could see much better what had to be done. Fortunately the directions in my B.S.A. handbook were easy to follow. But it seemed as if *every* vital part of Oppy had to be disconnected to get that wheel out. First the stop light and speedometer cable, then the brake, and the perfectly filthy job of finding the connecting link in the grease-laden chain. Finally I slackened the axle nuts, and with a great heave from Billy Blue Jeans and myself the wheel slipped out.

Then he filled the tube with air to locate the leak, but he was a little bit too enthusiastic about it, because immediately there was a loud explosion. Small particles of inner tubing scattered across the ground and Matelot took off as though he'd been shot.

"Inferior rubber these days," grinned Bill sheepishly.

Luckily I had a spare tube in my tool kit. Bill got the tube and tyre back on the wheel rim, but I was left with the headache of trying to get the thing back in place again and assembled correctly. I thought I did everything the handbook recommended for rear-wheel alignment, but still the tyre touched the fender on one side as it spun erratically around. So I tried shifting the axle nuts, adjusted the chain, and even gave poor Oppy a few hefty kicks.

All this labour took place under the fascinated gaze of several local kids and motorists who had pulled in for petrol. This small, interested and at times helpful crowd kept my temper fairly smooth, but as the evening wore on I grew dirtier, hotter, and began to doubt whether I would ever get the wheel to rotate properly.

Oppy sat with her back end hoisted up on two wooden crates, looking pathetically naked under the bright light above her on the wall. Matelot was fast asleep by the pile of assorted luggage, and then as sundown came and went the last of my sympathetic audience left for home and bed.

Pretty soon Bill came out dangling a bunch of keys, "I'm just going to lock up for the night. If you want to use the rest room——"

Hastily I rummaged around in the luggage for my toothbrush and towel, and decided I'd better sleep right here outside the petrol station. As I scrubbed off the black grease under the hot-water tap I promised myself optimistically that in the morning everything would seem different and I would have no trouble at all assembling that rear wheel.

Bill turned off the station lights, tested the locks and then, shouting good-night, strode off into the darkness. I looked around; I had certainly slept in worse places but never in a more conspicuous one. Spreading out the ground sheet on the concrete floor against one of the garage walls, I blew up my air mattress and arranged Matelot as close as possible to me on his rug. Gnawing pains clutched my stomach and I realized then for the first time that I was desperately hungry. But because I was already inside the sleeping bag I merely pulled over the food bag without even getting up, opened a tin of pineapple and made myself a cheese sandwich. This woke up Matelot, so I had to share my midnight feast.

I suppose I ought to have felt very depressed with poor broken-down Oppy's silhouette beside me, but instead I felt strangely content, because a big pale moon was coming up over the top of the dark mountains and stars were shining brightly in the sky above.

I had just dozed off when a large truck drove into the petrol station and stopped less than a yard from my face. I kept my eyes tight shut. A voice said, "Jeez, look at that guy sleepin' down there. Sure looks rough." His companion with a strong Brooklyn accent replied, "They say they breed 'em tough in the west."

Then, after both of them were apparently satisfied that the station was closed for the night, they slipped into gear and roared off. But I wasn't left in peace long; a few minutes later a car packed with gay merrymakers pulled in, and one of the them nearly fell over my feet as he looked for petrol. But the sight of Matelot scared him and he hurriedly retreated to his car.

"Brother!" he shouted, "one of them cayhotes from the hills got loose in town!"

At this point I began to wonder if I'd have to put up with such disturbances all night long, but around one in the morning the last tourist seemed to have departed for his hotel.

When the first pale light of dawn crept over the dark hills I awoke and hurried to make myself presentable before the town around me came to life. By the time Bill and the proprietor had arrived my coffee was made and I was stirring a bubbling tin of hot beans on my little stove. Somehow that hot coffee and beans worked wonders, because the very first time I tried to assemble the wheel everything slipped into place in perfect order. So perfect that I could hardly believe my fumbling despair of the evening before. I felt quite delirious with my success, and Bill said, "Just shows what you can do when you try hard enough."

After that I packed the luggage on to Oppy as quickly as possible, so anxious was I to get out of the town and on to the road once more.

The day promised to be hot as I set off across the vast, lonely cattle ranges. Alpine had been like a small green oasis with its green hills and soft wooded slopes, set in the midst of this harsh desolate landscape. At first I drove very cautiously, not daring to believe that the rear wheel was safe. I kept waiting for some sign of a wobble or rubbing noise, but it never came.

As I drove steadily all morning through the dry heat, the blue mountains ahead became less distant, and then after a bit the road wound gently up through a narrow rocky canyon. Up we went across the barren land of west Texas. There was nothing green in sight, the hard dry earth was scorched brown, and the grey mountain sides were scattered with yellow sandstone boulders. The sun poured down increasingly hot every hour. After about fifty miles driving across this lonely country I was very glad to reach the small town of Sanderson around lunch time. This little community was plumped down in the middle of very barren rocky country, hemmed in by the treeless mountain slopes.

There wasn't a scrap of shade in sight, and judging by the country I had just passed through, I doubted whether I would find any on the road ahead. I felt that I just had to get out of the burning sun for an hour or so for lunch. Passing an ice-cream stand, I caught sight of a table set in the shade against a wall. The friendly young woman who served Matelot and me with cups of ice cream came outside to chat with us as we sat panting under the shadow of the building.

"Why don't you come inside out of the heat?" she offered.

I followed her into the small kitchen at the back of the freezer unit, which was delightfully cool. So I settled down in a chair and caught up on a little clothes mending that I hadn't found time to do because of the heat. My companion, who introduced herself as Mrs. Rhoades, was very talkative and gay. She gave me an account of how she had come to the United States as a child from Yugoslavia, which seemed a very far cry from Texas. She tried very hard to persuade me to stay overnight at her home, but I felt the cool of the coming evening was the best time for driving.

Although I had to decline her friendly invitation I certainly didn't refuse the use of her wash house for my laundry. But I had to be careful to keep the wash-house door shut, because Mrs. Rhoades was taming a baby racoon there and it was clinging to one of the pipes on the ceiling. Of course Matelot smelt the racoon immediately and nearly went mad when I locked him outside.

So, as I scrubbed away at my clothes, a little bunch of brown fur looked down at me from above, its wild beady eyes watching my every movement. Then I put my dress back on wringing wet, and with my hair still dripping, I stood in the sun and hung up my spare clothes to dry. In the space of five minutes my hair and all the clothes were bone dry!

When the cool of the evening started to fall, I set out once more, waving thanks and goodbye to Mrs. Rhoades as I turned the corner.

The drive on across that rough rocky country was made enchantingly lovely by the warm night air and the enormously bright moon that rose in the star-covered sky. My headlight was still very poor for night driving, but now I hardly needed it, because moonlight flooded the road that wound ahead of me like a long white serpent. I had the impression I was driving very fast; the miles seemed to spin away as we rode along. About halfway to Del Rio, the next town, I came to a small lighted café and petrol station and decided both Matelot and I needed a drink.

So I left Matelot lapping water out of a large can under the petrol pump and went into the café. I'll never forget the man who served us coffee. It would have been fun to sit there all night and listen to that wonderful westerner telling stories of the good old bad days, but it was already ten o'clock and we were still a long way from Del Rio. My fellow coffee drinkers warned me to drive slowly when I came to Pecos Canyon, a few miles down the road, where the highway dropped very steeply.

I set off once more in the moonlight and after climbing for a few miles reached the summit of the road where I could look down far below into the rocky canyon. Just at this minute I ran out of petrol! This seemed impossible, for I had checked the tank at Sanderson. Oppy must have got thirsty in the heat too! And now after I had discovered that the petrol in the emergency can had evaporated, there was nothing left to do but look for a camping site near by. Coasting down the road a short way, I saw a small park on the left of the road and overlooking the canyon.

It was literally hanging to the edge of the cliff—certainly a dreadful spot to pitch a tent with the wind blowing so hard. On closer inspection the ground proved to be covered with large rocks, and what land had been cleared was solid rock and most unyielding to tent pegs. But somehow I managed to tie the back guy rope to Oppy's frame and the front one I secured under a large boulder. Then I placed heavy rocks all round the edge of the tent and crawling inside after Matelot, I prayed that we wouldn't hurtle off into the canyon below during the night. The tent walls billowed out around us and I could hear the wind howling through the canyon. It was a strange contrast to the still heat of the day!

The next morning I was quite stuck until I could get hold of some petrol. There seemed to be very little traffic on the road, so when a large truck finally turned the corner I rushed out and waved at the driver. The poor man had a lot of trouble finding me a cupful of petrol. His huge forty-gallon tanks on the rear of his truck were in a most awkward position, and he had to kneel down in the dusty road and try to siphon out the liquid with a piece of hose. But he insisted upon filling up both Oppy's tank and the emergency can as well, and when I protested that he was far too generous, he laughed and said, "I'm not paying for it, ma'am —thank my boss!"

Another day and a half's driving across the lonely Texan countryside brought us one Sunday afternoon to the outskirts of Laredo, on the border of Mexico. Now that I was at last so near the Mexican border I was beginning to feel distinctly nervous at the thought of travelling alone through a country which was unknown and new to me. Having been in Spain I did have a working knowledge of Spanish. But I also knew how incredible the spectacle of a girl travelling alone would seem to a Latin. With this in mind I had decided not to camp out in Mexico. Instead I planned to take advantage of the favourable rate of exchange and stay at inexpensive hotels.

I lay awake longer than usual in the tent that night, thinking of the following day, and wondering what kind of strange beds I might find in Mexico.

CHAPTER X *South of the Border*

NEXT morning I was still brooding over my lack of courage when I entered Laredo. This small city was quite different from any other American town of its size I had seen. It almost seemed as if I were being broken in gently for Mexico and the different way of life that lay ahead. For here at least fifty per cent. of the population was Mexican. Shop signs and film advertisements were in Spanish and everywhere I heard the excited chatter of that lovely language.

Stopping by the little park in the centre of town, I started to check off the list of vital things to be done before leaving the States. The post office had already been asked to re-address my mail to Mexico City, but I was a little doubtful of its safe arrival, because my recent letters had been reaching me forwarded from eight different places scattered from Canada to Texas. The food bag and every spare corner beneath Matelot was stuffed with tinned dog food and fruit juice and vegetables for myself. At the chemist's I had purchased a container of water-purifying tablets and a large bottle of medicine guaranteed to cure any intestinal disorder. I had been told so many stories of Mexico's insanitary food conditions and germ-ridden water that for once I decided to be prudent and take no chances.

All my United States road maps were at the bottom of the map case and an exciting, illustrated one of Mexico was folded on the tank in front of me. My last dollar was spent and my purse was bulging with what looked like a fortune in paper bills, but what was in reality only about twenty dollars in pesos. So, checking the straps on my luggage, I gave Oppy a hasty wipe with a rag, boosted my courage with a little extra lipstick, and then we were off for Mexico!

Matelot didn't enter Mexico like a proper British dog at all! As we crossed the bridge which separates Laredo, Texas, from Nuevo Laredo, Mexico, he decided to leap off and chase a passing cat. He dodged between the legs of screaming Mexican peasants returning home with their arms full of American goods. The bridge was narrow and the traffic in both directions was heavy. Bus loads of Mexican workers and American cars packed with tourists jostled their way from border to border, and amid all this busy throng a bulging and stationary Oppy caused a definite block in traffic.

Somehow I managed to back up off the bridge and return to the U.S. customs house under the disapproving glances of the stern officials. Then I found Matelot sniffing furiously beneath a stall of fruit, with a ring of intimidated and excited Mexicans keeping a respectful distance from him. When I got hold of him I told him in no uncertain terms exactly what I thought of him, and his brown ears drooped sadly.

My first sight of Mexico was an impressive archway over the customs house, with the flag of the republic fluttering on either side of the building. When I drew up outside the customs house, parked Oppy and walked inside with Matelot and my passport, shrieks of laughter and excited jabbering greeted my ears. *"Mira! Mira! La señorita, Madre Dios!"* I looked back to see a bunch of hysterical porters dancing round Oppy with a mixture of disbelief and mirth, and pointing fingers at our retreating figures. Then inside the building I gave my passport to the tall grim-faced official. He grabbed it, muttered something at me rapidly and disappeared.

Now I followed the other bewildered tourists to a row of wooden benches against the wall. The room was indescribably stuffy and my mouth was as dry as a bone, but the coke machine was out of order.

We sat there for half an hour, during which time I suddenly remembered that I had left a twenty pesos bill in the back of my passport. At the current rate of exchange this was just over two dollars, but a far larger sum than I was allowing for my entire daily budget. So I hurried into the office to try and retrieve this nest egg before it was too late. The chief official and I had a heated conversation in Spanish, with me explaining that I was not a filthy-rich tourist and him explaining that his clerk had considered the twenty pesos a tip and stressing how insulting it would be to ask for the money to be returned. But I waved my hands in the air in my best Latin style, becoming more and more excited until my half-forgotten Spanish was strained to a maximum, and finally I managed to squeeze out a few tears and dabbed my face with an already sweaty and soaking piece of Kleenex.

"*Momento, momento, señorita,*" the official said now, patting my shoulder and re-entering his office. Then there was a torrent of furious Spanish and I caught a glimpse of an angry young man, and soon after that my kind official came back with the twenty pesos in his hand.

However, my little success was short-lived, because when I reached the next official who wanted to check Matelot's paper, I found that the Mexican consul in Los Angeles had forgotten to stamp my visa allowing for importation of a dog. This, I was informed, was absolutely necessary, and I would have to go all the way back to Los Angeles and attend to it there.

I was about to fling my hands in the air once more, when the official smiled slyly and said that he thought something could be arranged here, but that naturally this would entail a special consular fee.

"How much?" I asked in Spanish, as he put a small stamp on my visa.

"Twenty pesos!" he replied without looking up.

After that a very bewildered customs inspector checked Oppy's frame and engine numbers and asked a few vague questions as to the contents of her packs. Then with a careless shrug, followed by a polite bow, he welcomed me to the freedom of his country.

Now at long last I threw Matelot aboard Oppy and glanced around to see that everything was in order. My companion settled himself in his box and stared haughtily at the still giggling porters. Every eye was glued on me, watching to see how a girl would mount a motor-cycle. And as I seated myself, my black divided skirt billowing out decorously down either side of the tank, I heard someone whisper in Spanish, "But she's wearing trousers!"

Good old Oppy started up at the first kick, producing an "*Hombre!*" from the spectators. The crowd became braver as I gathered speed. They shrieked and yelled and this of course drew the attention of the townspeople as well. I hardly noticed what Nuevo Laredo looked like, I was so embarrassed by the shouting population and small barefoot boys who ran along in the gutter trying to keep pace with Oppy, as we bumped over the rough cobblestones.

"*Mira! Mira! La señorita y el pero!*" they yelled.

A Ride in the Sun

At the outskirts of the town I stopped by a little fruit stand to buy some bananas. For about ten cents I got half a dozen fat ripe fruit, which I stuck on the tank in front of me and ate as I drove down the road.

The town was behind us now and the road ahead lay as straight as the eye could see, due south, across an arid plain of scrub and cactus plants. The sun was pouring down mercilessly hot and there was not a scrap of shade in sight. We drove for several miles without seeing a single vehicle, house, or even a road sign. Then gradually a few tourists' cars from the States began to overtake us, all their occupants frantically waving and calling. To me those cars from California, Illinois and Texas seemed like dear friends from home. I was no longer the foreign tourist that I had been. Mexico had already brought about an Anglo-American union!

After about an hour the last of the cars from the States passed me, and once more the road was almost deserted. A few ancient jalopies rattled past, or an occasional sleek sedan with a Mexico City licence overtook us with elegant Mexicans gazing out of the rear window, disbelief in their eyes. Now I began to feel very lonely. What on earth would I do, I wondered, if I had another flat out here in this isolated dry wilderness?

But at last I came on my first glimpse of civilization, a small mud hut by the side of the road sporting a large red Coca Cola sign. A big truck was parked outside and from the interior came the sound of hearty laughter. I pushed aside the rough curtain screening the doorway and entered. There was a deathly silence and four wild-looking men gazed at me open-mouthed.

They wore smock-like shirts held inside their baggy trousers by a wide band round their waists. On their feet were primitive rope sandals, and their wide-brimmed straw hats were pushed back to show curly black hair and a good week's growth of beard on their brown faces. A woman rushed forward and pulled out a chair for me. She was dressed in a vivid striped skirt and shawl flung over her shoulders.

I pointed to her coke freezer, which dwarfed everything else in the small hut. But of course it was used for storing drinks—and not for cooling them. The brightly coloured liquid which was served to me in a lukewarm, unrefreshing state was my introduction to "Bimbo," a soft

94

drink which I found rather repulsive. Later I learned that it came in four horrible bright shades, the most palatable being orange.

Now I sipped the tepid mixture from a crude earthenware mug and compared my primitive and colourful surroundings with the chrome and polish typical of most American lunch counters. Deciding that here was an ideal place to practise my Spanish, I made a few bright remarks about the weather to the four truckers who were still gazing at me open-mouthed. This amazed them even more and there were whispers of "*Americana,*" so I replied, "*No, Inglesa,*" and then the ice was broken. After that we chatted away happily, and whenever I became stuck for a word they helped me search my little pocket dictionary until there were bursts of "Oh! *Si, si, si, señorita.*" I began to feel positively brilliant in Spanish, but at last reluctantly got up to say good-bye and go on my way.

I left amid much shouting of "*Adios, adios!*" and then a few minutes later the quartet overtook me, all hanging out of their truck and waving madly. So I felt warmed and heartened to all Mexicans as we sped on up the straight road.

Far away in the distance I could see a range of mountains outlined against the sky, but the land around me was still a barren wilderness. The first village we came to was La Gloria, but a less glorious place I have never seen. It consisted of a dozen scattered mud huts, and the only stone building was a dirty, down-at-the-heel petrol station.

After another hour's steady driving we started to climb gently into the mountains. Round and round we went, the road wound up above us like a ribbon, but the gradient was easy and gradual and Oppy took it in second gear like a lady. The air was lovely and cool and the country was a diverting change from the dry, monotonous desert land. The steep mountain sides, covered with boulders and craggy rocks, shut us in on all sides, causing the sun to cast great shadows across our path.

The road reached the highest point in the mountains and then wound down steeply until we passed a small village of flat-roofed, rough stone houses. A lovely little church with a tall square tower perched on a side of the hill above, and the small winding street was planted with shady, overhanging trees. Women sat on benches outside their houses knitting, while the men gathered together in groups talking. I looked around for a petrol station, but I couldn't even find a shop. There seemed to be only the little groups of stone houses clustered round the base of the churchyard.

Oppy was drinking up petrol faster than usual, and even allowing for the heat I felt there must be something wrong with her. And I was worried now that I might run out of petrol, because the service stations seemed so far apart. Luckily the next village proved much larger, and even boasted a small hotel and several cafés. Here I found a petrol station and pulled in for my first gallon, or rather litre, of Mexican petrol. Being a two-cycle engine, Oppy's lubrication system works directly from the tank, and this entails the messy job of mixing a heavy-grade oil with every gallon of petrol. The trick of shaking petrol and oil thoroughly together resembles the making of a milk shake. I had a special little tin for doing it and an old spoon to see that the job was well done. Whenever I was too lazy or too clean to bother with this messy job I always regretted it, for then the heavy oil sank into my carburettor and clogged up the whole engine.

Now there was the added complication of converting litres into gallons if I were to gauge the exact amount of oil I needed. And in his excitement the young boy filling the tank let the hose slip and the petrol shot out all over the tank and down my clean skirt. A big swarthy man rushed forward, pushed the boy aside and, taking the hose from him, shouted *"Idiota, idiota!"* After that the service was superb, and rags were produced to mop up streaming Oppy and my dripping skirt.

The small crowd of onlookers pressed forward curiously and someone produced an air hose. Luckily just in time I saw that fifty pounds of air were going into my rear tyre, and before the inner tube shattered to pieces I managed to let out the excessive pressure. The crowd was growing every minute now, and the garage proprietor was furious at the inconvenience to his customer. He yelled and waved them away, but still they pushed closer, their dark faces alive with excited laughter and curiosity. Small ragged boys, barefoot and dirty faced, stretched out hands with cries of *"Dinero, dinero, señorita,"* and I had to pretend that I couldn't understand what they meant. They tried other words like peso and dollar, but still I looked blank. Others pushed forward holding bananas or a single pear in grubby outstretched hands, but I shook my head stubbornly.

96

With my limited funds I knew I would have to start hardening my heart as the way I had been forced to do when travelling in some parts of Europe. Nevertheless when I finally set off again all the children raced us down the street.

The country about us now was rich farming land. I passed field after field of corn and neatly planted green vegetables surrounding large farmhouses. The day was drawing to a close and I found many new companions of the road. Small donkeys, heavily laden, jogged along placidly. Some carried huge bundles of faggots loosely roped together, while others dragged small trees in their wake. Then sometimes we would see a tall, lanky-legged peasant astride one of these small sturdy beasts, the man's long legs hanging down almost to the ground on either side; and often his wife would be seated in front of him, riding gracefully side saddle with billowing skirts. It was really quite a sight—the long straight road with its background of blue mountains, and the tiny grey donkeys jogging their way along under the tall avenue of trees, carrying their masters home from work in the fields.

And then we came upon proud horsemen on their graceful steeds, prancing along the grassy edge of the highway. In the gathering dusk I overtook two of these picturesque *caballeros*, and presently I heard behind me a thundering of hooves and wild cries of *"Ola! Ola!"* Then Oppy and two wildly galloping horses were racing neck and neck down the straight highway. I shut my throttle a little to get a better look at my pursuers, and caught sight of flashing white teeth beneath the brims of two wide sombreros. The hooves pounded and Matelot stood outside his box in furious excitement, balanced precariously on one of the suitcases.

I longed to stop and ask one of the riders to change saddles for a moment; it would have been such fun to let a wild Mexican steed whirl me through the warm darkness. But I suppose I was becoming too mechanically minded, because at last I pulled back my throttle, gathered speed, and with a wave of the hand and *"Adios, amigos,"* I drew ahead of them into the night.

The high mountains were very close now; they were silhouetted against the starry sky, and away off in the valley the bright lights of a town beckoned. I was approaching Monterrey, the second largest city in Mexico; the streets were cobblestoned and bumpy, and poor Oppy's packs bounced up and down over the rear wheel, and Matelot must have felt as if his spine were being dislocated.

We passed several huge lighted factories and then reached what looked like the main street of the city. There was a long avenue of trees planted in a small park running down the centre of the street. The stone benches were crowded, and throngs of laughing, gay people overflowed from the park and pavements into the roadway. So I pulled over to ask the way to a cheap hotel. The cobbled streets had recently been washed, and as I turned Oppy's front wheel too sharply, she skidded on the greasy surface, and the next thing I knew I was sitting in the middle of the road, with the luggage scattered in all directions and the engine screaming away beside me. I sat there in humiliation for a few seconds and then many willing hands were pulling me to my feet and dusting down Oppy. Cars shrieked their brakes just behind us and a wildly jabbering crowd gathered on the pavement; Matelot had performed his usual emergency jump and was staring at me in utter disgust.

I felt as if I were in the midst of a comic opera. Dark-skinned young men pressed forward to look at Oppy's engine, children fingered every part of the machine they could lay hands on, while the women hung back on the edge of the crowd, chattering excitedly.

Two gorgeously dressed policemen beat their way through the throng of people. I got out my little hotel guide book and pointing to the least expensive hotel listed, I asked *"Donde?"* This question started everyone yelling and pointing, quarrelling and shouting at one another. The hotel seemed to be in every direction at once—north, south, east and west—so, amid the pandemonium, I kicked Oppy over and she burst into life apparently none the worse for her fall. At the sound of the engine everyone jumped, and soon a path was cleared for me.

I rode off amid yells of *"No, señorita, este direccion!"* With the help of a street map I located the hotel myself, but the young clerk behind the desk refused to allow Matelot into the hotel. He was kind enough to telephone all over the city for us, but the answer was always the same— No dogs. Feeling rather dejected, because it was now nearly ten o'clock at night, I drove through the dark, narrow streets until I came back to the main avenue, where I turned into a large service station situated on the corner. By this time I realized that my only hope lay in finding a room in a private house. The mechanics were trying in vain to be helpful, when a well-dressed man of about forty appeared, and a torrent of rapid Spanish ensued.

One of the mechanics wrote an address for me on a piece of paper, which read "Casa de Huespedes Reynosa, Calle Reforma." The well-dressed man crossed the road and beckoned for me to follow him. All the garage men nodded and grinned, so putting my faith in the tall figure striding ahead, I slowly followed. Down the dark street I wobbled, and round two corners, and then my guide came to a halt outside a large stone house with a huge wooden door and a wrought-iron grating set in one of the panels. I read "Casa de Huespedes" over the doorway, lifted the heavy knocker and let it fall with a resounding bang. Presently the iron grill was opened and my Mexican protector leaned over my shoulder, making rapid explanations in Spanish. The door was flung open and a large fat woman in a bright print dress and carpet slippers peered out at me.

I waved a hand at Oppy and Matelot sitting against the kerb, and then a young man joined the woman on the top step. All at once a terrific argument seemed to be going on between these three people, and I just stood by quietly waiting for a lull in the conversation to put in my plea for a night's lodging. Then the young man addressed me in fluent English; "I'm afraid my mother thinks we'll never be able to lift your motor-cycle up all these steps into the hall, but I know a garage which would look after it for the night, if you like."

I sighed with relief, that this was all that they were worried about. Oppy was soon installed in a shabby little garage around the corner, and the son carried my things back to the house.

Señora Reynosa showed me to my room, which was a box affair with no window, but a large double door which gave out on to an open patio. All the rooms opened out on to this tiled courtyard, which furnished little privacy since everyone was forced to leave his door wide open for air. My neighbour opposite lay sprawled on his bed in nothing but his under-shorts, but the heat was so terrific that I am sure nobody thought anything of it. However, not feeling quite so informal, I closed my door and prepared to stifle. Even this gesture didn't give me great privacy, because the glass door was only thinly covered with a net curtain. The main feature of the room was a huge comfortable bed which took up exactly half the space.

After I had enjoyed a shower in a large stone room which resembled a prison cell, I changed into a dress and joined the *Señora* in the patio. It was not yet eleven o'clock and the night was still young in Mexico. When I had paid seven pesos for my room, which was only about eighty cents, I chatted for a moment to Señora Reynosa and her son, and then we were joined by a couple of the guests, who were curious about me.

A bottle of wine was produced, and sitting there in the wicker chairs under the starry sky, we toasted in turn the Republic of Mexico, President Truman and Queen Elizabeth. A fat, tubby man, whose stomach wobbled like jelly every time he laughed, got quite hysterical at my frenzied attempts to hold a discussion in Spanish. But his own stuttered words in English seemed to be restricted to—"hamburger," "hotdog" and "I love you, baby!"

At last I remembered the long journey stretching ahead of me next day, so shaking hands with everyone and murmuring *"Buenos noches,"* I started off for bed.

Next morning at five o'clock Señora Reynosa knocked on my door, and by the time I had packed Oppy and was bumping my way through the streets of Monterrey, the sun was just beginning to come up over the mountain tops. By the light of day I could see the city much better. Down each narrow street, between the grey buildings of stone and wrought-iron balconies, I caught glimpses of the craggy mountains outlined against the clear blue sky; in every direction I looked I saw these rocky summits.

For breakfast I stopped at a small café with gay red-and-blue table-cloths and a radio playing wild Mexican songs. Reasonably good coffee and two sweet buns cost about five cents. When no one was looking I sneaked a water-purifying tablet out of my purse and into the coffee, feeling extremely prudent but a little guilty of bad manners as well.

The city was just beginning to wake up now, as I drove across the southern suburbs on the way to the main Mexico City highway. I stopped at a small street fruit stall. There I augmented my breakfast with a huge juicy pineapple costing about ten cents.

All that day I drove southwards across the rolling plain lands of orchard and fields. Small barefoot boys, wearing hats almost as large as themselves, carried long sticks to drive herds of goats along the highway, and men bore buckets of water, coolie fashion, suspended on long wooden poles across their shoulders. The highways were alive with every type of domestic animal, and Matelot was itching to jump down into their midst. Chickens and ducks strolled across the road in a suicidal fashion, often tempting me to speed up so that I might acquire a tempting free supper. Donkeys of every shape and size were my constant companions, while herds of cows, goats and pigs continually blocked our way. But Matelot was especially infuriated by the galloping horses, who kicked dust in our faces as they tried to overtake us.

When it grew dark, we once more approached a city, and this time it was Ciudad Victoria, where I planned to spend the night. I pulled in at a petrol station for hotel advice and immediately a young boy rushed across the road.

"Hotel, *señorita?*" he grinned, pointing to a brightly lighted building opposite.

I nodded, so he led the way to a large door which he held open for me. I found myself in a wide open courtyard where I leaned Oppy against a wall of the hotel. Then I took out my most precious belongings and sent up a prayer for the safety of the rest.

The entrance to the hotel looked awfully palatial, but it was too late to turn back now, so I followed the boy inside. The walls of the entrance hall were beautifully painted with scenes of Mexican life and a map of the Pan-American Highway was drawn on the wall beside the staircase. This stone staircase boasted a banister of fine wrought-iron work, and curved up gently towards the ceiling delicately set with mosaic.

My room looked like something out of a medieval castle, and I could hardly believe that the price was little more than one dollar. It was enormous, with a high ceiling and thick stone walls and floor. The bed was huge and solidly built like the rest of the dark, richly carved furniture. In contrast the shower-room with its pile of fluffy white towels and chrome fittings was ultra-modern. But a family of large brown cock-roaches rather ruined this last touch of luxury. I had intended to go to bed early in order to get off at dawn the next day, but it was such a wonderful night that I went out on my balcony to watch the street scene below.

The air was sweet and balmy and above a thousand stars shone down on the softly lit streets. The cobbled pavement wound between over-hanging grey houses with iron balconies and shuttered windows. There was gay chatter from the passers by, and across the way a small fruit stall, lit by flickering candles, was doing a roaring trade in fruit juice. Guitar strumming sounded faintly on the night air, and a small café opposite was ablaze with lights and alive with the melodic rhythm of a tango.

Girls strolled by with their dark hair coroneted about their heads or flowing in long tresses down their backs and caught with a bright hair comb or ribbon. Their full skirts flounced and long gold earrings swung to and fro, catching the dim street lights, as they passed by on the arm of their escorts.

The men were no less fascinating with their wide-brimmed hats, graceful walk and dark faces. And as I sat on the edge of my balcony I imagined that a trio of guitar players would come along at any moment to serenade the dark figures of the girls on the balconies opposite. For, like me, they were hanging over the railings staring with envy at the gaiety down below.

CHAPTER XI *Mexicana Enchantment*

WHEN I crept into the courtyard next morning, just before dawn, I found my young friend of the evening before stretched out on a camp bed beside Oppy. I don't know whether this was part of the hotel service to guard our property or if the boy always slept in the courtyard. The noise I made packing Oppy brought him springing to his feet, slightly embarrassed to be caught in such a position. I gave him a peso as he held the gate open for me to ride out. His bright eyes gleamed and he almost did a little dance.

Gasoline Gypsy

As I bumped over the rough cobbled streets an early-morning house-wife was scrubbing her front steps and an old man was pushing his barrow of fruit down the road. The street cleaners were already hard at work, while showers of bedclothes were flung to air over the balconies above. The air was fresh and cool with the merest suspicion of warmth from the burning sun to come. The road wound up into soft green hills, and the view back over my shoulder to the old grey city of Ciudad Victoria, with its many beautiful church towers, was a lovely sight.

Not far south of Ciudad Victoria I came to the crest of a hill, and beside a small drinking booth built of stout palm leaves I saw a large notice that read "Tropico de Cancer." It seemed a very exciting moment when I realized how far south on this continent we had already driven. I looked down at slim-framed Oppy bursting with all her packs; in my imagination she had taken on an almost human air so I patted her with affection and said "You're a good girl." Jealously Matelot leaned his head on my shoulder; I stretched up and scratched his soft brown ears so he wouldn't feel left out. In return I received a big wet lick on my cheek.

As if the surrounding countryside wanted to prove to me that it was indeed south of the Tropic of Cancer, it began to take on a very sub-tropical look. The vegetation was dense with thick overhanging bushes and plants; palm trees dotted the landscape, and for the first time I saw bananas growing wild. Again we climbed into a small range of moun-tains, and the view out over the wide lush valley was such a contrast to the dry, arid desert lands of Texas and Arizona. I saw several of my old hand-waving tourist friends from the border. They had evidently stayed a day in Monterrey to sight-see. For it didn't seem possible that anyone would travel quite so slowly as Matelot and I. The Cadillac from California, the two young men from Texas and a family from Illinois all roared by now waving and shouting "See you in Mexico City."

The villages became more picturesque with every mile. The small huts clustered beneath the shady palm trees, their roofs made of shiny, closely woven leaves and the walls full of holes from loosely intertwined branches. I had been told that the palm leaves made such a completely weather-resistant roof that not even the strongest tropical rain penetrates these fragile-looking abodes. It was the first week in August and well into

Mexico's rainy season, although up to then I had seen no rain at all. I had been warned that this rain fell between the hours of four and six in the evening with the regularity of a Swiss wristwatch. This daily downpour was supposed to be strong enough to halt the traffic on the road and soak anyone to the skin in a matter of seconds. However, after my experience on the desert I felt this sounded almost like a joke.

Climbing into the hills north of Mantes, I was overtaken by a motorcyclist even more laden than Oppy. This large machine was driven by a heavily built man who had a small boy perched in front of him on the tank, another child clinging round his waist from behind, and a youth hanging precariously on to the rear seat. In the sidecar was seated a woman with a baby on her lap, and three more small children were packed in beside her. This was the first time I had seen nine human beings on one motor-cycle outfit!

Now, I have already said the comradeship of motor-cycling is international; anybody who owns a motor-cycle seems to belong automatically to a recognized yet non-existent club bound together by two wheels. So we both pulled to the side of the road and began talking like old friends. My conversation with this enormous motor-cycling family was very amusing, and all the kids crowded round to stroke Matelot. But because their parents were in a hurry to reach Mexico City all the kids were soon fitted in again, like sardines in a tin, and off they went all waving and screaming lustily.

I entered Mantes about noon, which was a bad time of day for shopping, since all provincial Mexico stops its business from twelve o'clock until three in the afternoon. Siesta time was in full swing now and most of the shops were closed. I was forced to waste nearly three hours before I could buy for my camera the film which was only carried in the larger towns or tourist stops.

In Mantes' small post office I tried to mail some letters to Europe, and this caused a complete crisis in the life of a bewildered young clerk. He had never heard of a place called Denmark, although I pointed to the Spanish translation in my pocket dictionary. I had to produce a small map of the world before he could reckon the necessary postage. England was a little simpler, but not much. Still, I was rather pleased at this few hours' delay in Mantes, because my long rides between towns were so isolated that I often held one-sided conversations with Matelot to make up for my lack of human contact.

Now I sat drinking coffee in a little open-air café and chatted with the pretty *señorita* who waited on me, and the other customers at the tables alongside. I found it was up to me to break the silence and unwavering, embarrassing stares that my obviously foreign appearance created. All the Mexicans I talked to were curious and interested beyond words about their neighbours across the border and their mother country of Spain. Anything I told them about the rest of Europe and how it differed from Mexico fascinated them. Most of the people I met had talked with few, if any, foreigners and were shy with me at first.

So I was forced to start stuttering away in my poor Spanish, and then they became so eager to help me in my simple phrases that they soon lost all self-consciousness and chatted away with real Latin animation.

I planned to spend that night in a small town called Tamazunchale, which nestles at the foot of the great Sierra Madres, about seventy miles from Mantes. It seemed prudent to start climbing into the mountains early next morning, because this was going to be an all-day endurance test for poor Oppy. Some of the villages I drove past that afternoon looked far more prosperous than in northern Mexico. The walls of the huts were of stone and roughly whitewashed, which contrasted delightfully with the shining palm-leaf roofs. I saw many women working outside their homes, who looked like full-blooded Indians. Their brightly striped skirts fell almost to their bare feet, and their hair hung in long dark braids down their backs. Half a dozen flashing gold bangles hung on their arms and their ears were pierced by exotic dangling earrings. They looked happy and gay people, and as I sped past they lifted their hands in greetings and some shouted "*Ola, ola!*" Then I would wave back and toot Oppy's horn.

Little children would come running into the road beside me, shouting, some naked as the day they were born, and all as brown as berries. Oppy's little toot always brought forth grins and shouts of merriment, but if I stopped to take their picture they ducked shyly and ran screaming back to Mama. I have never found any people so camera shy as the Mexicans; they act as though you are pointing a gun at them, not just a camera.

The road surface ahead of me now was wet, and in the distance I could see a beautiful rainbow outlined against the sky. Apparently I had just missed the evening downpour, because the trees were soaked and dripping with moisture. The air was quite fresh as I rode into the red-and-gold rays of the sunset.

Pretty soon I came upon the two young Texans to whom I had waved so often on the highway as they sped past me. But now they were both lying on their backs trying to mend a flat tyre. By this time I felt I had become expert at changing tyres, so I stopped and asked if they wanted any help. But they only laughed and said I'd better hurry on to Tama-zunchale, warning me that the roads at night in Mexico were full of bandits. What nonsense, I thought, as I rode along in the gathering dusk.

But little seeds of doubt laid in one's mind always ripen faster in the darkness, and I began to think of the horror-struck face of the Mexican consul in Vancouver when I had told him about the motor-cycle trip I proposed to take by myself through his country. He had implored me above all not to travel at night after dark, because Mexican roads are lonely and deserted and anything might happen to me. That night it was very dark; the moon was hidden behind the mountains into which we were climbing.

I drove head on into a blinding wave of small bugs, and had to stop and get out my goggles and a scarf, which I tied over my lower face like a gas mask. Halted there on the side of the deserted dark road made me feel very creepy, so just as quickly as I could I kicked Oppy's engine over and got under way once again. We were climbing higher every moment. As the road twisted and turned upwards I had to drop into second gear. My lights were poorer than ever and the night inky black, lit only by numerous fireflies.

All at once the road dropped steeply, and I was flying round sharp hairpin bends. The dim lights of a small town showed far below in the darkness. Figures dressed entirely in white suddenly loomed up in front of the machine, walking placidly all over the road. Had it not been for their light-coloured dress I would surely have run into half a dozen of them. But they seemed quite unconcerned as we flew past, missing some of them by no more than inches.

Driving slowly through this little community, I never felt so strongly that I had stepped into a dream. All the men were dressed in pure white from the top of their wide-brimmed sombreros to their white canvas sandals. Their light clothes contrasted with their dark skin, giving them a theatrical appearance. No hotel was in sight, although I'd been told that Tamazunchale was a fair-sized little town and that it contained several inns.

Along the village street there were flocks of little open-air drinking booths, lit by the soft flickering light of candles. There was in fact no other lighting in the street, and it made the place seem even more like a scene from a play. The tiny houses were of whitewashed stone with thatched roofs, and the narrow winding street was flanked on either side by tall overhanging trees that completely shut out the night sky. The air was warm and heavy with the scent from tropical night flowers. Men squatted on the ground or leaned against the wooden counters of the drinking booths, drinking wine and Bimbo. The women were separated from the men and many sat knitting on the benches outside their houses.

As I slowed down looking for some sort of hotel, Matelot jumped off and chased a small dark shadow that was hopping down the pavement. I gave chase too, and found he had cornered a huge pouchy-looking toad against an old stone wall. An old man and his wife, sitting in the doorway of their cottage, were laughing and pointing at his frenzied barkings. I have a horror of toads, so I kept well away.

But by this time Matelot's barking had attracted most of the village, who gathered curiously round Oppy. When I asked the old woman if this was Tamazunchale, she couldn't understand my accent. Then the most beautiful dark-haired girl came forward out of the crowd and, pointing on my map, indicated that Tamazunchale was farther up the road. I wondered if she knew how lovely she looked standing there in her simple white blouse and gay coloured skirt, which fell just above her brown bare feet. Her hair was a dark cloud hanging to her waist, while her face would have been her fortune anywhere outside of that small Mexican village.

Once again we climbed up into the darkness of the silent mountains and the warm night. Then I gradually came into the light of the moon, which was steadily rising over the summit of the mountains. The road ahead was lit like a silver ribbon, winding up and up round the dark mountain sides. The beauty of the night was intense, and I wished that drive would last for ever. But after about half an hour of steady climbing the road dropped steeply once more, and the bright lights of Tamazunchale shone ahead in the valley below.

I felt far too grubby and untidy to enter a hotel, so on the outskirts of the town I stopped by the side of the road. There I made a few half-hearted attempts to freshen up, washing my face out of the water bottle, and dragging a comb through my hair, which was thick with small night-flying insects.

Then, farther down the road, I passed a long, low-lying lighted building and after that the road seemed to wind off into the depths of the country again. Tamazunchale was certainly an elusive place! I turned Oppy round and went back to the lighted house, where a small group of people were sitting round an oil lamp in front of the tall pillars running the length of the house. When they all peered forward as I approached, I shut off the engine and asked them the way into the town. A small dark woman of about forty jumped up and asked if I needed a place to sleep that night; because if I did she could give me a very nice room. By this time I was dreading the thought of searching for a hotel in a strange town, so I didn't hesitate for a moment.

Lupez introduced herself and then, turning in the direction of the house, she let out the most piercing scream, "Simon, Simon!" She stamped her foot in impatience, and finally Simon appeared on the scene. He was a tiny man just over five feet tall, with curly black hair and a winning smile. He stood by patiently as Lupez gave him a torrent of orders in Spanish, and then hurried back inside the house.

I put Oppy inside the courtyard, and then as I started to remove my typewriter and overnight bag Lupez once more yelled, "Simon, Simon!" He came hurrying out again as fast as his little legs would carry him, and seized all my things; I wasn't even allowed to carry the camera. Then I followed him along the beautiful green-and-white tiled porch with its stone pillars and gracefully arched ceiling.

Two sides of my room gave out on to this open cloister-like corridor that ran most of the way round the house. The furniture in the room was richly carved, and a huge mirror hung on one of the pale-green walls.

Gasoline Gypsy

On a low table by the sumptuous bed was placed an oil lamp which gave off a soft pleasant light, and cast shadows on the high ceiling above. A little maid was already making up the bed with snowy white linen, and Simon lowered my rather shabby luggage on an exquisitely carved chest in front of the window.

By the time I got to the shower room I was beginning to worry about the price, but when I signed the guest book, brought in by Lupez, and paid only eight pesos, I was agreably surprised. Then I looked at the departing figures of Lupez, Simon and Maria, the maid, and thought there weren't many places on earth where one could get such luxury and service for less than a dollar a night.

Presently Simon came back struggling under the weight of two enormous buckets of water, and I wondered if he thought Matelot was that thirsty! When I discovered there were some repairs going on and the running water had been shut off, my thoughts of a delicious cool shower disappeared. But who was I to be so fussy? Only four days before, in the middle of the desert, I had been brushing my teeth with a dab of water out of a bottle and relying on service stations to wash out my socks.

In a few minutes Lupez came back to see that I had everything I needed, and then, looking critically at one of the brocaded curtains, she let out another yell. Poor little Simon came running at the double, and she poured forth a torrent of words; he disappeared, only to return a minute later under the burden of a ladder twice his size. Then with a nod of approval she left me with a *"Hasta mañana, señorita."* I don't know what poor Simon was doing to the curtain, and I personally couldn't have cared less how they looked for one night. But evidently he was satisfied at last when he crept gingerly down the steps to the floor and surveyed his handiwork.

"Muy bien, muchas gracias, señor," I said smiling and he flashed me a delighted grin. Then, murmuring inaudibly, he staggered out under the swaying ladder.

I opened up a tin of fruit, spread out some cheese on a roll, and lay down on the bed to eat my unusual picnic supper. The night was deliciously warm, not the stifling heat of the last couple of weeks. A lovely balmy air drifted through my screen door, and lying between the cool sheets I decided that Mexico was a holiday-maker's dreamland, and fell into a contented sleep.

The morning sunlight fell in little lacy patterns across the green-and-white tiled floor, and I could look out through the screen door straight on to the highway beyond. I felt deliciously lazy not to be springing to my feet in the half light, or wriggling around inside a cramped tent. As I watched, a small boy appeared driving a herd of goats up the road. He was followed by a tiny black donkey jogging along under the weight of a huge man whose bent head nodded under a large straw hat. Two girls carrying water pitchers passed, their primitive sandals making a flip-flop on the hard road. Beyond the highway and jungle-like vegetation the green mountains looked cool and inviting. I could have lain there all day, but the long mountain highway awaited me, so I sprang out of bed.

Lupez came in to tell me breakfast was ready; there would be no escaping the Mexican food this time! Up to then I had eaten nothing in Mexico but bananas, bread, and a few tins of fruit and vegetables brought in from the States. I couldn't afford to take a meal at a good hotel, and I had been warned against eating the food in small cafés.

However, I really love to try new types of dishes, so I approached my Mexican breakfast with curiosity. Before me on the plate sat some dried-up, thin, cold pancakes called *tortillas,* and a dish of beans. These beans were a squashed brown mess and tasted just as awful as they looked.

Following the example of Lupez, I picked up a *tortilla* in my fingers, rolled it round in the messy beans, and flung the dripping object into my mouth. I nearly choked! The *tortilla* was dry and tasteless and the beans had a horrible rancid oily taste. I flung some hot chili over the rest of the food and succeeded in burning my mouth, but anything was preferable to that first nauseating taste of *tortillas* and beans. The coffee arrived, and I couldn't help noticing the half-washed cups and the flies floating on the top of the cream pitcher.

And unfortunately Maria opened the kitchen door just at that moment, so I caught sight of the cat drinking out of the milk can. The *tortilla* dough sat in an ancient metal bucket on the floor, and two chickens were pecking at a cockroach which scuttled out of the kitchen and into our eating room. I could feel my stomach turning over, so, excusing myself, I rushed back to my room, where I gulped down a couple of swigs of my foul-tasting stomach remedy.

I was all ready to leave when Oppy started playing up, and I had to dirty my hands changing her spark plug.

At last I made a late start, but it wasn't until I had got to the bottom of the hill that I happened to look down at my left hand and saw that my engagement ring was missing. I was horror-struck, then I remembered that I had taken it off outside in the courtyard and put it on the edge of one of the packs while I was changing the spark plug.

I drove slowly back up the road searching every inch of the ground hoping to catch a glimpse of it shining in the sunlight. Maria and I searched every corner of the courtyard and the roadway in front of the house, but I never saw my ring again. Perhaps it rolled into a crack or under a rock and may still be sitting there to this day, but more likely some jubilant child had the find of his life.

That ring meant so much to me that I still feel as if a part of me stayed behind in that small Mexican mountain town. Although Tamazunchale is an ancient and beautiful place dating back to early Indian time, set against a background of steep mountain sides, jungle vegetation and a wild, flowing river, its winding streets full of quaint shops, cafés and a beautiful old church were almost wasted on me. I was so sad about the loss of Carl-Erik's ring.

However, after a bit I perked up enough to go bargain-hunting down in the street market. Every type of basket and bag, hand woven in natural and brightly dyed straw, hung from the stalls. Pottery of every shape and size covered the uneven cobbled streets, and handsome hand-woven blankets and rugs were spread out to display their wonderful colouring and design. As I strolled along examining one beautiful article after the other, the merchants shouted their wares at me. I was looking for a small bag to serve both as a camera case and as a purse to use when I reached Mexico City. I found a beautifully made one in natural straw, and when I was asked only fifty cents, all ideas of bargaining disappeared.

The road out of the town didn't lead us gently over low foothills before beginning the great mountain climb; instead, it rose boldly above us and led steeply into the rock face at a rather alarming angle. I dropped immediately into second gear, and could feel the back wheel dragging under its terrific weight and this sudden steep hill. Our road clung to the side of the mountain and wound above us in three long hairpin bends. Gazing upwards it was hard to believe that we were actually going to climb to those heights. By this time the traffic above us looked as small as ants. The climb over the Canadian Rockies had been gradual, but this road over the Sierra Madres was overwhelming with its sudden altitude.

And as we climbed slowly into these beautiful mountains I realized what a feat of engineering skill the Pan-American Highway was, and marvelled at the width and perfect surface of this road hacked out of pure rock. Below, the valley lay green and distant, while the mountains ahead looked just as green and gentle too; yet as I climbed I saw we reached the summit of one mountain, only to start climbing farther and higher to the next range. How deceptive were these mountains with their gentle, rounded formation, but with altitudes far greater than those of famous European Alpine passes. After a bit I stopped at a viewpoint that was breathtakingly lovely. I could look down on the road I had just climbed, far down below to where it began to twist up from the valley. The mountains in the distance were a purple-blue against the paler sky and green slopes, lovelier than any painting. I was sitting on a stone parapet now and revelling in all this beauty, when a car from Illinois stopped and three young men from Chicago introduced themselves.

They were certainly bearers of bad tidings. First I learnt that it was already nearly five o'clock in the afternoon. Then they told me that the road climbed just as steeply into the mountains for the next hundred miles! And the nearest town with a hotel was fifty miles away!

At the pace I was creeping along, barely twenty miles per hour, I realized that I should find myself out on the mountain highway when darkness fell. Fifty miles, even on low-powered Oppy, is nothing on an ordinary road, but on this terrifyingly steep hill fifty miles might require over three hours driving time.

Oppy crept more and more slowly up the road, and on the steep hairpin bends I was forced to throw her into first gear. She became so overheated that I was worried that her piston might expand and freeze in

The journey begins. Halifax, Nova Scotia.

Matelot dons his goggles on a snowy road near Vancouver, January 1952.

With Janie and Eric Reed of Penticton. Peggy and Matelot, hats on for the cold Rockies.

Daytripping in the mountains.

Go west, young woman.

Peggy decokes the Bantam.

A fine vista, but sometimes a dog has something else on its mind.

Back on the road after working in Montreal.

The perennially popular Matelot.

Dirt roads and the magnificent scenery of the Rockies.

the cylinder, so I stopped and put some more oil in the tank. A glance at my speedometer needle showed that we were climbing now at a rate of less than ten miles an hour! Even the heavy trucks which seemed to crawl up the road like snails passed me with much hooting and grinning from the drivers. I listened to Oppy's spluttering feeble engine and guessed that her piston rings must have expanded, or perhaps one of them had broken with the heat. There was nothing I could do about it until I got to Mexico City and found some spares. So I settled down to try and enjoy the magnificent scenery about me and forget my worries for the time being.

Occasionally I passed a lone figure walking along the side of the highway, a roughly dressed peasant or barefoot child. I wondered where they came from, since the towns and villages were so far apart. Then I caught sight of several small clusters of primitive huts perched on the sides of the mountains, almost obscured by the dense tropical undergrowth. I passed one small hut village of full-blooded Indians. Apparently they were living just like their ancestors had some hundreds of years ago. Some of them had set up rough stalls by the side of the road, to sell bananas, which hung in great bunches on tall poles. I bought one variety which measured over a foot long, while another kind was a queer orange colour. Bananas in Mexico were so very cheap that they were fast becoming my steady diet.

Presently Oppy developed another symptom—a distinct wobble in her rear wheel. Driving so slowly had made it difficult to steer and unavoidably we had hit a few bumps in the road. Now I was sure that my wheel-changing in Texas hadn't been able to stand this added strain. There wasn't much I could do about it out there alone on the highway, so I went on hoping against hope that the wheel would hold out somehow until Jacala, the next town, before collapsing completely.

With a sinking heart I steered a now drunken Oppy up the steep road. The sun was fading behind the mountain and the most glorious sunset had fallen over the rock face, turning it, in a matter of minutes, from fiery red to soft pink. The air was suddenly cold, the cold of a mountain night; there was a sharp tangy feel to the atmosphere. I piled on a couple of sweaters and longed for my slacks and warm socks. My blood was thin and my body conditioned to extreme heat; this return to cold night air was quite a change for me.

Then suddenly the worst happened—wobble—wobble—wobble— the rear wheel did a snake dance, and I only just managed to drop my feet to the ground and steer Oppy to a safe halt. In the last fading light I found that half a dozen of the wheelspokes were loose, and two or three had broken off completely. I wondered, too, if perhaps the second bearing had not worn under the tremendous load it was carrying. The dark night was dropping all around me now and my broken-down motor-cycle needed a skilled mechanic.

All at once the beautiful mountains weren't friendly any more. They seemed to loom above me with a sinister air, while the thick jungle on either side of the road appeared ready to close in. I thought again of how I had laughed at the idea of bandits on the roads at night, and the tales of wild animals that were supposed to inhabit the subtropical jungles of Mexico. Then something seemed to move in the undergrowth; I was positive I heard a distinct rustling noise! I hung on to Matelot's collar for protection, but nothing happened, and I was still alone on the dark moun-tain. Perhaps I was already watched by unseen eyes from some of those small hidden huts? That thought stopped any idea of camping.

Then up the long highway came the deep rumble of an approaching truck, climbing slowly under a heavy load. There was only one course for me to take and I didn't even stop to think of the consequences. As the truck's piercing headlights played over the scene of our breakdown I flung myself in its path and waved both hands frantically. At that moment I was lucky to be a girl, because no vehicle would have stopped on that lonely mountain highway for a man.

But the huge truck came to a stop beside me, and peering through the darkness up into the cab window, I looked into the face of a swarthy young Mexican.

CHAPTER XII *Latin Chivalry*

TWO figures jumped down from the back of the truck; they were joined by the driver and his companion from the front. Four roughly dressed, brown-skinned Mexicans regarded me for a moment in utter astonishment, then all at once they burst into an incomprehensible dialect, all of them shouting at the same time.

I beckoned them over to where Oppy was propped against the stone parapet, and they gathered around the machine, excitedly pointing to the wheel and throwing their hands into the air. Then, making a few gestures to explain that the back wheel would not turn properly, I pointed to the back of the truck.

Almost at once all four men started to nod their heads and chorused "*Si, si, si, señorita.*" Then they began to lift Oppy over to the rear of the truck. I put all my loose belongings into the back of Matelot's box and secured them with the groundsheet and a couple of straps.

Meanwhile a furious argument was going on among my four rescuers. It seemed that there was a cargo of several hundred kilos of oranges on the back of the truck, and they didn't like the idea of Oppy sitting on this crop destined for the Mexico City fruit market. In any case it would have been almost impossible to hoist my machine on to the back of that high truck.

Finally a huge rope was produced and the young driver lashed this round Oppy's middle, and with a heave and a ho! two of the men and I pulled with all our might until the machine was nearly in the hands of the two other men on the truck above us. The idea was to suspend poor Oppy from the back end of the truck by means of the stout rope, and leave her hanging in mid-air. The first time we hoisted her up, she came crashing to the ground again. "*Caramba!*" exclaimed one of the men in horror at the weight of the stout little motor-cycle.

But at last the Mexican on the truck grasped Oppy and secured her

A Ride in the Sun

firmly until she lay dangling over the side of the truck, swaying precariously. The young driver offered me the seat beside him at the wheel, but I preferred to stay where I could watch out for Oppy's safety. The two men already seated on the pile of oranges in the back of the truck pulled me up beside them, while the driver gave Matelot a boost. He came up fighting miserably every inch of the way at this undignified handling. I sat myself down on the huge, sweet-smelling mass of fruit and looked about me.

Beside me huddled a strange figure beneath a large, beautifully coloured poncho. Two beady eyes looked at me out of a dark wrinkled face. "*Buenos noches, señorita,*" quavered the old man politely. Apparently Matelot and I weren't the only hitch hikers that night.

We started off slowly up the winding road, and I hung over the back, watching Oppy as she swayed back and forth with the motion of the truck. However, she seemed to be perfectly safe, so I settled back on my pile of oranges and prepared to enjoy the trip. Then I began to see the humour of my situation. Here I was sitting in the back of a truck rumbling through the night over the Sierra Madres of Mexico, with five strange Mexicans for companions.

At first I made no attempt at conversation; it was so pleasant just to lie back on my elbows amid the scent of oranges, and gaze up into the starry night sky. Now the moon had risen and was shining over the valley far, far below us; above the road was traced like a band of sequins by the traffic moving slowly ahead of us. Gradually we climbed farther and farther into the mountains, until I felt that if we didn't lose height soon we would reach the sky itself. Tiny lights gleamed here and there out of the dark jungle, reminders that huts belonging to Indian mountain folk were all about us.

One of my companions had produced a guitar now, and he was gently plucking at the strings and humming a little tune. Then he started singing in a low, rich voice; the rhythmic strains of his instrument accompanied the little folk song. This fitted into the romantic scene about me. The old man pulled his blanket farther over his shoulders and nodded in time to the music.

Next the young guitarist played a catchy, gay little tune that made me want to jump up and dance all over the oranges; then he sang a tender

116

love song, sweet as only such a song can sound in Spanish. We rumbled on through the moonlit night to the strains of that Mexican music, and I don't think I had ever made such a lovely and unusual journey.

After all this entertainment, our guitarist's friend decided that he needed some refreshment. Pulling a huge knife from his belt, he picked up an orange, divided it into two halves, one of which he handed to me with a polite gesture, saying "*Señorita?*" and the other half he gave to our singer. Picking up a second orange, he cut once more with the flashing blade of his knife and shared the fruit between the old man and himself. Those oranges tasted like pure nectar. I had eaten nothing since my appalling breakfast with Lupez, except for a couple of bananas on the roadside. My stomach was positively rumbling with this first touch of food. I ate orange after orange, all carefully split in half for me by my chivalrous companion.

During this time I had been chatting with both young men, as best I could. The old man had long since buried his head under the blanket and gone fast to sleep. My two companions told me that they would be delighted to carry me all the way to Mexico City. They added that the trip would take the whole night and they would be arriving in the city in time for the early morning fruit market. Probably I should have gone on with them, but I felt I just couldn't miss the sight of the Sierra Madres by daylight. Also I wanted very badly to drive the rest of the way myself. So I politely declined their invitation and asked to be put down at Jacala.

This small mountain town was supposed to have a large garage attached to a tourist court. And by the light of day I hoped to fix up the rear wheel so that we could limp the rest of the way into Mexico City under our own steam.

Now, after two hours' steady climbing higher and higher into the mountains, we suddenly turned a corner and started to drop rapidly downhill. The slope was so steep that our driver slipped into low gear to give his engine the maximum braking power. My companions began to tell me cheerful little tales about the dangers of this part of the road. Many trucks, they said, had gathered up so much speed that they had failed to make the sharp hairpin bends, and crashed down into the precipice below.

As they were telling me of these horrors, far away down in the valley I could see the lights of Jacala twinkling. Gradually we wound our way down, our ears popping with the drop in altitude and all of us bouncing up and down on the oranges whenever the driver suddenly braked the truck on the worst curves. Now every time I see oranges for sale I think of Matelot, the three Mexicans and myself jumping around on all that fruit.

Presently we drew up beside a large modern garage and tourist court, ablaze with lights and full of people. Half a dozen willing hands started to disentangle Oppy from her humiliating position, while a rather terrified garage mechanic received a wildly struggling Matelot, very anxious to get off the truck. There was a tremendous amount of excited jabbering and argument as Oppy was gently lowered to the ground; everybody called everybody else names for not being more careful with the *señorita's motosicleta*.

Then a very important-looking stout man in a superb brown uniform with shining buttons and badges stepped forward. He bowed slightly and, speaking in English, introduced himself as head of the local police. I had no idea, he informed me, what a terrible fate these kind fellows had saved me from. He raised his hands in horror as he told of the wild animals and rough characters who frequented that road at night.

Then I begged him to ask my gallant saviours discreetly whether I might give them something for their trouble. After the translation there were cries of protest, and with much shaking of heads the four embarrassed men started back toward their truck.

"They say you owe them nothing, that they were delighted to be able to help a *señorita* in distress," explained the police chief.

As the four men were climbing aboard the truck, I rushed up to each in turn, shaking him warmly by the hand and wishing him a profitable sale of the oranges. Four pairs of white teeth gleamed in their dark faces, and with a chorus of "*Adios, señorita,*" they were borne into the night.

This time I was unavoidably caught in an expensive tourist hotel. My room lacked the charm of Lupez's El Patio court but the price was triple. However, the view from my window next morning would have made it worth even twice as much again. The hotel lay clinging to the side of the mountain, with a terraced garden falling away beneath. The little town of Jacala nestled, white and gleaming, in the green valley below, while on every side the mountains rose sharply into the sky. The green slopes looked soft and gentle, but they were misleading; actually in places they are more than seventeen hundred feet above sea level.

When I went in search of my breakfast coffee I found the dining room already packed with hungry tourists. The most delicious-smelling platter of ham and eggs swung past under my gaze, and came to rest in front of a portly American at the next table.

"What, ham and eggs again! Don't these Mexicans think we eat anything else back in the States?" he grumbled.

If he'd only known how close I came to whipping the plate from under his very nose! Of course I had the price of a dozen plates of ham and eggs, but New York was an awfully long way away, and it was better to pull in my belt now than to starve later on. So I hurriedly left the dining room before I gave way completely to the smell of food and became weakminded. Back in my room I made myself a banana sandwich.

Two of the mechanics helped me hoist Oppy's rear on to a couple of wooden boxes, and I went ahead with the task of removing her wheel. I wasn't at all sure what I was going to do after that; perhaps I should try to tighten up some of the loose spokes and find out whether the other bearing had worn. Then, becoming really rash, I was about to take a look inside the hub for the bearing, when two impeccably dressed city men came over to watch me at work. I must have looked rather absurd to them as I sat there on the concrete floor, with the motor-cycle stripped down, my hands as black as soot and my face pouring with sweat. In any event, ignoring their beautifully tailored suits and manicured hands, these new arrivals immediately took hold of the wheel, spun it expertly and instantly gave their verdict in perfect English.

"You have nothing wrong in the wheel except a few broken spokes," one of them said. "If you drive carefully you ought to be able to make Mexico City."

"If I were you, I'd definitely try to take some of the weight off the back wheel," added his companion.

Then, rubbing their hands clean on a rag, both of them wished me luck, stepped into their low-slung convertible and drove off in the direction of Mexico City.

Fortunately one of the service station men who had overheard this good advice offered to carry my heavy luggage to Pachucca. He said that he was going there that afternoon to pick up a load of petrol. From the map I learned that Pachucca was a good-sized city just off the Pan-American Highway before reaching Mexico City. So I gratefully accepted this offer. If I could drive to Pachucca and get the spokes repaired, then I might be able to make that triumphant entry into Mexico City after all!

When we had stowed away the two heavy side packs, suitcases and tent in the petrol tanker, the driver wrote out the name of a garage where he would leave the luggage and handed me the piece of paper. This left Oppy with just the weight of Matelot and the overnight bag, and she looked almost streamlined now. Still, I felt just a twinge of anxiety for the rest of my precious possessions, and thought how awful it would be if they got lost.

Anyhow I soon managed to get the rear wheel back in place, but it was nearly lunchtime when I set off downhill for Jacala. It was the most horrible feeling careering down the steep winding road with the back wheel swaying beneath me. At times I thought I was going to lose all control of the machine, but luckily we had the inside of the road. It would have been terrifying to be wobbling near the edge of that high precipice!

Jacala proved to be even more picturesque than Tamazunchale. The cobbled streets were narrow and steep, and old houses hung over on either side, shutting out the bright sunlight and casting shadows across our way. There were several attractive little inns gathered round the open market square, and I wished that I hadn't had to waste my money staying in the tourist court. There was a brisk business going on at the market stalls, which were hung with all the usual gay Mexican merchandise of rugs, bags and blankets.

Stopping at one stall to buy bananas for lunch, I asked where I could get some fresh meat. Poor Matelot had eaten his last tin of dog food the day before. The banana man pointed down a steep little street. So I walked on until I came to a rough open stall covered with ancient carcasses of meat. They were black with congealed blood and a hundred flies buzzed round the revolting mass. An old man with a long, matted grey beard was scraping away at a piece of flesh with a long knife and grimy fingers. There were several Mexicans in wide straw sombreros and vivid ponchos flung over their shoulders, standing by this primitive butcher's stall, so I waited patiently for my turn to be served. Everyone stared at me curiously and then went back to discussing the day's business. At last it seemed to me that I was being deliberately ignored, for the old man went on hacking away at his meat and heaping it up into unappetizing mounds on his counter. And nobody appeared to be buying anything at all. Impatiently now I pushed nearer to the evil-smelling stall, wondering if Matelot would survive such a poisonous-looking dinner.

When the old man finally realized I was a prospective customer, and not just a curious tourist, he gave me a toothy grin and heaped his scales with some of the stringy lengths of meat. His price was very expensive, but after all a dog has to eat, so I settled for a pound of meat, which the old butcher wrapped up in a ragged piece of newspaper. Then, clutching the bloody package and vowing to look for tins of dog food in Mexico City, I hurried back to the place I had parked Matelot and Oppy.

But of course Matelot found that horrible meat the best meal he had eaten for ages, and devoured the whole packet in one fair swoop. A chattering mob surrounded him as he licked the last cobblestone clean as a whistle.

No sooner had we left the village behind than the road climbed steeply once more. It twisted and turned up the mountain in dizzy-making heights. And now not only was Oppy's back wheel wobbling worse than ever, but also the motor was coughing and spluttering and nearly giving out on every turn. Thinking of my loss of power and the trouble the carburettor had given me in Olympia, I decided to check that part of the engine here and now.

As I sat there on the side of the road, Oppy's carburettor in pieces, a truck passed me, pulled in ahead and stopped. A very Mexican-looking Mexican climbed down and came over to me. He was tall and well dressed, with a neatly clipped moustache, sunburnt face and the inevitable wide-brimmed sombrero. He wore very dark sun glasses, completely hiding his eyes; in fact, he looked like a villain out of a bad Hollywood grade B film.

But he introduced himself as Juan, an ex-motor-cycle cop. Then, throwing my dismantled carburettor a professional look, he asked if I wanted any help. After I had put the carburettor together again, he told me to ride up the road so that he could listen to the sound of the engine. Then, when Oppy and I had done a few turns up and down the road, he confirmed my original diagnosis.

"Compression in the piston rings," he said. "You're out of luck until you find new ones in Mexico City." He looked up at the road rising steeply ahead. "You won't get another two miles out of that engine. But I'll be glad to take you to Mexico City."

This kind offer seemed the answer to my predicament, so I thanked him and started preparing Oppy for another upheaval. I was just wondering how the two of us alone would ever hoist Oppy into the back of the truck, when I remembered that most of my worldly possessions would be left behind in Pachucca if I took off now for Mexico City. Then, by an extraordinary piece of luck, who should round the corner just at that moment but my friend of the petrol tanker! When he saw me he stopped at once, grinning with delight at my latest hitch-hiking success. Then he sprang down and helped Juan and me lift the machine into the back of Juan's truck. It was full of great bales of paper and we only just managed to squeeze in Oppy. When my luggage had been transferred, and Matelot settled on the floor of the cab, we were ready to start off. So, thanking the kind petrol truck driver, who wished me luck, I climbed up beside Juan and we were on our way to Mexico City.

The load on the back was heavy, and we crawled slowly up the road, which seemed to be getting steeper at every turn. Even a brand-new Oppy would have found this climb a terrific strain.

Poor Matelot was getting terribly tied up in the gear shift and brakes. This was dangerous, because with the great drop into the valley below Juan had to shift gears and brake very rapidly. So I pulled the dog on to the seat beside me and he hung his head out of the window and breathed in the fresh air with happy relief. He seemed to miss his back seat on Oppy and was probably mystified by this sudden change in vehicles again.

Juan was most talkative, and he stretched my Spanish to its utmost as we chatted about his country and all the things around us. He told me how this section of the Pan-American Highway was really a feat of sheer human endurance. It had been engineered and built entirely without modern equipment, by pick and shovel in the hands of hundreds upon hundreds of labourers. Then Juan went on to explain the customs and history of his country, its politics and coming presidential elections, and their last war over one hundred years ago. My head was bursting with trying to comprehend all this in Spanish, but I managed to make Juan understand in turn some of the things I told him about Europe. He knew a little English, so whenever I got stuck in Spanish I substituted a few words in my own language and many wild gestures with my hands.

The journey was passing all too quickly. Night fell amid an exquisite sunset, and then the moon came up like a great orange pumpkin and hung in the midnight-blue sky.

The road was dropping now steadily, and after about half an hour we reached a small town, where Juan stopped for supper. It was about eleven o'clock at night when we entered the large noisy restaurant. A long counter and bar stretched the length of the room, but we chose one of the small tables dotted across the room. The most fiery Latin-American music was blaring forth from a juke-box and the air was blue with smoke. This was just the sort of place I had been longing to see but hadn't dared enter alone.

The floor was scattered with sawdust except for a small space swept clear for a few couples dancing to the strains of a tango. The conversation around us was excited and noisy; swarthy men flirted outrageously with beautiful *señoritas*, a table of youths next to us shouted for another bottle of wine. There was a large family eating an enormous meal, and I gazed astonished at the small children busily gorging themselves at this late hour on meat covered in peppers and hot chili sauce!

Presently our waitress came over and I wondered what typical hot Mexican dish I would dare to order. But Juan wouldn't hear of it.

"You'd better have ham and eggs," he said. "It's the best thing they do here."

Suddenly I remembered that I had eaten nothing all day again except for a few bananas; in fact, I hadn't bothered much about food for the last two days because of all these mechanical breakdowns. So now as I tucked into the large plate of ham and eggs I also realized that this was the first hot meal I had had since the supper with June Caldwell in Tucson, ten days before.

With the ham and eggs we drank a dry red wine, which my host told me was made locally. Over coffee Juan lit up a long thin cheroot. The atmosphere was so typically Latin, with the animated voices all around us, the smell of hot Mexican cooking and the wild music, that I would have loved to tango with Juan just to get in the spirit of the evening. However, the hour was already late and Mexico City was still over two hours away, so, stuffing a couple of sugar-coated buns into my bag for Matelot, we hurried back to the truck.

The road stretched over a very gently sloping plain. The high mountains of the Sierra Madre were left behind now, but as Mexico City itself is more than seven thousand feet above sea level we had not left the mountains altogether. The truck was tearing along down the dark road, and we seemed to be making excellent time. Then suddenly ahead of us a light was swinging across the road and a couple of uniformed police signalled us to stop.

"This is the first police check-station for contraband," explained Juan.

The police examined his papers carefully, and then, when they caught sight of me, a flood of questioning began. I got out my passport and explained what had happened, so then the back of the truck had to be lowered in order that Oppy might be examined too. They seemed satisfied with my story and let us proceed up the road. I never quite understood why there should be such check-ups all down the road leading to Mexico City, but it certainly made the journey more exciting. By the time I had explained myself and passport for the third time I was practically word perfect in my Spanish phrases.

We were just entering the outskirts of Mexico City when a car with a California licence plate passed us. Juan gave an excited exclamation and speeded up his truck. When we overtook the car Juan leaned out of his window, yelling at the driver in pigeon English. Both vehicles pulled over to the side of the road, and two young American couples got out and started wringing Juan by the hand and saying, "Well, what d'y know, Juan!"

It seems that Juan had found the young people stranded with engine trouble near Tamazunchale the night before, and had towed them into the nearest service station. He certainly was a real Good Samaritan of the road. Not content with all he had done for these Americans already, he now insisted on showing them how to find an inexpensive hotel, and led the way in his truck.

We dropped the Californians off at a hotel, and then continued on through the city. Once we were stopped by a policeman when he caught sight of me sitting up beside Juan. Apparently there is a law in Mexico prohibiting female passengers in commercial trucks; but when Juan explained that I was a foreigner in distress, the policeman gallantly waved us on. We came to a large wide avenue with tall trees planted down either side, and this, Juan told me, was the Avenida Juarez, the main street of the city. Very beautiful it was too, with its floodlit buildings, large mansions and luxury hotels.

I was just thinking about the problem of getting a hotel room at two in the morning, handicapped as I was by my travel-worn appearance, a broken-down motor-cycle and large shaggy dog, when Juan came up with a good suggestion. He must have realized that I had to save every peso. Anyway he offered to let me sleep in the truck, and said that in about six hours he would be driving to the warehouse to drop off his load, and then there would be plenty of men to help us lift down Oppy. Juan added that his truck would be parked the rest of the night in front of his apartment, and I would be quite safe because I could lock the doors.

Certainly the idea of sleeping in a truck in the deserted streets of an unknown district in Mexico City sounded rather wild, but I was too tired to feel either nervous or excited. The truck stopped in a small ill-lit street beside an old grey stone building. Juan pulled out a flat and rather grubby pillow and a blanket, and with a *"Muy buenos noches, Señorita Peggy,"* he disappeared into the dark house.

I snapped the two doors locked, pushed Matelot on to the floor and looked out into the dark street. There was not a soul in sight, and somewhere a clock chimed the half hour softly. Then, placing the pillow under my head, I wrapped the blanket round me and tried to stretch out. For a girl of five feet nine to try and lie full length on a short cab seat, without her knees almost touching her chin or her feet hanging down on to the floor, is an impossibility. I felt like a contortionist. Finally, after a lot of wriggling around, I pushed my head up against the door as far as possible, and with my legs in the air, I wrapped my feet round the opposite door handle. But I pushed the blanket away from my face because it smelt strongly of cheroot.

Now for a moment I lay there thinking of the past two days' events. Mexico City was a far cry indeed from Vancouver, British Columbia. Perhaps this was the start of the trouble everybody had warned me was bound to catch up with us sooner or later. But, even with such pessimistic thoughts turning around in my head, I pushed my toes harder against the window, closed my eyes and slept.

CHAPTER XIII *El Maestro*

WHEN I woke up I ached in every bone in my body, I had a foul taste in my mouth, and for a moment I wondered where on earth I was. The atmosphere in the cab was hot and stuffy, so I quickly opened a window and peered out. All around me the street was beginning to stir now, and the clock across the way showed that it was just after six o'clock. A man from a small grocery store opposite was brushing the pavement with a long broom, and two women in black passed carrying metal milk cans and small, flat loaves of bread. I felt horribly grubby and untidy and not at all like facing a day in the big capital. Then, because I couldn't get to my water bottle, I cleaned my face and hands as best I could with cold cream and combed my hair.

On the corner of the street a baker's shop had just opened, so I jumped down from the truck and went across the street with Matelot to buy a few buns for breakfast. The dark-haired young couple who served me immediately threw up their hands in delight at the sight of Matelot. The wife rushed to fetch a bowl of water, and I stood there in the little shop and we talked about dogs, while Matelot gratefully lapped at the cool water. Then I picked up my bag of buns and went back to the truck. The sun was just beginning to strike the roadway between the tall houses, and the street was full of activity. A long line of school children accompanied by a nun passed on their way to early mass, and a young servant girl appeared walking a snooty-looking poodle on a long red lead. Sitting up in the front of the high truck munching my breakfast, I felt rather conspicuous, for many passers-by were staring at me curiously. Then I remembered the law about women not being allowed on trucks and hoped a policeman wouldn't come along and ask some embarrassing questions.

About eight o'clock my friend Juan showed up looking clean, rested and well shaved. We set off once more across the city, and presently we turned into a wide cobbled street and stopped outside a shabby warehouse. At the hoot of the truck's horn several men came running out.

They shouted their amazement at the sight of Oppy in the back of the truck, but soon calmed down enough to lower her carefully to the ground under the sharp orders of Juan. Apparently he was not merely a salaried truck driver but the owner of his own trucking business. I tried hard to thank him for all his kindness, but he wouldn't even listen to me. Like a true gentleman, he felt he had merely shown me conventional politeness.

And now, after telling me how to find the motor-cycle shop, he swept off his wide straw hat with an elegant gesture, shook my hand warmly and wished me a happy stay in Mexico.

I set off carefully over the wide bumpy streets, trying to avoid the broken patches of cobblestones. Suddenly I hit a dreadful hole, the rear wheel leapt into the air and Oppy almost turned upside down. Then a pinging noise warned me that a few more spokes had fallen out of the wheel. Now the only way I could steer the machine was with both feet dragging on the ground. So I had to crawl across Mexico City at about five miles an hour. It was the most embarrassing drive of my life.

I found myself on a busy main street packed with rushing taxis, cars and rumbling trams. Matelot couldn't stand this wobbling snail's pace; he jumped down on the pavement and disappeared into a delicious-smelling café. An awful disturbance was coming from inside the café, so I hurriedly threw Oppy against the kerb reserved for taxis and dived through the entrance to capture Matelot.

Inside I found he had caused a complete uproar among the customers, who had been so astonished at his sudden arrival that they had mistaken him for a wild beast escaped from the zoo. Matelot had cornered a spitting cat under the table and the furious proprietor was swatting at him with a table napkin and shouting with rage. Dodging the cowering breakfasters and gripping Matelot's collar I yanked him back between the tables, scattering my apologies as I went. Then I dumped him back into his box on Oppy and looked him in the eyes, ready to give him the scolding he deserved. But he was so cute and pleased with himself that I didn't have the heart to say a word.

We seemed to sway for hours through the busy city streets until at last we reached the motor-cycle shop. Then I found it didn't open until ten o'clock in the morning! I passed the waiting time by looking at the shining new models in the large showroom window.

At last a dapper little man in a well-cut business suit came along to open the shop. He bowed me through the entrance and into the large showroom full of toys, sporting goods and motor-cycles. I explained as best I could that I needed several spare parts for my machine. But after several telephone conversations he told me there were no spare parts for this model B.S.A. in the whole of Mexico City.

I felt quite desperate, and I must have looked as if I was about to burst into tears, because the shopkeeper put his hand on my shoulder and told me to cheer up. Several other salesmen had come into the shop by this time, and they all discussed the problem with Latin enthusiasm.

Then in halting English one of them suggested that I go and talk to their head mechanic, who was sure to be able to fit parts from some other similar make of machine. Their service department was several blocks away, but he shouted to a young boy at the back of the shop to show me the way.

I set off behind a large, powerful machine, with poor Oppy wobbling worse and worse with every turn of the wheel. When we reached the service department I drove up the slipway and into the workshop at the back, where we were soon surrounded by three excited mechanics. A portly little man, who looked like a bull frog, pushed forward and with a regal air asked me what was wrong.

Now, I find it difficult enough to use technical motor-cycle jargon in English, but in Spanish it was an impossibility. I hunted furiously through my little dictionary, miming whenever I lacked words for my explanation of Oppy's sick condition.

First the mechanic shook his head firmly, and when I explained that I had to find some type of piston rings as well as spokes for the wheel or I couldn't move another yard, he threw his arms in the air and shouted *"Impossible, no hay!"*

Finally I went out to the front of the shop, where a calm elderly man and a young girl behind the counter listened to my frenzied attempts at explanation, which were getting wilder and less coherent every minute. I felt more Latin than the Latins as my voice rose higher and higher in excitement. The dark-haired girls said something to the man in rapid Spanish and then, smiling, she told me she was sure they could find parts to fit my motor-cycle from a German model of similar design.

But then the fat little head mechanic, whom everybody addressed as "Maestro," waddled in, and there ensued a furious argument. Precious minutes were slipping by; it was a Saturday morning. I didn't want to spend the whole week-end motor-cycleless, so I tried to hurry matters up a little. Finally it seemed settled that not only did they have the correct-sized piston rings in stock, but also a rim and spokes which would fit Oppy perfectly. However, El Maestro stolidly returned to his other work and seemed to take no further interest in us.

Whereupon I rushed over to where he was busy reboring a piston on a tool-scattered bench, and asked if he couldn't possibly fit the wheel at once. He grinned all over his fat brown face and said *"No es possible, señorita."*

"But why?" I shouted in Spanish. He explained to me that there would be no time because they closed the shop at two o'clock in the afternoon and didn't open again until Monday. Over three hours, and they couldn't change the wheel in time! I was so mad I shouted that if he was such a slow worker then I guessed I had better fix that cylinder head myself.

So I went ahead with the now fairly familiar operation of removing the cylinder head. All three mechanics left their pressing jobs to gather round to watch me working on Oppy. Under their professional gaze my hands trembled and my wrench kept slipping.

El Maestro graciously waved his hand toward the bench of tools and indicated that I could borrow anything I liked; this made the job much easier. I found the piston rings had expanded as Juan had told me, so I pushed in the new pair hoping that they were really the correct size. Next I took off the rear wheel, and pushing it under El Maestro's eyes I said "Monday—*Lunes*," in a loud voice. He nodded and grinned, while the other mechanics giggled and pointed at my greasy black hands.

There was nothing else I could do now, so leaving Oppy to a lonely weekend in the shop, I took the luggage I needed and walked through to the front of the shop. I asked the girl there if she knew of an inexpensive hotel nearby, and she wrote something on a piece of paper and handed it to me.

I felt very conspicuous trudging down the street under the weight of my typewriter, overnight bag, food and camera, while Matelot strained at his leash and made every step worse than the last. At last I found the Hotel San Pedro, a shabby building with a flight of dark stairs leading to the second floor, and a stuffy atmosphere of stale cooking odours. The place seemed deserted, but soon after I had rapped impatiently on the counter a grubby-looking man in his shirt sleeves and several days' growth of beard came through a door from the back. I didn't like the atmosphere of the place at all, so I only paid for one night.

My room was an agreeable surprise, because it was quite clean and light with a large window giving out on to the main street. I went to take a shower to rid myself of all the motor-cycle grease, and when I got back to my room the rain was beating furiously on the window pane. Within five minutes the bright hot sunshine had disappeared and a heavy tropical downpour had taken its place. This fierce rain storm lasted for about two hours and it stopped just as suddenly as it had started, and the sun shone through once more.

Next morning I decided to go on a little walking tour of Mexico City, because with Matelot I was unable to get on any buses or trams. It was Sunday, which is a very gay holiday in Mexico, and the streets were alive with people strolling along in the sunshine. I spent the whole morning wandering through an attractive street market which stretched for at least thirty blocks. After that I needed a rest and found a beautiful park in the centre of the city. Here Matelot seemed tireless as he romped over the green grass, but I took off my shoes and found I had already worn a hole through each sole. And how I missed Oppy as I watched the traffic whirling down Avenida Juarez, and thought of the long walk back to the hotel.

By the time I reached my room that evening I must have walked at least fifteen miles on the hard pavements, and I was so tired that I dropped on to the bed in all my clothes and fell asleep.

Next morning, promptly at ten o'clock, I was sitting on the doorstep of the repair shop. El Maestro greeted me unenthusiastically, making it quite clear that he had more important jobs on his hands. I left Matelot in the shop and hopped on a bus going downtown to the main post office. Eight letters forwarded from the States awaited me. It had been nearly ten days since any of my mail had caught up with me, and I could hardly wait to get to the park opposite and read my letters. And because this took so long it was lunchtime before I got back to the shop.

Now I expected to see my new wheel being assembled, but Oppy stood alone in her corner and everybody was busy working elsewhere. I almost hit the ceiling—"Didn't you promise faithfully to do my job first thing in the morning so that I could get away to Veracruz? Don't you realize I can't afford to stay any longer in the city?"

"*Si, si, si, señorita, mañana, mañana,*" soothed El Maestro.

Tomorrow! I had already caught the Latin habit of flinging my hands in the air and shouting the roof off. So I exploded now with a vengeance. Everyone thought it a huge joke and roared with laughter. The girl from the parts department came out to calm me down and to explain that they were searching at the main shop for a rim and spokes. Why they couldn't have done this on Saturday I do not know, except that Latins seem to love to put off until tomorrow what ought to be done today! And when the rim finally arrived, El Maestro refused to get to work on it! I tried every-- thing from tantrums to false tears.

Then suddenly for no apparent reason, just when all seemed lost, the temperamental man downed the tools he was using and, picking up the new aluminium rim, he fixed it on a lathe and very slowly started to work. This time I stayed right in the shop and insisted that he keep on the job.

I don't think I have ever seen anyone do so little work in such a long space of time. But I wanted the job done properly, so I didn't dare hurry him.

The next day found him still at it! Now I decided to be tactful, and summoning as much patience and cheerfulness as I could manage, I asked how the work was going.

El Maestro's conversation was full of technical terms which I finally translated to mean that the new rim called for another size tyre and inner tube. Then he added cheerfully that there were none in stock of this size at the moment. *Mañana*, he informed me, they would start to try and find me one elsewhere.

I counted to twenty-five rapidly before trusting myself to reply. Then, instead of picking up the nearest wrench and hurling it at El Maestro's tubby figure, I sang him a little song that I had once heard in Madrid, which says that *mañana* is another day. This musical comment appealed to him very much, and he grinned broadly and the other mechanics took up the chant. "*Si, si, señorita, mañana, mañana!*"

Now they were teasing me. But at the same time they made it clear that they were doing everything in their power to get the *señorita's* machine fixed as soon as possible. Did I see that machine over there in the corner? The owner had been waiting for three months.

Oh! *Madre Dios!* how infuriating those Mexicans were! Yet I couldn't help liking them for their gay childish laughter and unpredictable behaviour! I decided that all my pleadings were in vain and the only thing to do was to sit back, calm myself and let them work at their own pace. After all, beyond *mañana* there was always another *mañana!*

However, I felt too restless to sit down quietly, so I decided to clean Oppy. I hadn't done this task properly since Vancouver, and she lay under a thick layer of black chain grease, mud and dust. I had just loosened all this filth with a special solution and was ready to wash it off with the hose when the water was suddenly cut off! Fortunately the usual evening downpour was already beating down on the roadway outside. So, dragging Oppy on her one good wheel out to the street, I let the waters of nature wash her clean, and a very fine job they did too.

Wednesday dawned, this was my fifth day in Mexico City! I didn't seem any nearer to leaving than when I first arrived! But a surprise was awaiting me at the shop. The wheel had been respoked and fitted with a used tyre that was perfectly satisfactory, and the big assembly job was about to get under way!

It was late in the afternoon when Oppy was once more packed and ready for the road, and I could hardly believe that once more I was finally free to go where I pleased.

In pesos the repair bill seemed staggeringly high, but a quick reckoning in dollars made me realize that all those hours of El Maestro's work had come to less than $3.50, while the parts cost about $25. Everyone came out on to the pavement to see us off. El Maestro shook me warmly by the hand and said it had been a pleasure to meet an English motor-cyclist, but added that he thought I was a very impatient and excitable girl.

CHAPTER XIV *On the Road Again*

IT was wonderful to be back on the open highway now, spinning along in the sun with all my cares left behind me. The road out of Mexico City, leading east to Veracruz, lay under an avenue of tall straight trees.

Then a bend in the road brought us into full view of the most magnificent snow-peaked mountain. In the far distance I could see other peaks shining in the sunlight. My map told me that some of these were over eighteen thousand feet high. As I climbed gently into some low-lying mountains, I left these giant peaks away across the valley to the south.

At the bottom of a steep winding hill I stopped for petrol in the small village of San Martin Texemelucan. The pump was very old-fashioned and the young boy who served me had to operate it by hand. When the time came to pay I saw that there was no meter on the pump to register either the price or amount of fuel sold. I had never given too much attention to the price of petrol, since Oppy was so economical, but usually a full tank cost me less than a peso. So when this cheekly little urchin calmly asked me for six pesos, thirty centavos, I felt most indignant. A couple of bystanders drew in their breath in atsonishment and waited for me to behave like a gullible tourist who doesn't care what the correct price should be or is too timid to ask.

Now I was certainly one of the most budget-minded tourists that ever entered Mexico and I didn't dare waste a peso. So once again I exploded in my best and most fiery Spanish. Neither the boy nor I gave ground, not one inch. I said that I had never met such a cheat, and just because my Spanish was bad did he think I was a halfwit to be hoodwinked by such a cheap trick? The rich Spanish language lends itself perfectly to such theatrical outcries, and both the boy and I were really enjoying ourselves. Certainly the crowd that was fast gathering around us was having a wonderful time too.

But after a bit the boy dropped his air of bravado and whined as he pointed to an Oppy that was bursting with baggage and equipment, and said "*Americanas muchas* dollar."

This remark made me look around at the rather poorly dressed and in many cases shoeless people, and almost caused me to feel like a "heel."

Then, remembering my fast-diminishing funds, I made my last stand.

"The police," I shouted, "the police shall decide. Where are they?"

This was a pure shot in the dark, because I did not really believe such a small village would have a police force; but the boy's face dropped instantly now.

"Four pesos, *señorita*," he said, grinning in defeat.

"Nothing," I said, getting ready to leave. "For your dishonesty I will give you nothing!"

"Oh! *Señorita*, two pesos, and I will say prayers for you." His bright little black eyes gleamed at me; no girl could have resisted them.

As I handed him two pesos I said, "You thief, you are being paid twice over," and tried to hide a smile.

Everybody looked pleased and there was a lot of chattering and laughter. After all, the *señorita* was a *little* stupid, everyone knew she owed only about fifty centavos!

And as I drove off down the village street, with two small boys and three dogs infuriating Matelot as they pursued us, I noticed two large police motor-cycles parked outside the café opposite. Two uniformed figures lounged on a shady seat drinking a bottle of wine. As I passed they both lifted their glasses in mock salute.

All afternoon I drove through the lovely green countryside, rich in subtropical foliage and sunshine. Just outside the city of Puebla I stopped Oppy under a shady tree and started to tidy myself up before hunting a room. And I was sitting on the grass tugging the wind and dust out of my hair, when a very old man in an ancient hat, and swamped by a blanket on his shoulder, hobbled up the road leaning on a stick. After we had passed over the first polite preliminaries about the weather, he sat down beside me on the grass and fixed his eyes on Oppy.

"The *señorita* carries more than my donkey when I go into the forest to look for firewood," he said in his quaint peasant's speech.

"I can go much faster too," I laughed, and he cackled in agreement.

From the basket I had bought down the road, I offered him an apple, and he took one with a polite bow of the head. We sat munching apples under the shady tree and watching the cars as they rushed by us on the highway. Both of us agreed there were nothing like donkeys and motor-cycles or your own two feet for getting you around in God's good fresh air. And as I bade my old friend goodbye and started off on the road once more, I looked back over my shoulder to see him standing there on the grass. He had raised his hat in farewell and was waving it furiously in the air; soon he was just a small speck on the horizon.

In the Puebla Tourist Bureau two friendly young men advised me in faultless English of the most reasonable hotel suitable for tourists.

It turned out to be a lovely old grey building built round a cobbled courtyard. There was a wide gallery encircling the second storey with ferns and creepers hanging down through the iron railings. Down the outside staircase came the hotel keeper, running to greet me. Then he bowed me upstairs and into a large high-ceilinged room opening off the gallery. Matelot flopped to his usual place under the large cool bed and I took a shower.

Next morning I got up early, because I wanted to have a good look at the city before taking the road over the mountains to Jalapa, the last town of any size before reaching Veracruz on the coast.

Turning down a small side street, I came on the open market which ran the length of two narrow cobbled lanes. I strolled along looking at the different stalls and was offered everything from squealing little piglets to hand-woven rugs, from freshly cooked *tortillas* with chili sauce to finely chiselled silver bangles. You could pick out a style in baskets that took your fancy, and if you had the time you could wait for your basket to be woven to order under your very eyes.

Live bundles of chickens and geese tied together by their feet, and squawking pathetically, were thrust in my face. One small boy chased me down two streets insisting that I buy one of his gruesome-looking chickens.

"Now, where on earth would I carry such a thing?"I said, appealing to the grinning crowd around me.

"Perhaps a nice *amigo* for your dog?" suggested one wit, so I had to begin my argument with the small boy all over again.

On the outskirts of Puebla I was stopped by two brown-uniformed policemen standing beside their motor-cycles on the side of the highway. I produced my passport, but it didn't seem to interest them in the slightest; they wanted to inspect Oppy. And after peering under all the luggage and examining her small cylinder head, they fingered the twist grip with a professional air and then gasped as they read out the number of miles on my speedometer.

The mountains stretched now far away on both sides of us, and the road followed a wide rolling plain thickly covered in tropical plants. The sky on the horizon had clouded over and the sun was obscured by a great black sheet of rain that was rapidly darkening the whole sky. I had just entered the outskirts of a small village when a torrent of rain streamed down. Blinking my soaking eyes, I caught sight of a low stone building that looked like a café. I pulled Oppy under the half-shelter of an over-hanging roof and, grabbing my camera and Matelot's chain, I lost no time in getting inside the door.

The room into which I stepped had a long lunch counter running down the length of one wall, and there were several tables and chairs scattered over the rough floor. A young woman with a baby in her arms came forward smiling, and I asked for some coffee. When she had brought me a cup of rather weak grey liquid and an assortment of dust-speckled buns, she sat down opposite me and stared very hard. As she bounced the baby on her lap she showered me with a torrent of curious questions. Two other women and a curly-headed young man all gathered round the table. I seemed to be the only customer, and they told me no tourists ever stopped there and that most of their regular customers were the night truck drivers, who made it one of their stops on the way to Mexico City.

It was quite dark by now and I began to wonder how I would ever drive the sixty or so miles to Jalapa in the darkness and rain. I asked the girl if there was anywhere I could spend the night in the village.

"There is no hotel, *señorita*, but you can sleep in our bar tonight when it closes," she told me.

Sleep in a bar! Before entering Mexico I had been nervous of even the idea of staying in a hotel. But here I was caught miles from any city with night coming and a fierce tropical downpour making motor-cycling impossible.

Still, sleeping in the bar of a rather primitive Mexican village seemed to be just a wee bit too adventuresome. At least when I sat on the back of the orange truck we had been on the move. And sleeping in the streets of Mexico City I had been able to lock the truck door.

But there was no other choice now, and the faces around me were friendly, so I thanked the girl and accepted her invitation. Oppy was wheeled inside and put in a small room between the kitchen and the café.

It promised to be a boisterous night, because presently several great heavy trucks roared up and stopped outside, and a crowd of noisy, wild Mexican truckers burst through the door. They all stopped short and gazed at me sitting at a corner table, trying to catch up on my neglected diary. There was much whispered explanation from the café owners and nodding in my direction, before everyone settled down to the latest gossip from Mexico City.

Gradually the café filled until I was all alone in my corner, feeling thoroughly conspicuous. The girls had left the café and were busy in the kitchen, from where they were sending forth the strongest odours of frying oil. By this time the night help had arrived to take charge. He was a large elderly man who wore a white apron tucked round his fat tummy, and the tilt to his chin gave him a certain resemblance to Mussolini. He seemed to glory in his position of authority, and every order shouted to the girls in the kitchen was given with the air of an officer on the parade ground.

My peculiar "case" had been explained to him, and presently he pushed himself importantly through the mob standing round the counter and came over to me. With the air of a Parisian head waiter, he waited for me to order supper. Actually I was feeling very hungry, for my staple diet of bananas and bread was beginning to pall on me. Long before this I had thrown away the water-purifying tablets and forgotten all about germs. And now I decided to be completely reckless and indulge in the most typically Mexican meal I could order.

The night help was throwing his hands up in the air ecstatically to explain what delicious dishes the girls were cooking, while I was searching my head for the Spanish equivalent of "give me the works." Finally we both compromised with nods, shrugs and *si, si, si's*.

Then I sat back and waited, my mouth fairly watering at the prospect of my first hot meal since the ham and eggs with Juan six days before. Meanwhile more and more fascinating characters pushed their way into the crowded smoke-filled café. Apparently half the village had come over to have a look at the strange foreign *señorita*. I didn't even have the support of Matelot, because I had left him in the other room to guard Oppy, not quite trusting the timidity of the children that had been wandering around the café all afternoon. So I found myself gazed at from all sides by the weirdest and most incredible-looking men.

Their large sombreros were pulled low over their dark faces, and over their shoulders were slung gorgeous coloured striped blankets. Several of these characters stared unwaveringly at me with dark piercing eyes between the small space of hat brim and blanket edge; the most sinister scrutiny I had ever encountered. I was so fascinated that I think I also stared back unwaveringly. Actually it was their wonderful woven ponchos or blankets which fascinated me, but I kept catching the eye of a poncho's owner, and judging by his knowing glances I am afraid he thought I was fascinated by him!

At last Mussolini arrived with my supper. He flung a rather grubby check tablecloth in front of me like a matador swinging his cape in the bull ring. Then he gave a terrific performance, flourishing knives and forks and a glass of water on to the table, while all the spectators peered forward to get a better view.

When he came back bearing the first plate I was sure the meal was going to be stupendous after all these preliminaries. I looked down at the plate he had set before me; a thin bone hanging with a few threads of stringy meat was swimming in a thick gravy-like soup. It tasted even worse than it looked, so I didn't dare try to guess its origin. I dowsed it thoroughly in hot chili sauce, which left me with nothing but a burning sensation in my throat and a desire for about a gallon of water. The inside of my throat felt as though it had developed prickly heat, so that when Mussolini came bearing the next plate high in the air I was totally unable to speak.

At once I seized whatever was before me and stuffed it into my mouth, nearly choking, because I had swallowed one of those vile-tasting *tortillas* made of maize flour and fried quite dry. It was a good deal like eating a thin piece of cardboard. To go with this delicacy there was, of course, more of that famous backbone of the Mexican cuisine—beans. Horrible, gooey, mashed beans mixed in rancid oil.

The meal was even worse than Lupez's breakfast, but I was so hungry that I had to eat *something*. When I had unstuck my throat from all this horrifying mixture, I managed to attract Mussolini's attention for a glass of water. Then I finished the evening's banquet with a cup of coffee and two buns, and that was definitely the best part of the meal. By this time my stomach was beginning to protest. The chili was quarrelling with the beans, and the beans were jumping around on the *tortillas,* and the coffee and buns only added insult to injury.

When the café began to empty Mussolini came over, all full of smiles and inquiries as to how I had enjoyed my supper. I didn't want to hurt his feelings, so I just gave him a weak smile and said nothing.

The bar, he informed me, was about to close, so if the *señorita* felt like sleeping he would show the way. I followed him through a door into a small smoke-filled room which reeked of alcohol. A young man was clearing away the last glasses and Mussolini swept three tables together against a wall, indicating that this was to be my bed for the night. It was around midnight, so even three hard tables in a bar looked pretty good to me. I hurried back through the café to collect my sleeping bag.

But I was a little undecided about Matelot. Should I leave him with Oppy to protect our precious luggage, or take him along to guard me? I soon decided on the latter course. There was a small basin in the passage way near Oppy, and I tried to brush my teeth and soap my face before going back to my bar. But I seemed to be directly in the way of a continuous stream of traffic, which somewhat cramped my style.

So I shrugged at the thought of spending the night with a grubby face, and went back through the café trailing my sleeping bag, air mattress and Matelot behind me.

I had just blown up the air mattress when I discovered that the stopper to the air tube had been left behind in the luggage. I couldn't face going through the café any more, so I stuck a pencil into the tube and hoped it would seal in the air. Then I placed the air mattress on the tables, and with the aid of a chair hoisted myself up and crawled into my sleeping bag fully dressed. There was a little hissing noise near my ear and gradually and painfully the mattress began to sag under me.

After that I kept changing my position this way and that, trying in vain to get comfortable. Finally, after tossing and turning from one side of the tables to the other, I lay on my back and tried to sleep. The air was heavy with smoke and reeked of stale beer and wine, and the continued stopping and starting of heavy trucks just outside the window, mixed with the noise and clatter of the café, was hardly an incentive to sound slumber.

All my moving about had caused a rift in the tables, and presently I found myself nearly falling on to the floor between a gap in two of the shifting tables. So I rolled down from my wrack of pain and pulled the tables back together again; it was then that I noticed the dark faces pressed against the window on the other side of the bar. There was a brightly lighted sign swinging outside and this illuminated the whole bar fairly clearly, so I found myself looking into three brown faces squashed closely against the window pane. As I gazed indignantly at the window three pairs of eyes, three large sombreros and three enveloping, brightly coloured ponchos disappeared from sight.

I had never felt so glad of Matelot's presence as at that particular moment. Fine watchdog that he is, he lay stretched out beside the bar, as dead to the world as a bearskin rug. However, I always tell myself that he would be ready for the attack at a second's notice! So now I settled myself once more on to the tables, and even though I sensed my Mexican friends were probably still staring at me outside the window, I fell asleep at last.

I awoke to a bright light in my face, and Mussolini gently shaking my shoulder. "*A la seis, señorita,*" he murmured, and I sat up with a start. The grey light of dawn was stealing through the window and the air was cold and damp. I jumped thankfully off the hard tables, and Matelot leapt up begging to get outdoors. On my way to the café I nearly tripped over the prostrate and snoring form of a young man who was sleeping under the bar. Somehow I wiped the bar aroma from my face with a pocket hand-kerchief and cold cream, fixed my hair, and finally piled on a couple of sweaters against the sharp morning air.

When I started off across the village of San Salvador El Seco, the mist was still lying in white patches across the green valley, the highway was wet and shining and the air penetratingly cold. After a few hours' driving we reached Jalapa, at the bottom of a steep winding hill and surrounded by mountains. I immediately liked it even better than Puebla. It was much smaller but built in the same colonial style. The streets were more winding and narrow, the flowers seemed more wonderful, and the view of the snowy peaks was closer and even more entrancing. I sat in the shadow of an old church wall and ate my lunch; Matelot snoozed contentedly at my feet and a little ring of barefoot boys regarded me curiously from a distance.

As soon as we left Jalapa the countryside changed again sharply. The trees became more closely packed together and more thickly overhung with creepers; the undergrowth was dense and entangled. There were long stretches of sugar cane and coffee under cultivation, and always the air seemed to get hotter and hotter. The nearer we got to the coast the more tropical was the vegetation around us. Matelot leaned over my shoulder panting with the heat, his long pink tongue dripping wet saliva down my neck.

"It won't be long now, boy, before you can cool off in the Gulf of Mexico," I told him, and he gave me an answering pant of anticipation. I too was looking forward to my first swim since leaving the Pacific coast.

CHAPTER XV *Veracruz*

IN the centre of Veracruz, overlooking an old square bright with flowers, I came upon the State Tourist Bureau of Mexico. I went inside to find out if I could get an immediate passage for New Orleans or any of the other gulf ports in the United States. But I was politely informed that the last passenger boat for the United States had left the day before, and the next one called in ten days.

I had set my heart on sailing into New Orleans, and certainly didn't want to retrace my steps through the mountains of Mexico and then the hot desert of Texas. All I wanted to do was to flop down on a nice ship's deck and do absolutely nothing for two days. But visions of us drifting over the blue gulf to the United States seemed to be going up in smoke.

However, I determined not to give up so easily and decided to wait until the week-end was over. Then I would start inquiring for a passage on a freight ship. The gloomy-faced man in the tourist bureau told me this was a very unlikely possibility. But I paid him no attention and went out to find a hotel for the week-end. I was dropping with fatigue after my poor night's rest in the bar.

Welcomed into the Hotel Brena by two dapper elderly men in white suits, I found conversation with them easy; both had spent their youth in the merchant navy, where they had acquired a fairly good knowledge of English. We had quite a job lifting Oppy on to the pavement to wheel her into the courtyard, and the poor hotel keepers got their suits covered in grease. However, they were all smiles, and so happy to have a *señorita* on whom to practise their English.

My inside room boasted no window, but only the door which gave out on to the open-air gallery overlooking the courtyard. It was possible to get cool for a few minutes if one stood under the cool shower and then flopped on the bed. An electric fan on the wall above kept the air circulating. As for Matelot he just crawled under the bed and lay panting loudly on the tiled floor.

Having spent the whole weekend loafing on the beach doing nothing more energetic than swimming in the incredibly warm waters of the gulf, by Monday morning I was ready for action and determined to find a passage for New Orleans. But in every shipping office the reply was the same. They didn't book passages on freight boats and I would have to wait eight days for the next passenger ship. Finally one of the employees took pity on me, and taking me aside whispered that it was a lot of bother making out special papers for one passenger. If I went down to the docks myself, the official continued, and spoke to some of the captains of the different vessels, they might arrange something for me.

So I returned to my room and got ready to try my wiles on some foreign sea captain. Putting on my least creased cotton dress, I dug out my only pair of gloves and pinned my hair down a little more tidily.

The policeman guarding the dock gates scrutinised my passport, listened to my story and finally let me pass. I had no idea which ship to try first, and my original cocksureness was rather waning as I picked my way over the dock littered with packing cases and metal piping. Every Mexican along the wharves stopped whatever he was doing to stare, and remarks were hurled at me from all sides. I tried to ignore them and act as though I knew exactly where I was going. Then I caught sight of the Norwegian flag fluttering from the stern of a small cargo vessel, so I made my way over to the gangplank.

A row of blond heads surveyed me in silence as I scrambled up on to the deck with Matelot just behind me. After the swarthy Mexicans with their excitable manners, these tall blue-eyed Scandinavian sailors seemed strangely calm. One of them took me down to the captain's cabin, where I found a grey-haired, gruff-voiced Norwegian drinking coffee. He waved me into a seat and called to a young seaman, who fetched another cup for me.

The captain was polite but firm. His ship had no sort of accommodation to carry passengers. "But I wouldn't mind sleeping on the deck," I begged. The captain shook his head smiling.

"Why don't you try the large Dutchman lying in the end berth?" he suggested. Thanking him for the coffee and the advice, I went ashore again and hastened to the other ship.

Now a young Dutch sailor led me down a maize of corridors to the doorway of a large smoke-filled cabin. Half a dozen men were seated there around a table drinking and smoking long cigars. A large, fat elderly man addressed me. "Vell, vell, vat do *you* vant?" he asked sharply, giving me a sweeping look from head to toe.

I was so upset that I completely forgot my carefully rehearsed little piece about being an English girl stranded in this tropical Mexican port. I forgot too the choice part where I told about my having been in the British Navy and not minding where I laid my head on a ship. As a matter of fact even my few words of Dutch escaped me.

"I want to go to New Orleans," I stammered feebly.

Everybody stared, and the captain put down his cigar, gulped his glass of whisky and barked, "Vell, vhy don't you go to the proper authorities? I don't book passages." I fled from the ship feeling a perfect fool.

A hundred eyes seemed to be boring into my back as I rallied my flagging spirits and walked toward a beautiful, shining white vessel flying the blue-and-yellow flag of Sweden. At the bottom of the gangplank an elderly woman was chatting with the policeman on guard. "What are you selling, *señorita?*" she asked politely, looking at my bag. Apparently she thought I was selling souvenirs from ship to ship. The idea was embarrassing, but this Swedish ship looked like my last hope, so I shrugged my shoulders and climbed up the gangplank.

The spotless deck was being enthusiastically scrubbed by two tall Swedes in white shorts. They ushered me politely down to a beautifully furnished cabin, where a white-uniformed officer was seated behind a large desk. I was certainly seeing a lot of captains' cabins! By this time I felt like a grease spot, and even Matelot forgot his manners and dropped to the deck with a sigh of relief. I was bowed into a chair and for a moment there was dead silence. My reception was certainly polite, but the answer to my request was firmly in the negative. The very last thing this Swedish captain wanted on his tidy ship was a travel-worn female, a shaggy-looking dog and a dirty motor-cycle. But he was gallant enough to refuse us on the grounds that it was against ship's regulations.

All that afternoon under the hot sun I trudged in vain from ship to ship, trying another Norwegian ship, then two Mexican coastal steamers, and finally an Italian oil tanker. Finally I returned dejectedly to the hotel. The shipping office had informed me that no other vessels were docking until Wednesday, so I spent the whole of the next day wondering if perhaps I shouldn't just turn round and go back through Mexico, the way I had come. But the thought of those Sierra Madres always made me more determined than ever to find a ship.

On Wednesday morning I was welcomed back on the docks like an old friend by the police, who wished me good luck in my further search. The only ship I could find now was a newly berthed Norwegian freighter bound for Cuba; it looked as though I was doomed to hang around in Veracruz another whole week. I drove away from the docks, and as I started up the street the usual stream of children followed, shrieking and whistling behind me. "Here comes the *Señorita Motorsiclista,*" chanted the small boys, and people on the pavements grinned and pointed. I had become such a well-known sight that I couldn't stir from the hotel without attracting attention. If I left Oppy behind, kids followed me down the street yelling ,"Where's the motor-cycle? Where's the motor-cycle?" It looked as if I were fast becoming a permanent resident of this small port, and I didn't at all enjoy my notoriety.

Across the street from the dock gates I suddenly noticed a familiar coat-of-arms, with "British Consul" written beneath it. Now, I was under the impression that one of the main jobs of Her Majesty's consuls is to help her subjects when in distress, so I parked Oppy outside the building and walked inside with Matelot.

The room opened directly on to the pavement, and it was full of workmen hammering and banging on the walls, sending clouds of plaster and dust into the air. Under the window, and behind a sea of books and papers, sat a man at a large desk. When he looked up I saw he was a good-looking, squarely set Englishman in his thirties. The noise and pandemonium of the Mexican workmen seemed to leave him quite unperturbed.

"Sorry about all the racket, we're getting new bookshelves," he apologized, standing up to greet me. After I had explained the details of my predicament, I asked him if he couldn't use a little influence in finding me a passage.

"Well, I'll do my best to get you out of the port, because I always think motor-cyclists are a hazard," he smiled. "I suppose you've got money for the passage?" he added.

"Not too much. I wish I could work my passage."

"That's out of the question, but at least you've got *some* money, which is more than I can say for a lot of the odd characters who come in here claiming British citizenship with no money and lost passports." Then he wrinkled up his brow as he asked, "Have you tried any of the ships in the harbour?"

"That," I nearly shouted, "is a closed subject. I'm so well known on the docks right now that the police don't even ask what I want."

"That's strange. The captain of the Belgian boat in port is a very nice bloke. His wife is English, so I should have thought he'd be glad to help you."

"B-Belgian boat?" I stuttered. "What Belgian boat?"

"She's lying in number three berth, flying a yellow, black and red flag."

"Thanks, I'll let you know what happens," I said, already half way to the door.

And now at last Captain Nellens was sympathetic and slightly amused as I poured out my story, first in French and ending in a torrent of English.

"Well, if the agent has no objection, I don't see why I shouldn't take you as far as New Orleans," he said. I could hardly believe my good fortune!

"You'll have to hurry up and arrange everything, because I'm sailing tomorrow afternoon." I assured him that I would be on hand in plenty of time.

"Why don't you stay for lunch? It'll be ready in a few minutes," he said, getting three glasses and a bottle of sherry out of a cupboard. I agreed, and he rang the bell and told the steward to set another place in the dining saloon. A big fat man with a red face and a deep laugh joined us, and the captain introduced him as the first officer.

"Vell, you came to the right ship," the mate said in a thick Flemish accent. "Ve are all married to English girls."

Lunch on board that day was simply wonderful. The soup was terribly hot for such weather, but so good that I would have drunk twice as much. When the steak and mushrooms arrived, I tried hard to conceal my hunger.

At that moment the captain looked down at the table and laughed.

"A clean tablecloth—we don't usually get one until Friday. What has come over Jacques?"

The little steward was nearly falling over himself to give perfect service. He was shy, and hardly dared to address me in his broken English with its charming French accent. "More coffee, mademoiselle?" he whispered when our meal was coming to a close. As I went up on deck the captain pointed to a door, from behind which we heard the sound of a lot of cleaning.

"Jacques is getting your cabin in order already," he smiled.

The shipping agent seemed so glad that I was really leaving Veracruz and wouldn't be bothering him any more, that he promised to have the special one-woman passenger list drawn up by early the next morning.

It was with a rather sinking heart that I paid for a first-class passage, which, including Oppy and Matelot, came to over one hundred dollars. I stuffed the book of travellers' cheques back into my purse quickly, not daring to count how many I had left to finish the trip.

I should have known that my conception of "early morning" was vastly different from that of a Mexican. When I arrived outside the shipping office at eight o'clock, the shutters were still over the windows and the door locked. I went across the street to a café to wait, and it wasn't until I was on my fourth coffee that the agent arrived. Luckily the necessary paper was already drawn up, signed and sealed officially, so I grabbed it and rushed off to clear myself through the Mexican Emigration Authorities.

A fat, sleepy-looking Mexican, about to pop the last button on his already gaping tunic jacket, couldn't understand why I wanted to leave Mexico at that time in the morning. After studying my passport, he slowly began to make out what looked like half a dozen detailed forms. Thirty minutes later he handed me two copies and told me to go and get my belongings cleared at the Customs and then bring back the papers for his signature. Unless I got this signature, he informed me importantly, I couldn't leave Mexico.

The customs house was a huge shabby building sprawling along the now very familiar docks. A foreign girl trying to clear a motor-cycle, a pile of luggage and a dog through the customs was an unprecedented event. We were tossed from department to department, and in every new office I had to start my stuttered explanations all over again. When I reached one counter for the third time, and saw there was only about three hours left before the *Gand* was expected to sail, I put my papers firmly on the counter and said I wasn't going to move until they took care of me.

As he reread the papers, light seemed to dawn in the eyes of the little official; he gave a gasp of recognition and asked me where I had left my motor-cycle. I led the way outside to Oppy, who was surrounded by an admiring throng of stevedores. Their hats were pushed back on their heads, and they were chattering and pointing to the different posters stuck on Oppy's fender which told of the places we had already visited. The foreman yelled furiously at them to go back to work, but they stayed there, scratching their heads and giggling like small children at a party.

The little official didn't quite know what to make of the luggage-laden motor-cycle. It was definitely the first one that had come under his authority. The workmen were shouting advice to him, but he was trying to keep his dignity and not let them realize that he was slightly perplexed. Finally he rushed back to his office and returned with two of his colleagues and a pile of forms. I was made to crawl under Oppy and scrape away the mud clinging to her engine and frame so that her numbers could be checked with those on the two forms. The crowd of workmen bent down to have a look too, shouting advice and infuriating the officials, who yelled at them to mind their own business. At last with a few flourishing signatures on my papers, the filling out of two more forms, and a large label saying "*Salido*" stuck on Oppy's front fender, the affair seemed to be at an end.

Then someone said "What about the dog?" and more forms had to be filled out, and then another *Salido* label was put on Matelot's curly-haired back, amid howls of merriment from the crowd. Even the three officials grinned.

Matelot and Oppy had now officially "left" Mexico, so only I could leave the docks to go back to the emigration office. It was infuriating to have to walk the length of the hot town, with Oppy lying idle just inside the dock gates.

When I reached the office I found everybody gone for lunch, so I sat down on a seat in the passage to wait. It was then that I noticed that it was nearly two o'clock, and Captain Nellens had told me he was sailing some time in the afternoon. I felt panic-stricken at the thought that he might leave without us.

At last, promptly at two o'clock, the emigration officer waddled back to his office. He studied all the signatures on the papers until I thought I would scream. As soon as he had added his name to the form, I grabbed it and raced across the town as fast as my legs would carry me, under the scorching sun. And I drove Oppy across the dockyard like a maniac, dodging frightened workers who got in my way, and skidded over the railway tracks, narrowly missing a pile of unloaded packing cases.

But, rounding the corner, I saw that the *Gand* was still in her berth and there were few signs of departure. So I drew up alongside her with mingled feelings of relief and excitement.

Several heads hung over the railings above, curious to have a look at the novel cargo coming aboard. The captain was on the bridge, so I shouted up to ask him "Where should I put my motor-cycle?"

"The first officer is going to have it pulled up with the crane and stowed on the aft deck, so leave it over there against the wall," he advised me.

"Be careful, *mademoiselle*," shouted a seaman from above, as I steered just a little too close to the edge of the ship. Suddenly Oppy's rear wheel slipped for a second on some grease; I righted her quickly, but there was a loud splash—then a cry of "Oh! *mon Dieu!*" from above. My typewriter with its case full of exposed film had slipped from the back of Matelot's box and fallen into the filthy water between the ship's side and the harbour wall. It had sunk like a stone to the bottom of Veracruz harbour!

I dropped quickly to my knees and peered down; I was just in time to see my even more precious diary floating away under the dock. Weeks of intimate travel memories were disappearing under my very eyes.

Two dockside hangers-on were as quick as lightning; they heard the splash and cries of anguish, and within thirty seconds they had stripped off their trousers and let themselves down into the narrow strip of filthy water. I hung over the edge, encouraging, imploring, and was just preparing to go over the side too when one of the men came up with the dripping book in his hand. The other was swimming about under the dark wharf chasing my scattered collection of maps. Of the typewriter there was no sign, it had completely and truly disappeared beneath the slimy dark water.

No sooner had the two dripping swimmers clambered back on to the dock than they were clamouring for money. After I had given them a ten-peso note each, which in a reckless moment I felt they deserved, they began to climb back into their clothes.

"Oh! Don't put your pants on yet!" I wailed. "How about the type-writer?" They fingered their ten-peso bills lovingly.

"That is a very difficult job, *señorita*," said one slyly.

"Don't you offer them more than twenty pesos, *mademoiselle*," said a young bearded sailor beside me. He was joined by a dozen of the crew from the ship, who were all peering down into the murky waters and asking me the exact spot where the typewriter had fallen. Everyone made pessimistic remarks about the chances of finding the lost machine.

I had hoped to come on board as quietly as possible, so that the captain wouldn't regret his decision of taking a woman passenger on his ship. Now I found myself in the midst of a noisy and embarrassing situation. All the ship's crew and officers were diverted from their work, the dock was fast becoming crowded with excited Mexicans, and I was cursing myself for carrying the typewriter loose in the back of the box. Generally it was stowed carefully in one of the side bags, but I had brought it out ready to take down to my cabin.

Soon there was a crowd of volunteer swimmers milling around in the dark waters, and making attempts to dive to the bottom. There was talk of easy pesos to earn, in the air, and everybody wanted to get into the act. Small piles of clothes lay all along the edge of the dock and a lot of splashing was going on below with shouts of excitement when someone found a piece of an old map or sheet of paper.

The second engineer, a slim, serious-faced boy, took me aside and suggested that I go down to the fishing jetty and try and find some professional boy divers.

"They're no good," he said pointing his finger at the gasping faces of the different men all frantically vying with each other to swim under water. It was impossible to dive properly owing to the lack of space.

Gradually the swimmers' enthusiasm died and the dangerous current of water under the keel of the ship became the main subject of their excited discussion. By this time they were demanding one hundred pesos for the recovery of the typewriter, so I accepted the suggestion of the second officer, and we set off across the dockyard.

Luckily the ship wasn't sailing until four o'clock, so I had an hour and a half, but I quickened my steps at the thought of having to sail without my precious machine. The salt water must have already ruined all my films. We rounded up every likely-looking boy hanging round the fishing boats, and returned to the ship with a strange little band straggling behind us. I felt like the Pied Piper of Hamelin as more joined in when we marched back to the docks. The police stared speechlessly as we came through the gate, but I waved the lads forward and told them to hurry.

When they saw the narrow space of water between the ship and harbour wall, the experienced diving boys shook their heads and said it was too dangerous to dive so near to the ship. They were further demoralized by the crowd of dripping and unsuccessful men who had got nothing for their pains, and were anxious to try and make me raise the price even higher.

At last a young boy stepped forward and said he would try. The water was cleared of the other swimmers, and then suddenly he muttered something and hung back. Everybody shrieked with laughter and I asked what the trouble was.

"He says he has no under shorts and he is ashamed that everyone should know this," whispered one of the crew.

"Well, I'm willing to lend him my corduroy shorts if only he will dive," I said.

But someone off the ship had fetched him a pair of swimming trunks. There was further delay until I turned my back, and then at last the boy descended into the water. He stayed under a long time and I began to feel nervous and wished that I hadn't asked him to take the risk. At last he came gasping to the surface to say that although he had reached the bottom, which was about six fathoms deep, he could see nothing and only a diver with proper equipment could search properly.

Now I asked if there was not a professional diver somewhere in the port, and the crowd of swimmers all started yelling at once. Finally I understood there was only one such person in the whole of Veracruz and he was working on the other dock, two miles away.

Just at that moment Oppy rose off the dock, wrapped in chains, and dangling precariously in mid-air on her way aboard.

"Don't worry, everything's under control," grinned the first officer, who was bossing the proceedings.

"We're sailing in an hour," reminded the captain as I prepared to rush off in search of the diver. Outside the dockyard I found a taxi and hurriedly explained to the driver where I wanted to go.

When we got to the other docks, the driver got out to help me look for the diver. We both picked our way across a pile of rubble to where a gang of men were working down by the water's edge. A good-looking young man with a mop of curly-black hair and a cheeky grin was sitting on the side of the dock, with a diving helmet near him.

At first he refused to help me, because he was already working on a job and he hadn't got a portable air pump. I pleaded with him, and finally, encouraged by the fat taxi driver, the diver said he would have to ask his boss first for the necessary equipment. Precious minutes were ticking away as he climbed into his trousers and laced up his shoes. Then he and his two seemingly indispensable buddies let themselves be bundled into the taxi, and off we dashed again toward the town.

Veracruz's only professional diver seemed to be enjoying his importance now. He pushed his blue cap to the back of his head, leaned back in the seat and asked details of the mishap, like a doctor diagnosing an accident case. The taxi screeched through the streets of the town, narrowly missing several pedestrians; the taxi driver had caught my spirit of desperation.

The diver's boss couldn't be found anywhere; we went from one address to another, until I saw it was less than three-quarters of an hour before the *Gand* sailed. After calling at the third address, I felt ready to give up, but the driver winked at me in the driving mirror and said, "Courage, *señorita,* courage!"

When at last the elusive man was found, the taxi driver hurriedly explained the situation in Spanish. The price for doing this job, the boss informed me, would be two hundred and fifty pesos, which made me nearly drop dead. But the taxi driver brought the price down to one hundred and fifty if the machine were fished out, and nothing if the diver were unsuccessful.

At the dock gates the policeman refused to allow the taxi to go any further. After a lot of shouting and argument on both sides, the chief of police was fetched out of his office, and when the taxi had been searched, he said he would give special permission for us to drive on to the ship. The *Gand* was all ready to sail now; the last of the cargo had been taken on board, and the agent was on the bridge with the captain, looking askance at the disturbance below.

There was a big crowd round the young diver, who seemed thoroughly to enjoy the limelight. Before an admiring circle, he donned the crude suit and iron mask, while his two buddies set up the air pump, which they operated by hand. At this point I suddenly remembered that I had no Mexican money to pay them if they did find the typewriter, and that I'd have to go somewhere to cash a cheque in the town.

With only fifteen minutes to sailing time, I flew back to the taxi driver, who was stolidly standing on the outside of the crowd, waiting for his forgotten fare. We drove rapidly past the astonished policeman at the gate, who waved and screamed for us to stop, but there wasn't a second to lose now. All the banks were closed, so I told him to drive to the Hotel Brena.

Here I shakily signed away another twenty-five dollars without even stopping to count my bundle of pesos. And just as we were starting off, the hotel keeper rushed out with twenty pesos which he had forgotten to give me. The policeman on the gate was simply hopping mad, and I expected him to draw his pistol or at least arrest us. However, once again his chief came out and saved the day, and we tore back across the dock, arriving with exactly five minutes to spare before sailing time.

All my efforts had been in vain, because there was no sign of the typewriter, and the diver said he doubted if anybody would ever find it, since the harbour bed was so dirty. He didn't care a bit about the loss of profit for his boss, but it was obvious that he expected a good tip for himself and the price of a taxi fare back to work. The meter charge on the taxi by this time was staggeringly high, and with so much money flying around everybody wanted to profit by it. I was surrounded by a clamouring bunch of Mexicans, all insisting they had risked their very lives looking for the *señorita's* machine.

By this time I was feeling so completely disgusted that I nearly threw the rest of the bundle of notes up in the air and let them scramble for it. But then I had sense enough to remember that I could change those pesos back into good green dollars when I got to New Orleans, so I stuffed the money back into my purse.

There was a deep, ear-splitting blast from the ship's siren, and untying Matelot from a hook in the wall, where I had left him during the excitement, I raced up the gangplank. The first officer greeted me at the top, "You're just in time, we almost sailed without you."

The ship began to pull rapidly away from its berth, and I leaned over the rails and gazed down at the churning waters over the fatal spot. Everybody on the dock was peering down too, and I wondered how many of them were speculating about the possibility of finding that hidden treasure as soon as the waters were still again!

They were all grinning at me and waving their hands in farewell. "*Adios, señorita, adios!*" they chorused.

CHAPTER XVI *Back with Uncle Sam*

THE *Gand* wasn't by any means a modern ship but just a small well-worked freighter. A comfortable deck chair with a foot rest had been placed on the shady side of the deck for me. After breakfast, armed with my still rather soggy diary and several magazines from Captain Nellens, I stretched lazily out on the chair.

My diary remained closed and the magazines forgotten on the deck beside me. Now that I had at last relaxed I unwound like an old gramophone, and stayed down. I found infinite pleasure in just watching the empty horizon, and looking out for the flying fishes that jumped and leapt up out of the shining blue water.

I could hear Matelot barking in a distant part of the ship. He had the time of his life racing from one end of the *Gand* to the other and he became a great favourite with the crew. The captain paced back and forth on the bridge above my head, the chief passed in his engine-room overalls; two seamen were painting the deck below—everybody had a job to do—everybody but me. I closed my eyes, kicked off my sandals and stretched my legs out into the hot sun.

Just at darkness of the second day we nosed our way slowly up the Mississippi river toward New Orleans. Ships lay anchored in mid-stream; a flash of green showed their starboard sides, and rows of lighted portholes gleamed across the dark water. The last reflection of pink light from the vanished sun lay like a haze across the harbour, and the silhouettes of the buildings were outlined against the sky.

Late that night I sat on my bunk in a sea of maps, travellers' cheques and my last pile of Mexican money. Financially my future didn't look too encouraging. I looked at the map of Florida again. Prudence demanded that I take the shortest route across to the east coast and up to New York, but I was determined to see Miami and the Florida Keys at all costs. Perhaps if I made myself go on an even stricter budget, where even a cup of coffee or ice cream would be taboo, I might be able to finish the trip on my present funds. But only by thinking of a nickel as being as valuable as a dollar could I hope to reach New York. There was no economizing on Oppy's diet of petrol and oil, and I certainly didn't intend to cut down Matelot's food; after all, he hadn't asked to come. But with three days of colossal, nourishing Belgian meals inside me, I thought I might cut myself down to one meal a day for a time.

Next morning after breakfast I went up on deck and watched Oppy being slung over the side of the ship by crane. My heart was in my mouth for a minute, as I saw her suspended in mid-air; how terrible it would be if she slipped and crashed to pieces on the hard dock!

Everybody on board was busy unloading the cargo, but I managed to say a few good-byes before leaving. I thanked the captain for all the extra bother of having us on board, and he told me to come and see him next time I went to Belgium.

It didn't take me long to slip my overnight bag and camera into place; as we set off the cop on the dock smiled and shook his head unbelievingly, the captain and first officer waved, and there were a few cries of "*Au revoir, bonne chance,*" from some of the crew on deck.

Although I didn't want to lose too much time before getting on the road to Florida, I did spend the whole day poking around in the old French quarter of the city. At last I tore myself away and headed east toward Alabama.

About ten miles out of the city we crossed a bridge and followed the straight road across the swamplands. Suddenly I became conscious of an unusual and disconcerting sound coming from somewhere inside Oppy. So I slowed down and bent my head to listen more carefully. As Oppy came to a halt, she sounded just as if she were about to fall apart. I checked everything on the machine, and then when I reached the magneto I found the trouble. This unit, which should be spotlessly clean and rarely touched, was covered with fine metal particles and it looked as though a bearing had worn.

And of course the sun had to choose just this minute to sink out of sight. However, the coming darkness wasn't bothering me half as much as the clouds of unmerciful mosquitoes which rose off the swamps like a plague of locusts. I looked down at my bare ankles, to see at least a dozen insects sitting placidly there making a meal out of my blood. I had never seen such mosquitoes, some of them were the size of my finger nail; they swelled on my blood before my very eyes. And even though I slapped and swotted at them, they bit worse than ever. When I flung on a jacket over my thin dress, they bit right through it. The more mosquitoes I killed, the more seemed to take their place, and the madder I became.

My wild and futile antics were evidently being watched. A fisherman on a boat tied up to a small jetty beyond the bridge was waving and yelling at me.

"Come on over, I'll give you something to drive those swamp bugs away," he shouted.

I left Oppy and a row of tools scattered on the roadway, and hurried over to the boat. I couldn't grab that bottle of mosquito repellent fast enough, and smothered myself in the oily, strong-smelling stuff from head to toe. It certainly seemed to work! Although a few mosquitoes still sat sleepily on my now bump-covered flesh, they had lost all inclination to bite. Two other fishermen, with strong French accents, came over to where we were standing.

"If you stay in Louisiana long enough, they'll get sick of the taste of your blood," said one of them, and he rolled up his sleeve to show me a sun-tanned arm without a single bite.

The three men followed me back to the scene of the breakdown. I was rather touched to find that a whole packet of cigarettes had been flung down beside my scattered tools in the road. Apparently some passing motorist had felt sorry for the "guy" with the motor-cycle trouble. As I don't smoke I exchanged them for the bottle of mosquito repellent.

Then one of the fishermen had a wonderful suggestion to get me back to New Orleans, because I wasn't keen to drive Oppy in such poor shape.

"A fellow from the market in New Orleans is coming to pick up our catch in a truck," he said. "If you stick around I'll ask him to give you and your stuff a lift."

We went back to the boat. Someone had made a pot of coffee and I was invited to come on board. I squeezed myself round the table in the small cabin, and four fishermen entertained me with tales of their shrimp catching. Presently a large truck drove on to the small jetty. There was a lot of palavering in a strange French dialect. I understood enough to realize the driver had agreed to carry us back to New Orleans.

Once that was settled, I helped the men load the barrels of shrimps into the back of the truck, and then five pairs of willing hands hoisted Oppy up into the small space that remained. She leaned rather precariously against a barrel, so I decided to ride in the back and stop her from falling.

We set off into the darkness toward New Orleans. The truck was old and rickety and the barrels rolled around, smelling strongly of shrimps, and not adding much to our comfort. Cars approaching us from behind slowed down and motorists peered out of their windows to get a better view of the girl and dog perched on top of an open-backed fish truck.

Within about twenty minutes the truck was speeding down the narrow streets of the French quarter, and then pulling up round the back of the market. The scene was busy with men unloading trucks, and the air was strong with the smell of fish. Several of the stall holders crowded close as I jumped down off the truck.

"That's a mighty interesting catch you got up there, Pierre," said one wit. Oppy was unloaded next, and then came the problem of what to do with her and where Matelot and I might find a bed.

One of the stall holders promised to look after Oppy during the night, but there was no tent-pitching area within sight and I was in no state to venture inside a hotel. My hair was blown in wild disorder from the truck ride, I smelt heavily of fish, and I had ripped my skirt jumping off the truck.

Then an old fellow came forward and suggested that if I wanted to find a place for the night he knew where I could get a cheap room. He wrote something for me on a scrap of paper and gave me directions for getting there. I managed to wash off some of the fishy smell under a hose, and someone produced a bar of soap. Gathering up a few things for the night, and securing Matelot on his chain to give the impression that he was a fierce beast, I set off across the dark narrow streets of the French quarter.

It was rather creepy and completely deserted in spots. I took to the middle of the street and strode along with Matelot trotting happily at my side. Then I turned down a street gay with cafés and night clubs and full of the sound of hot jazz music. The end of this street brought me into North Rampart Street, where the house with rooms to rent was situated. I found the house, which was a tall, shabby grey building with a long flight of steps leading up to the front door. Two men in down-at-heel-looking clothes sat on the top step; as I approached they gazed at me curiously. It took all my courage to lift the knocker on the door, and I listened to it echoing through the house with a pounding heart. This was really the last sort of place I wanted to spend the night in. I would have much preferred sitting bolt upright in the fish market beside Oppy.

Finally the door opened and a slovenly looking woman, her hair hanging down in grey wisps and a cigarette in the corner of her mouth, stared at me. "What d' y' want?" she asked me suspiciously.

I explained who'd sent me and she broke in to say, "Sounds like the guy that ran out on me six months ago—owed me a month's rent." She looked down at Matelot. "Don't take animals, but if you want a room on the top floor you can have it for six bucks. Take it or leave it," she added rudely.

"Thanks, I'll leave it," I said, thinking I wouldn't have stayed there if I were paid to.

As I trudged on up the street, a clock pointed to eleven o'clock, and I didn't want to wander round looking for cheap rooms much longer. I passed several dismal, squalid-looking houses with Rooms to Rent signs, but either my courage deserted me at the last minute or else some unsavoury character was hanging about near the bottom steps. Finally, at the next house advertising rooms, I forced myself to go up and knock on the door.

A young woman with a sour face opened the door, and in answer to my inquiry said I could have a room for two dollars. There was no mention of Matelot, so I hurried up the dark stairs after the woman. We climbed to the fifth floor, and then she led the way up a short flight of rickety steps which gave out on to an open-air corridor and a view to the dark courtyard far below. The room was even worse than I had imagined it would be, but I was too tired and hot to care. When I opened my purse to pay I realized that I had no American money, and the landlady refused to cash a travellers' cheque. So leaving Matelot in the room with the luggage, I made my way down the street again.

Trying to change a travellers' cheque that late at night was almost impossible. The café-owner man looked at me suspiciously and said he hadn't enough cash in the till. There were no other shops open in the neighbourhood, except a few dimly lit bars. In each one I was refused. Finally I found an all-night petrol station, but at first the attendant turned me down point-blank like everybody else. Then I explained about how I had just arrived from Mexico and about my trouble with a broken-down motor-cycle. At the word "motor-cycle" his whole attitude changed, and he began telling me he owned one himself. In no time at all he was counting ten green dollar bills into my hand.

When I finally reclimbed my five flights of stairs the hour was approaching midnight. The welcoming bang of Matelot's tail on the floor was reassuring as I looked round the sordid room. A large iron bed revealed grubby sheets and a threadbare blanket. Beside it was a table covered in dust and a pile of lurid-looking twenty-five cent paper-back novelettes. There were stacks of old newspapers on the floor, and a man's rusty black waistcoat lay forgotten on a hanger. Gingerly opening a closet door, I quite expected to find a body or at least blood-stained garments, but only a greasy old hot plate, several unwashed dishes and an empty milk bottle met my eyes.

A breathless hot atmosphere lay over the room and I was forced to leave the door open. The lumpy bed creaked and groaned under me, and the pillow smelled dreadful. I placed a scarf under my head and turned out the light. There was a step on the gallery outside and Matelot raised his head; the figure of a man was outlined for a moment in the doorway, then he moved up the passage. I heard a door open and then slam shut, and all was quiet again. The whole place looked and felt like the setting for a cheap murder mystery.

I don't think I was ever so glad to get out of a place as I was early next morning, when I hurried downstairs into the bright sunshine. Oppy was sitting safely where I had left her, surrounded by a pile of discarded, empty fish crates, and the market all around her was in full swing. I gazed at the rows of appetizing fresh fish, and Oppy's night guardian followed my hungry eyes.

"Would you like a piece for lunch?" he asked.

"If you'll fillet it for me, I'll cook it right now and have it for *breakfast*," I replied.

"O.K.," he said, producing a long sharp knife and slicing expertly at a large fish.

I got out my stove and frying pan and set it up in a small alley at the back of the market. In no time at all delicious aromas were wafting through the air, and a crowd of fish-stall owners had gathered around to watch me have breakfast.

"How can you eat fish at this time in the morning?" asked one man. "It's a common practice in England," I told him, and he wrinkled up his face in disgust.

As soon as I had finished eating, I jumped on Oppy and, driving very carefully, I weaved slowly through the market. Oppy's motor was still turning over, but it was making a horrible noise when I drew up outside a motor-cycle shop.

Inside I found a young man sitting on the floor beside a disassembled machine. He looked more like a college student than a motor-cycle dealer. Henry was full of sympathetic friendliness and jumped up to help me wheel Oppy inside. He and his partner Vance, a good-looking young fellow in neat T-shirt and jeans, both examined the sick magneto.

"Well, frankly I've never worked on this type of unit, but I'm willing to learn as I go along," Henry told me. I urged him to go right ahead, and sat down on the floor to watch.

It was a long, slow job, but at last the whole complicated mechanism was apart, and looking at the chewed-up bearing that had caused the trouble Henry told me he thought he could find a replacement. After that I didn't worry any more; Oppy was obviously in good hands.

During the afternoon I met the two young men's girl friends, who urged me to stay for the evening and go to some races that were being held nearby. I had never seen a motor-cycle race in my life, so I was easily persuaded. Late in the afternoon Oppy was ticking over again like her natural self and Henry and Vance started to close up shop. Trying to get a bill out of them proved impossible, they wouldn't even let me pay for the bearing!

Matelot and I followed Henry's car out to the race track, which lay on the outskirts of the city. The grandstand was already packed with people and there was the deafening roar of racing motor-cycles tuning up. The first half of the evening was devoted to hot-rod racing cars. But just before the intermission Rheba, Henry's girl, asked me whether I would like to do a stunt of my own round the track to show off overpacked Oppy and Matelot. I declined and she looked very disappointed.

"I was just talking about you in the judges' stand, and they said you would be such good intermission entertainment."

"It would be an added attraction for our motor-cycle races," added Henry.

Well, the idea of making a spectacle of myself in a public stadium didn't appeal to me at all, but if I could help interest the crowd in motor-cycles I couldn't very well refuse. Still, I looked at the large oval track with trepidation, and wondered what on earth I would do if we skidded on one of the corners. I could just imagine falling down with all the luggage and Matelot on top of me—what a humiliation in front of a packed grandstand!

"Take it slow," warned Vance. "The announcer wants to have time to explain about you and the trip."

After half a dozen racing cars had skidded and crashed their way through six races, the track was pretty badly ploughed up and muddy as well.

Henry nudged me, "Start up your machine, Peggy, you're on next."

I felt like bolting from the arena, but it was too late now. So, with Matelot looking the picture of dignity sitting up behind me, and with my heart in my mouth, I started slowly off toward the track. As I wobbled over the uneven dirt the announcer was shouting over the loudspeakers, "Ladies and gentlemen, we have a very unusual event this evening . . ." I wondered just how unusual it was going to be as Oppy wobbled round the first corner, her small tyres sinking in the tracks left by the skidding cars. Then I accelerated a little, and immediately realized I wasn't giving the announcer enough time to finish our life history. The next corner was even thicker in mud, and for one frightful moment I was sure I was losing my balance. Then at last we were coming into the straight and passing the now cheering grandstand.

When I got back to the centre of the arena my four motor-cycling friends were grinning their approval. "That was far worse than my whole cross-Canada trip last year," I said, flopping down on the grass. The rest of the evening I watched half a dozen noisy racing machines tear round the track, and decided that I preferred the open highway on a low-powered machine.

About eleven that night I waved good-bye to my young hosts of the evening and set off once more across the hot swamplands. It was already so late that I didn't bother to pitch the tent. A few minutes later I regretted this decision, when a great wave of mosquitoes started humming and singing over my unprotected face. I couldn't find the insect repellent, so I spent a suffocating night, buried as far down into the sleeping bag as possible. It was like slowly stifling; each time I came up for air the insects covered my face and I had to pull the bag of hot goose feathers further over my head again.

I woke up in a pool of perspiration and found I was lying right on the edge of a dense swamp. As I threw my things together I had to keep hopping up and down to drive away my tormentors. After that I decided to keep away from swamps when camping.

My road lay alongside the gulf for one beautiful mile after another. I was just spinning along in the hot sunshine and feeling very pleased with life, when I hit a large bump in the road.

There was a loud explosion from under me, and Oppy went into an uncontrollable wobble. I gripped the handlebars with all my might and waited for the crash that was bound to follow. We zigzagged crazily across the road and then Oppy just lay down on her side in the middle of the highway. Matelot was the first to pick himself up; then I crawled out from under the luggage feeling none the worse for the fall, but rather scared and definitely soiled. Poor Oppy just lay there with a tyre ripped to pieces, and what was worse the rim and spokes of her rear wheel were a mass of bent, squashed metal. The beautiful shiny chrome which had been El Maestro's pride and joy was no more!

It was an early Sunday morning and we were a good eighty miles from New Orleans. I dragged Oppy to the side of the road and sat down to think what I should do next. The road was deserted except for an occasional car packed with tourists, or a fishing-bound family out to enjoy their Sunday freedom. I probably looked as though I was enjoying a rest too, because I got several cheery waves as they passed me by. Then all at once, hurtling round the corner in the direction of New Orleans, came a large red truck. I jumped to my feet, rushed across the road and raised my thumb in hopeful anticipation.

CHAPTER XVII *Thumbing it—Motor-cycle Style*

THE large truck that was approaching me began to slow down. With a hiss of brakes and a great shudder it stopped exactly in front of me. The cab was so high that I couldn't see the driver, so, putting a foot on one of the huge front fenders, I grabbed the door handle and hoisted myself up. I looked into the inquiring face of a young Negro. He leaned forward and shouted above the roar of his engine, "Is you in trouble, ma'am?"

I pointed to where poor Oppy lay prostrate on the grass. The driver swung himself down from his seat and followed me across the road. "Sure does look a mess, ma'am," he said, studying the tangle of squashed metal which had been Oppy's rear wheel. I explained that I needed to get to the nearest motor-cycle shop, and he suggested taking me back to New Orleans. I was wondering how we would lift Oppy up on to the high truck, when a large motor-cycle appeared round the corner and the driver stopped and offered to help. So the two men let down one side of the truck, while I started to unstrap the luggage. The truck had drop sides and smelled strongly of cattle. Thank goodness it was quite empty now, and Oppy didn't have to share her space with a herd of cows.

The first time I staggered across the road with one of the bags, the coloured driver rushed over and seized it from me. When I tried to help lift Oppy on to the truck he reproved me, saying, "Oh, no, ma'am, this isn't woman's work." With the strength of Samson, he shouldered practically the whole dead weight of Oppy by himself, and motioned the young motor-cyclist to get up on the truck and pull from the front end.

The cab of the truck was crowded with several boxes and a bag of tools, so I put Matelot in the back with Oppy, then the two men closed up the sides. The motor-cyclist took off, with a wave of good luck, and presently we followed him down the road. Once more we were New Orleans bound, and I began to think that this city had somehow put a jinx on us.

Conversation with the driver was rather limited because of the roar of the powerful diesel engine, but I managed to scream a few remarks above the deafening noise. From time to time I glanced out of the rear window at Oppy swaying in the back. She had been securely lashed by a couple of stout ropes, so I didn't need to worry for her safety. Matelot was up on his hind legs peering over the side; with perfect balance he was gazing with interest at the countryside flashing past. He certainly was a more poised tourist than I would ever be!

A few hours later we pulled up at a large Gulf station on the outskirts of New Orleans. Here the driver explained apologetically that he didn't dare take me farther into the city, because his boss didn't allow him to pick up hitch hikers.

The attendants at the petrol station looked rather surprised at the paraphernalia that began to litter their tidy yard. Matelot was the first to leap down, then I began throwing the luggage to the ground; finally Oppy was lowered gently with the help of two mechanics. The coloured boy jumped back aboard his truck, protesting modestly as I thanked him warmly for his kindness.

Now I was left in the middle of the petrol station, with all my worldly goods in one untidy heap and surrounded by three bewildered-looking men.

"We don't know anything about fixing motor-cycles——" one of them began.

I explained that I was really on my way to the motor-cycle shop but this was as far as I had got. And since it was Sunday it was just about as far as I would get for another twenty-four hours. Then one of the men helped me drag Oppy into a corner of the backyard and the other two brought up the rear with the luggage. I knew that it was no good trying to get in touch with Henry or Vance today, because their shop would be closed until Monday. It looked as though good Gulf was stuck with us over the weekend.

Next to the station was a vacant lot with a rough patch of grass, and beyond that a café pull-up. This seemed like a possible place for the tent, even though it was in rather an exposed position. The afternoon passed quickly; I busied myself removing the squashed wheel. Next morning I planned to take it to the shop by bus, and thus save the expense of having the entire machine transported across the city.

Joe, one of the attendants, showed me how the pumps worked. And next time a car pulled in, just for fun, I stepped over the front window.

"Fill her up," said the driver without giving me a glance.

As I was waiting for him to pay, I leaned over and started to clean his windshield.

"Say," said an elderly man, sticking his head out of the window, "when did they start hiring girls here, anyway?"

"Oh, I'm new, just started today," I replied.

The other attendants sniggered as the car pulled away.

"He's a regular customer, so next time he comes we'll have to tell him you didn't work out," Joe laughed.

I had fun all the rest of the afternoon cleaning windshields, testing air pressure, and twice fetched drinks for thirsty tourist dogs. Later I sat in the backyard eating supper out of a couple of tins, and feeling as if I had put in a hard day's work. I shared the yard with four enormous double-trailer trucks with licence plates from such far-away States as New York and California.

The driver of a huge refrigeration truck came over to chat with me. When I told him I proposed pitching my tent for the night, he asked if I wouldn't rather sleep in his truck. He explained that the petrol station supplied the long-distance truckers with dormitories, so he didn't need to use the bunk in his cab. By now I was hardened to sleeping anywhere, even without the luxury of a bunk, so I agreed to this offer with delight.

"It'll be a bit noisy because of the refrigerator motor shutting on and off all night," the driver warned me.

Joe came out to say that if I wanted to use their shower I was very welcome. By that time I felt that I was getting first-class hotel service! And after a refreshing shower I sat on an upturned coke crate and wrote to Carl-Erik to tell him of our latest adventures.

The bunk in the truck was very comfortable and the sheets looked as though they had just been freshly changed. The driver showed me how to push open the screen window for air and pointed to a blanket on the seat in case I felt cold in the night.

It was lovely lying out full length on the bunk; this time there were no ship's engines throbbing under me, only the sound of the traffic out on the highway and an occasional shout from the mechanics still on duty. I was dozing off when suddenly there was the most hideous noise! The whole truck shook and shuddered and I nearly fell out of the bunk with fright. Then I remembered about the refrigeration unit on the trailer at the back, and sank down with relief. Several times during the night I was awakened as the huge, noisy engine started up again, making the truck throb and shake.

Early next morning I set off to catch the bus, clutching Oppy's squashed wheel in one hand. The bus driver gave me a look of surprise as I fumbled to find a dime with the greasy, heavy wheel leaning against me on the floor. The rest of the passengers stared at me in disgust and horror. I suppose girls don't usually carry dirty wheels on buses!

Henry and Vance listened to my tale of woe with a mixture of laughter and sympathy. Setting up the wheel on the bench, Henry inspected the mass of crushed metal. "Well, your Mexican friend must have had a mighty weak wrist, because all these spokes are loose. And when you had that blow-out the whole thing just collapsed," he explained.

The main difficulty now was trying to find a new rim and spokes to fit Oppy, and after a long search Vance came back with a used one. Although it was not the correct size, it could be made to fit.

Later that afternoon one of the boys drove me back to the petrol station to assemble the new wheel. Then once more all the luggage was piled on to Oppy's willing back, and Matelot jumped joyfully at signs of our departure. All the petrol station men came to wave us off, and Joe said to be sure and come back to my windshield wiping job if I had another breakdown.

So once more we set off down the now too familiar road, and I wondered if this time we had left New Orleans for good; three is supposed to be my lucky number. I drove along the shores of the gulf, fighting sleep as the hour drew past midnight. One stretch of white sandy beach looked particularly inviting, so I stopped and propped Oppy against a palm tree. I had meant to drive all night and catch up on the two days already lost, but as I sank down on the soft sand I decided to sleep until dawn. I made a pillow of sand, scooped a hole for my hip and for once fell asleep even before Matelot.

The sun on my face woke me up, and I went down to the sea to wash my face and hands free of sand. It was good to be back travelling along the coast again. Matelot tore across the sand after the sticks of driftwood I threw for him, barking furiously.

All that day we travelled in the hot sunshine; on through Mississippi and Alabama as fast as Oppy would carry us. During the afternoon we crossed into Florida. I was bowling down a long straight road flanked with palm trees, and feeling so content with life that I burst into song. I had just got to the line "this is a lovely day," when I noticed that horribly familiar wobble beneath me. Slowing down carefully, I discovered that Oppy's rear tyre was as flat as a pancake. So I got off and looked down the road behind us; a truck was approaching at a good speed. I raised my thumb in the air in best hitch-hiking style. The driver stopped and promptly offered to carry us to Pensacola. Together we managed to lift Oppy up on to the low, empty trailer. The driver had no means of securing her, so I said I would stay on the back and hold her steady.

I could hardly believe my good fortune at being rescued so quickly; the American Automobile Association itself couldn't have given me swifter service. Matelot was walking from one side of the swaying trailer to the other, watching the ground rushing away from us a couple of feet below. I felt rather nervous that he might decide to hop off and get left behind. This is exactly what did happen when the driver stopped for petrol. I had to bang on the window and shriek for him to stop, otherwise poor Matelot might have been left alone in the middle of Florida.

Pensacola's motor-cycle shop proved to be down a narrow street, and the great long trailer hardly had room to turn the corner; but the driver insisted upon taking me right to the door. Amid the unbelieving eyes of the motor-cycle dealer, we lowered Oppy to the ground once more.

"Thanks a million, you were wonderful," I said, jumping up to shake the driver's hand over the steering wheel.

"You're very welcome, ma'am." He let in his clutch and roared away.

A little later a mechanic pulled a large bent nail out of Oppy's tyre, like a dentist extracting a tooth, and said, "There's your trouble."

After an hour we were on our way again, and with the sun gone the best of the day was over. The highway I chose was not the main one, for I wanted to stay along the coastline. The beach lay a hundred yards away screened by a dense undergrowth growing on both sides of the road. The night was dark and starless. I had only gone about another twenty-five miles when once again the machine wobbled, and with a sinking heart I stopped.

It was pitch dark by this time and I had no flashlight; the headlamp gave off only a dim light, and I had to inspect the rear tyre by feel alone. One touch told me the tyre was soft and airless. It was a creepy spot with the dark trees close together on the narrow road. And I couldn't camp because on either side of the road there seemed to be a ditch of swampy water. I could hear Matelot splashing about and thought what an ideal breeding ground it was for snakes. Since we were off the main truck route it looked as if we were truly stranded this time.

As these thoughts were going through my mind, the bright headlights of a vehicle were approaching, so I held up my hand. A car flashed by with gathering speed. Five minutes later another light blazed ahead, and it too shot past me into the darkness. The road had very little traffic and apparently nobody was going to stop there in the middle of the night to help us. I began to wonder what on earth I should do and how a passing motorist could help us anyway. For after all I couldn't very well leave Oppy lying in the swampy ditch with all my precious belongings, and I certainly hadn't any money to spare for a breakdown car.

Then another headlight appeared out of the darkness; automatically I lifted my hand and this time a car stopped.

"Having trouble, ma'am?" asked a voice with a slow, soft southern drawl. I had barely finished explaining our predicament when a tall figure climbed out of the car, let down the trunk at the back and pushed a few tools aside.

"Do you think we could fit her inside here, ma'am?" he asked.

The idea seemed absolutely impossible to me, but my kind rescuer insisted that we try. Somehow Oppy was lifted up, front wheel first, and pushed sideways into the back of the car. A couple of straps secured her to the lid of the trunk, and there she lay on her side, little trickles of petrol and oil seeping out of the carburettor all over the poor man's nice clean car. Then my grubby luggage and Matelot were put on the back seat, while I climbed in the front with the driver.

After driving about forty miles we came to the town of Niceville. My friend turned the car off the road and drove into a yard packed from one end to the other with old, disused motor-cycles. "You'll be all right now," he said, helping me lift Oppy to the ground. He went off into the darkness, protesting against the thanks I tried to shower on him.

There was no light burning from the small house across the yard, and the workshop facing the street was dark also. So I picked a spot between two large rusty motor-cycles, blew up my air mattress, and went sound to sleep the instant my head touched the pillow.

When I opened my eyes next morning the first thing I saw was one of the monster machines about three inches from my face. For a moment I wondered if Oppy had grown in the night! Then I sat up and looked around me. The large yard seemed to be a cemetery for old motor-cycles;

there must have been at least fifty scattered over the grass. Oppy lay propped against a rusted jeep, and beyond her I saw a small wooden house. There weren't any signs of life anywhere, so I washed under a hose I found lying on the ground and then started to make coffee.

I was sitting on the edge of the air mattress sipping the first cup, when I heard a footstep behind me. Turning round I saw a powerfully built man, over six feet tall, regarding me with a look of utter astonishment. I knew at once who he was by the motor-cycle-embroidered T-shirt he was wearing.

"Hello. Have a cup of coffee?" I asked.

He burst out laughing and shouted over his shoulder in the direction of the house, "Hey, Adie, come on out. We've got a squatter in our backyard!"

A slim blonde in a bright gingham dress came running out of the house, followed by a small boy and girl. "Well, come on in and have some *real* breakfast," she said, glancing at my mug of coffee and roughly sliced bread.

Then her husband suddenly caught sight of Oppy leaning against the jeep, and burst out laughing even more loudly.

" You don't mean to say you *ride* that *thing*?"

Over a huge breakfast of ham and eggs I told Adie and Chuck about my adventures of the night before. In between their laughter they scolded me for not waking them up to demand a bed. We sat at the table a long time exchanging motor-cycling experiences and gossip. And the two children had a fine time outside playing with Matelot.

Adie wouldn't hear of me leaving that day, and I am sure that was the reason Chuck was so slow about repairing Oppy's flat. As always when meeting wonderful people, the inclination to hurry on always dies. Most of the day I sat about in the workshop, looking over the machines and talking to the different motor-cyclists who came in.

The next morning I wasn't allowed to leave before I had eaten another enormous breakfast. Then at the last minute Chuck suddenly remembered he hadn't given me a ride on his racing machine. I got up behind him a little nervously, because he had a wild look in his eyes; also I never feel really safe on a motor-cycle unless I am doing the driving myself. We were cruising down the straight road at a gentle twenty miles an hour, when Chuck suddenly pulled back the throttle and the machine almost leapt into the air.

We shot off down the road at about seventy miles an hour. The machine's pick-up was so rapid that I nearly fell off myself. All I could do was watch the ground hurtling past at a frightening pace. With no control over the machine I felt helpless and had a bad attack of the jitters. Then suddenly we slowed, and I was just going to lean over and tell Chuck not to dare speed like that again, when it happened once more! I closed my eyes but that only made me feel worse. And this time we slowed down so rapidly that I was jolted up in the air, and felt as though I'd left my stomach somewhere behind on the road. Chuck looked over his shoulder and grinned, "That's how you tune a bike for racing, you gear her down, which gives more rapid acceleration. Don't you think she's a honey?" he added.

"No, I don't; it feels frightful," I quavered, still shaken.

The sun was just disappearing over the horizon of the water when Matelot and I drove past Panama City beach. There was a large park area stretching for several yards along the beach of picnic shelters and a few palm trees set down in the fine sand. Almost every table was occupied by cheery parties of noisy holiday-makers eating their suppers on the beach. One family made room for me and fed Matelot all their scraps. He became their slave and sat up on his haunches begging, a habit he taught himself and which I find ridiculous in a large, husky airedale.

As I sat over my plate of salad, the map I was studying took off into the night, and I had to chase it across the dark beach. Near the water's edge I could see that the calm waves were now being whipped into a mass of angry white foam and the sky above was overhung with fast-gathering clouds. I felt a drop of rain and then another. After the heat of the last few days, I thought how refreshing a small cloudburst would be. By the time I had returned to my supper the rain was pattering gently down on the shelter roof. The beach was fast becoming deserted, as the last carload of picnic-makers packed up and drove off into the windy night.

When I prepared to camp down on the sands I had quite forgotten Florida has a rainy season. It was impossible to erect the tent, so I just rigged up a small shelter between Oppy's handlebars and a palm tree to keep the rain off my face. I was confident that the little shower wouldn't last long. By the time I had got into my sleeping bag the rain was coming down quite hard, so I covered myself with the ground sheet and wrapped a towel round my neck. Matelot had crawled in beside me and was curled up miserably close to my head.

The wind howled through the palm tree above, and the heavy dark clouds suddenly opened up and thick tropical rain poured down on us. In a matter of seconds everything was soaking wet. The wind blew the rain drops, as large as pigeon's eggs, into the last nook and cranny which had escaped the downpour. Water was dripping in a steady flow down my neck from a crack in the ground-sheet shelter above. Every second the sheet became heavier as it gathered more and more of the falling rain, until finally the whole collection of water fell with one mighty splash on top of my head. As I lay there in the teeming rain, soaked to my skin through the sodden sleeping bag, I could look up above to the highway where the cars were splashing through the small floods of water already gathered on the roadway. There was nothing I could do but lie there and hope that if I didn't move a muscle I might feel a little less wet.

As the wind howled even more ferociously, I began to wonder if this wasn't the beginning of a hurricane. I remembered then hearing that several such storms had been veering off the coast during the last few days. Earthquakes and sandstorms seemed infinitely preferable to this howling tropical gale. I was quite certain that I was going to end up in hospital with a good dose of pneumonia, and Matelot would be taken to the local dog kennel with a doggy virus.

It was the longest night of my life, and when the dawn finally broke over the windswept beach the storm had died down to a gentle patter of steady rain. Gradually the drops decreased until the wind chased away the last scurrying grey cloud and the sun began to break through. Matelot rubbed a cold, wet nose against me and crawled out of his soaking shelter. He stretched, then shook his curly coat, sending a shower of water all over me. I got up very stiffly because half the bones in my body felt paralysed. Luckily the clothes in my suitcases were dry, so I pulled out my warmest sweater and a pair of jeans and changed out of my soaking garments.

By the time my coffee water had heated the beach was spread with a weird assortment of women's clothes, ground sheets and miscellaneous items. It looked like a rummage sale; my dress hung from the rafters of the picnic shelter, Oppy was decorated with my underwear and socks, while the sleeping bag flapped in the breeze from a branch of the palm tree.

But the sun was really out in full force by this time, and before I had finished breakfast everything except the sleeping bag was bone dry. This remained a bedraggled lump of goose feathers and cotton quilting. A dry, warm sleeping bag is a camper's most important possession, so the first thing I did on arrival in Panama City that morning was to take it to a dry cleaners. In about twenty minutes it had been spun dry, and the last proof of my night's misery had been wiped away.

A petrol-station attendant told me that last night's storm was one of the worst on record and in places the fall of rain had reached eighteen inches. The streets and gutters in the city were still flowing with water as I headed Oppy into the sunshine of west Florida.

At Tallahassee I branched south through a country of long straight highways and unending palm trees. I wondered when I was going to see all the Florida snakes I had been told about. Oppy spun steadily along at forty miles an hour, and I reckoned that if we kept up this pace we might reach Miami by the next evening. Then that darn wobble shook the rear wheel once again!

I felt like picking Oppy up and flinging her into the nearest ditch, and I probably should have, but for her weight. It almost seemed as if somebody were sabotaging our trip, scattering nails along the highway just ahead of us. But after all I couldn't really blame poor Oppy for that!

Recovering my temper somewhat, I sat down on the side of the road, first taking care to see there were no snakes near by, and awaited the appearance of the first truck. Here I was about to hitch hike through the Deep South for the fifth time in four days. But for that wonderful band of men, the truck drivers of the United States, I am sure I would still be stuck down in the swamplands of Louisiana.

I hadn't long to wait; a large double-trailer monster came snorting up the road. In answer to my raised thumb, the driver drew off on to the shoulder of the highway. A big man with a huge stetson hat and a broad

Texan drawl offered me a ride all the way to Palm Beach, four hundred miles away on the Atlantic coast. But I told him I just wanted to get to the nearest motor-cycle shop. So we looked at a map and the nearest city of any size was Lakeland, over two hundred miles from here.

By this time I had become an expert in the art of lifting motor-cycles on to trucks, so I was able to give the hefty Texan a fair amount of assistance. Oppy reclined against some huge iron structure bound for Cuba, and Matelot and I hopped aboard beside the driver. The engine of the huge vehicle turned over and our driver pushed his heavy gear stick forward; the wheels beneath us spun around, but we didn't move an inch! The shoulder of the road was made of soft earth, and the five pairs of wheels were firmly sunk, and embedding themselves deeper every minute. I felt very guilty for having made the driver stop in the first place, but Tex as he told me to call him said that this happened quite often when he was driving a heavy truck.

"Don't worry," he said calmly, "the first guy to come along in a truck will pull us out." Then he sat back in his seat placidly and lit a cigarette.

One truck driver will always stop and help another on the road, so we didn't have long to wait. The first truck that came along was going in the opposite direction but it stopped. Then the two drivers got down and fumbled around with a lot of heavy chains. In no time at all the second truck had pulled us back on to the firm roadway. After a little gossip about road conditions, weather and loads, Tex and the other driver climbed back in their trucks and both drove off in different directions.

By the time we reached Lakeland it was later afternoon, and Tex and I got simply soaked in a downpour of rain, just as we started unloading Oppy. But this good-hearted, patient Texan just shook the rain out of his big hat, and got back on the truck with his shirt and trousers streaming with water and took off as casually as could be.

By the time this third nail had been extracted Oppy's rear tyre was looking rather the worse for wear, so I had to dig down in my pocket and find the price of another tyre. Luckily the dealer had a fairly good used one which he sold me for six dollars. Still, with all these breakdowns my last remaining dollars were diminishing at an alarming rate.

It was dark by the time we set off again, and I only drove a few miles before looking for a camping site. At Winterhaven I found a lovely grassy spot beside a lake. For the first time in two weeks I pitched the tent and crawled sleepily inside. Next morning I startled an early-morning fisherman by brushing my teeth in the warm, muddy waters of the lake. He was rowing out in a boat laden with fishing tackle, and offered to bring back a fish for my breakfast. I thanked him but said I was in too much of a hurry. Actually I didn't even stop to make coffee, and hurriedly packed up and set off on the road to Miami.

I passed mile after mile of orange groves, and I wished that it had been the picking season. After all my experience apple picking in British Columbia, I was sure I could have made an honest dollar or two to take me to New York. I was beginning to wonder how I was ever going to even get out of Florida!

But now as always, in between her fits of temperament, Oppy was rushing down the highway on two steady wheels and the engine was ticking over without missing a beat. Twice we were caught in deluging downpours, but I found I soon drove out of them if I just kept on going at a steady rate of speed. Under the hot sun my soaking dress and hair dried in a jiffy. My sandals, however, were getting ruined, so the next time I saw black clouds ahead of me on the highway I took them off and drove barefoot. It was really lovely driving under the warm streaming rain—like sitting under a lukewarm shower. I knew the sun was just ahead down the highway, so I didn't mind getting wet at all. The passing motorists looked out at me with my streaming hair and face, sodden dress and bare feet as if I were a freak of nature.

After skirting Lake Okeechobee, the highway to Miami lay for eighty miles across the desolate Everglades, those vast swamplands that cover hundreds of square miles of Florida. Here is the home of the crocodile and many deadly snakes, but the only sign of wild life that I saw that day was the flamingoes. At the sound of the motor-cycle they rose off the marshes, tucking their delicate legs under them and flapping their graceful white wings in flight.

One part of the road stretched for over forty miles without wavering off its perfectly straight course. With nothing to look at but this vast stretch of flat swampland, an occasional car and the flamingoes, I found this the most boring road I'd ever been on.

However, I did have one small diversion travelling through the Everglades. No sooner had the sun faded than great clouds of June bugs dived out of the sky like fighter planes going to the attack. They were about four inches across in wing span, and if one flew into my face with full force it was enough to throw me off balance. Whenever I saw them coming directly at me I ducked my head, but they thudded and zoomed against my body with painful precision. I drove through clouds of them, my face practically buried on the tank. It was a good thing the road was so straight or I would surely have crashed.

As soon as darkness fell these pests disappeared and I was left alone on the road once more. The Everglades certainly didn't seem a very attractive place to pitch a tent, so I drove on, until about ten o'clock at night I reached the limits of the city of Miami. I decided to try sleeping on the beach again. It was exciting to think that I was going to see the Atlantic Ocean again—for the first time since I had left Halifax sixteen months before.

CHAPTER XVIII *Miami*

I DROVE down the wide glittering boulevard leading into Miami, and thought how artificial it all looked after the lonely drive over the Everglades. Along both sides of the street there was row after row of neon-lighted all-night service stations, restaurants and taverns. Entering the city, I turned east and drove across the MacArthur Causeway leading to Miami Beach. The wide, smooth highway was flanked by palm trees and grass lawns, and beyond them on both sides stretched the waters of Biscayne Bay. Looking back over my shoulder I could see the whole city of Miami with its tall lighted buildings illuminated on the dark expanse of water. The moon had risen over the waving palm trees, making Miami look exactly like a gaudy ten-cent postcard, the sort one never feels is quite real.

I stopped to enjoy the beautiful view a little longer and decided to have supper. First I leaned against the trunk of a coconut palm, kicked off my sandals and hung my feet into the warm water. Soon Matelot had joined me in a cheese sandwich, while behind us the traffic of gay holiday-makers streaked past on the way to Miami Beach. If only I could pitch the tent here, I thought; the grass was so soft and the view so perfect, while the gentle breeze that blew across the water was pleasing and warm. But just then a low-slung scarlet convertible filled with a merry crowd of pleasure-seekers stopped and yelled at me to join them, so I realized that such a camp site wouldn't have given me much peace or privacy.

Although I had heard as much about this famous Florida playground as I had heard about the Sunset Strip in Hollywood, I was none the less completely dazzled as I started to drive down Collins Avenue. The pavements were packed with a colourful gay throng, some in flowing dance dresses and tuxedos, other in shorts, halters and sandals. Even I, with my crumpled sun dress and fierce sun-tan, didn't look too out of place.

I drove for what seemed miles past countless luxury hotels, but not one tiny piece of open ground did I see for my tent. Then presently I came to a residential district full of large villas surrounded by gardens and high stone walls. This didn't look like good camping ground either, until I noticed a small vacant spot between two of these high walls. I was just deciding how to negotiate Oppy up on to the pavement when a car stopped beside me. A policeman poked his head out of the window and asked me what I thought I was trying to do at that late hour. I told him I was going to camp on the beach.

"You can't camp on Miami Beach!" he said horrified, and went on severely, "It's against the law! You'd better find yourself a hotel." And with that he drove off.

Well, after such a warning I wasn't quite so stupid as to pitch my tent on that particular spot, but neither did I intend to abandon altogether the idea of camping beside the Atlantic Ocean. Driving a little farther down the road, I came to another open space. Looking hastily both ways up and down the road, I forced Oppy up the pavement, then shut off the engine so as not to disturb the residents of the houses nearby. After this I pushed a very heavy Oppy across the soft sand and propped her against one of the high stone walls. It was after midnight and both houses that gave on to the beach were in darkness.

There before me was the Atlantic rolling in across the deserted beach, and I could hardly get out of my clothes and into my swimsuit quickly enough to reach the water. That night I lay down on the sand in my swim suit, under the shelter of a small sailboat. The ocean lapped over the beach a few yards away, and the breeze was hot across my face as I fell asleep with Matelot at my side.

The pink light of the dawn on the grey horizon woke me up. Within a few seconds I was at the ocean edge, unhampered by having to climb out of a tent or change my clothes. But I didn't dare stay too long on the beach in case some millionaire looked out of his bedroom window and telephoned the police.

It was Labour Day, and that morning some motor-cycle events were to be held on the outskirts of Miami, so about eight o'clock I drove past all those tall white hotels again on my way back to the city. As instructed by a leaflet given to me in the Pensacola motor-cycle shop, I drove down the Tamiami Trail, which is the main highway leading across the Everglades to the west coast of Florida.

It was a dreadfully hot day to watch motor-cycles roaring and tearing up the highway. They were all covered in mud from their endurance run through some of the less swampy parts of the Everglades. Matelot and I sat panting under a row of trees, which was the only shade for miles around. We talked with a lot of motor-cycling enthusiasts and some of the hot, dust-covered riders, so that the day was amusing in spite of the discomfort of the sun.

Finally, everyone headed back to the city, and the last of the powerful machines passed me with the rider waving goodbye. I was just thinking how pleasant it would be to get back to the beach for a swim when Oppy did it again! Her rear wheel wobbled and shook violently, and I thought—well, this is a fine time and place to have a flat, way out on the lonely Tamiami Trail and on a holiday too.

When I dismounted to look at the tyre, I found it to be in perfect order, but the wheel was wobbling loosely from side to side, with the tyre rubbing against the fender and making a horrible whining noise. It looked as if the whole axle must have broken, and considering the terrible weight poor Oppy was carrying I was surprised it hadn't happened before. The tyre was being ruined too, because I was driving on the burning hot road with it dragging against the fender. But the machine was far too heavy to push and the highway was too deserted for us to expect a truck to come along and rescue us again.

At last we came to a small café and trailer park. Leaving Matelot panting under the shadow of the building, I went inside for a coffee. I felt very depressed as I sat at the small lunch counter. For if I telephoned for a breakdown service and added it to the charge of dismantling and repairing Oppy's wheel I would be almost flat broke.

But good luck came to me in two forms; the first was a pretty red-headed girl with a mass of freckles and a cheery grin.

"Hello, I see you've got trouble with your motor-cycle," she greeted me. Soon I had told her what had happened and she was full of advice.

"Well, you can't get it fixed until tomorrow, so I suggest you come over and stay in my trailer for the night, and then we'll think about some way to get you to the city tomorrow."

Just then a big heavily built man in his forties leaned across the counter and said, "I don't like to see a girl in distress." He seemed rather tipsy. "Tell you what I'll do," he continued, "I'll take that motor-cycle of yours into Miami on my truck and then bring you back here for the night."

I looked at Veda and whispered, "I think he's drunk and doesn't know what he's saying."

"So what? It's only eighteen miles to the city, and it's probably your only chance to get the machine in there without paying a ten-dollar breakdown charge."

So pretty soon the burly trucker got to his feet and led the way to the truck. He was certainly a little under the weather, but looked as though he were fit to drive. With some help from the café people we hoisted Oppy on to the back of his empty truck. I was slightly nervous the whole journey to the city, because my driver kept speeding up and then stopping suddenly on the red lights with only about a couple of inches to spare. Fortunately we found a petrol station quite near the motor-cycle shop

that carried Oppy's spare parts, and left her there in charge of two attendants. The journey back to the trailer camp was equally hazardous, but
we made it safely and I thanked the kind driver profusely.

Then I made my way across the trailer park to where a small, neat
trailer was sitting beside a blue convertible. My hostess was standing on
the top step of the trailer waving a cup at me.

"I'm glad to see you got back all in one piece, come and have some
coffee for your nerves."

That night I slept on a comfortable camp bed outside the trailer and
woke to the smell of breakfast. As the blue convertible sped Matelot and
me towards Miami, Veda told me to be sure and ring her up if we
wanted any help; I thanked her and said we'd drive out to say goodbye
when Oppy was fixed.

That day I spent a most depressing morning in the motor-cycle shop,
where a very disgruntled man, who obviously loathed girl motor-cyclists,
kept me hanging about until after lunch before he would deign to look
at Oppy. Finally he found the axle was broken and that I needed a new
wheel, for which he would have to send away. I opened my purse and
found that I had just over forty dollars left. It looked as though we were
really stuck in Miami, and I sat on one of the upturned luggage bags in
a corner of the hot, dirty shop and tried to think how to get out of this
mess.

To borrow money seemed the last resort. First I wondered if I had left
anything up in Canada Bernice could sell for me, but I remembered that
there were only my skis and they wouldn't fetch much. Then like a
flash it came to me that I did possess some dollar assets, but they were
across the Atlantic in England. Nevertheless I pulled out an airmail letter
and wrote a frantic and hurried note to the editor of a motor-cycling
magazine in London to rush over the money owing to me in dollars.

Then Matelot and I wandered out into the sunshine to find a room,
because it looked as though we were going to be at least a week in Miami
even if the money was cabled from London. I turned the corner behind
the motor-cycle shop and walked aimlessly along, wondering where to
start looking first.

Then I noticed a large piece of rough ground dotted with ramshackle wooden cabins badly in need of paint, a couple of trailers and a small house. I walked up to the door of the house, which was marked "Office," and rang the bell. A short woman with a doughy face framed in frizzy black hair peered out at me suspiciously. Vainly trying to hide Matelot behind my legs, I asked her if she had a cabin to rent.

"I don't let cabins to single girls," she said in a thick Scottish brogue, glaring at me. I stood my ground and explained how depressing it was to be so far from home with nowhere to stay.

"I only want it for about a week," I pleaded.

Finally she agreed and led me across to one of the cabins, telling me how she had left the Old Country herself thirty years before.

"I didn't like to turn an English girl away, but the owner of these cabins doesn't allow single women or animals."

She fumbled with a key and then flung open the door. "You see, it ain't fixed up enough and decent for a girl to live in," she said.

I could understand what she meant. The place was unpainted and filthily dirty. On the bare-board floor sat a huge iron bed, with a rusty oil stove in one corner and a built-in cupboard above, while a table and two hard chairs completed the furniture of the cheerless room. But, after all, I was used to rough camping, and this looked like a very convenient place to keep Matelot. Besides, it was only a dozen blocks from the centre of the city.

So, after the manager showed me where to fetch water outside, and pointed out a clean toilet and shower house, I went back to the office with her and paid five dollars for a week's rent in advance. Then I borrowed a broom, a pail and a mop.

For the next two hours, in the worst heat of the afternoon, I struggled to get that cabin into some sort of decent shape to live in. Clouds of dust were brushed from the ceiling and also cobwebs full of spiders, which I killed with the head of the broom. The floor yielded half a bucket of sand and scraps of old paper, and the shelves were stuck with stale odds and ends of food. In the cupboard I found a family of scuttling cockroaches which I managed to discourage with a whole bucket of soapy water. By the time the floor was scrubbed I was sweating and tired. At least the whole place was reasonably clean, although nobody could have called it a home from home.

I rang Veda about five o'clock and she came over in her car and helped me move the luggage from the motor-cycle shop. When she had gone I looked round the bare, depressing room with its stifling atmosphere, no bed linen or curtains. I hadn't eaten since breakfast with Veda, but I was still too depressed to think of food, so instead I sat down and wrote a very miserable, sorry-for-myself letter to Carl-Erik. I couldn't sleep that night for the heat and I lay on the bare mattress and wondered what the next step was going to be. Obviously I had to earn some money while I waited for that bank draft to come from England.

Next morning I bought a newspaper and opened it at the Help Wanted —Female page. Well, I had no clothes suitable for temporary office work, cooking has never been my strong point, and I was sure that I could never add fast enough for a clerical job in a store, so I turned to the column advertising for soda fountain and restaurant help. There seemed to be a great many jobs open, but they all wanted experienced people.

Undaunted I set off for a café that was advertising for a grill worker. I had no idea what this job entailed, but thought at least I could try my luck. So I entered the large shining café, sat down at the lunch counter and ordered a coffee. But as I watched the different girls at work they all looked so efficient that I completely lost my nerve. Ten minutes later I found myself walking out of the door without having even dared to ask about the job.

This process was repeated in half a dozen lunch bars and cafés, and finally all this coffee drinking was becoming too expensive, so I boarded a bus and went back to the cabin. I still hadn't eaten anything solid for twenty-four hours. That evening I got out my stove, intending to cook myself a few sausages and fried onions. But I was furious to find that Florida rust had got all over the stove and nothing would make it work! I took the whole thing to pieces and then couldn't put it together again. The fact that the stove was useless proved even more disappointing when Mr. Jones, a big bronzed man living in the cabin opposite, came over to ask if I'd like some fish. I accepted a great pan of mouth-watering snappers just in case I managed to get the stove to work later on.

Mr. Jones told me I could have as many snappers as I liked, because he fished every night commercially and always had plenty of extra to distribute around the camp. In fact, he admitted that the other cabin tenants were sick and tired of his free fish. But when I looked at my cupboard of dwindling supplies I seriously contemplated living on raw fish if need be.

The next three days I spent pounding the pavements job hunting, until I had two large blisters on my hot, sore feet. I always confessed that I was inexperienced, and that admission always brought the interview to an immediate end. At the end of the week I telephoned Veda and she told me not to be so stupid as to say I had no experience.

"You'll never get a job being so honest in this town," she insisted.

That Friday I parted with thirty dollars in the motor-cycle shop, and when I got back to the cabin I emptied my purse on the table and counted the remaining coins. A quarter, two dimes, two nickels and five pennies—sixty cents in all! In the cupboard were a couple of tins of dog food, one tin of beans, half a loaf of bread and a tin of tomato juice. Most frustrating of all was the sight of another pan of delicious snappers, that I was unable to cook. Three previous pans had already gone into the garbage pail because of my inability to eat it raw. Even Matelot turned his nose up at raw fish, and although his bones weren't yet sticking through his fur, I knew they would be soon.

The following morning I scanned a newspaper which cost a precious five cents, and noticed a job asking for an inexperienced girl to learn to be a "car hop." I telephoned the number given in the advertisement and a male voice informed me he would give me a trial if I would come along that evening at six o'clock and be prepared to work until one in the morning.

"Don't forget to bring a pair of brief shorts to work in," said the boss before he hung up.

Shorts! Would I ever find the nerve to run back and forth between cars and the café in shorts, half way into the night! Oh, well, I thought this is Florida, where everybody wears shorts in the street at any time of the day or night.

Still, I didn't feel very happy about my prospective job, as I boarded the bus that evening with the shorts under my arm and the address of the road-house café inside my purse. Also I was worried that Matelot might bark while I was away and wake up the whole camp and get us thrown out on the street.

At the road-house a coarse-looking man with a leering grin and a soiled white apron showed me where I could change. When I came out in my corduroy shorts and linen blouse, he and a brassy-looking girl in a tight black dress sniggered at me, and I knew I didn't look at all like a car hop should.

The restaurant consisted of a long bar open to the pavement; beyond there was a small enclosed dining room which the girl in the black dress looked after. My job was to stand outside on the pavement under two blazing lights and attract the customers inside. In addition I was to wait on anyone who wished to eat in his car, and also I was expected to keep an eye on a small patio with three or four tables.

I felt frightfully conspicuous as I rested against the building under those bright lights in my shorts and waited for my first customer. Convertibles glided down the street and young men whistled rudely at me and invited me to take a ride. I tried hiding round the corner in the patio, and by so doing nearly missed my first customer.

As I rushed up to the car window the door was flung open and a young man and his girl, looking rather surprised at my breathless arrival, pushed past me into the restaurant, where the slinky blonde was waiting to serve them. So I went back to my lolling on the pavement wishing every minute the ground would open up and swallow me. At last a car pulled into the yard and this time nobody got out. Eagerly I hurried over and stuck a menu through the rolled-down window.

I fetched my customers' order of fried shrimps in the basket, and took at least five minutes to write out the order cheque properly in the coded letters which the leering barman insisted upon. Then I piled the tray with the food and staggered out across the pavement. But when I got back to the car I hadn't the faintest idea how to clip it on to the car. Trying to look very experienced, I dumped the tray on the window ledge and felt around furiously for the little legs underneath that are supposed to secure it to the customer's window. How awful it would have been if I had dropped the whole caboodle on the poor driver's lap!

Luckily my customer was a kind young man. He hopped out of the other side of the car and showed me the correct way to secure the tray to the window ledge. But later, getting it off the window proved just as complicated, and I was most surprised to find my first customer had left me a ten-cent tip for my inefficiency. At least I had already earned my bus fare one way!

Business wasn't very fast, and I had many a long wait standing under the lights doing nothing and trying to ignore the leers and whistles from the passing motorists. But after a while most of my late-night customers started ordering beer, and for a solid hour I was kept busy running back and forth to the patio with trays loaded down with glasses and great pitchers of foaming lager. However, we had too much competition from a noisy, dimly lit tavern opposite, so midnight found me all alone standing on the pavement like a lifeless dummy, holding a menu card in one hand and a price list of beers in the other.

Just before one in the morning I put my hand in my pocket and counted my tips; I had one dollar and forty cents. My customers hadn't been very generous, but I had certainly given them very poor service. At closing time I told the barman not to expect me the next evening, because I didn't think I was cut out to be a car hop, and he smirked and said he didn't think so either.

I was about three miles from the cabin, and after inquiring I learned that the last cross-town bus had left at twelve-thirty. I was just wondering if my sore and aching feet would carry me three miles through the dark city streets, when a young man at the counter got up and said, "Well, where's your motor-cycle tonight?"

At first I was very surprised until he explained that I had bought some petrol from him on my first evening in Miami. Pretty soon he offered to take me home, and I gladly fell into his car. With all the running and standing about I was so tired that when I got back to the cabin I just lay on top of the bed in all my clothes and fell fast asleep. About midday when I awoke poor Matelot was standing there regarding me quizzically. He was very confused by this strange new life we were leading.

My mail was being forwarded to the cabin regularly now, and I kept getting letters from Denmark and England saying, "What a marvellous tour you are having! How I envy you all those wonderful experiences!"

Well, I was out of a job again and my finances had improved very little. But before long I had a new idea and boarded the bus for the general hospital.

The nurse in the blood donors' clinic took all my particulars and looked at my donor's certificates from England and Canada, and asked me if I wanted to send my blood to Korea or credit it against myself or a friend.

I told her I wanted to sell it! She looked slightly shocked and said they had given up buying blood some years ago, because they had plenty of volunteers. She made me feel so mercenary that I gasped, "Take it anyway and I'll give it to Korea."

After a short wait I was shown into another office, where a nurse took a tiny pinprick of blood from my thumb. She came back a few minutes later and said that it showed a great deficiency of hæmoglobins and would be useless for transfusion. She looked at me sharply and said, "What's the matter—are you feeling run down? If so, it's no time to come and donate blood." She told me that I had better hang on to every pint I had, and in addition advised me to take a holiday and change my diet.

As I left the hospital I felt very depressed; except for forty cents I was saving for bus fares, I had spent the rest of my money on airmail letter forms and dog food, and I hadn't eaten a proper meal for three days. In desperation I studied the newspaper again and found somebody advertising an evening job in a milk bar on a temporary basis. So, feeling this was my last chance, I boarded a bus for Coral Gables.

A kind, motherly woman in a big white apron interviewed me at a table in the clean, shining dairy.

"Well, you won't get many tips at the soda counter, and the work is quite hard, because you'll have to lift a lot of heavy milk bottles. Also you only get paid twice a month. But I think you'll be happy if you don't mind hard work," she said candidly.

I didn't intend taking the wages anyway. But I hoped to live on my tips until my money arrived from England. When the woman asked me if I knew soda fountain work, I managed to mumble something vaguely truthful, and I found myself hired as a dairy girl. The woman said I could start work that evening. The hours were from four o'clock in the afternoon until midnight.

I remembered that Veda had told me how she had once worked in a soda fountain and how easy it really was, so that afternoon I rang her up. I begged her to tell me how to make a milk shake and what were the ingredients for a malted milk, and how you created a banana split. She told

me as best she could, while I took feverish notes. Then, laughing and saying she would love to see that first banana split, she wished me good luck
and rang off.

Promptly at four o'clock I arrived for work, and was given a large
white apron which I tucked round my middle and tied at the back.

"This is where we keep the hot fudge, and the nuts are in this jar and the
sauces are up at the top," said Mrs. Hunter, showing me the soda counter.
A small, bouncing little man with beetling eyebrows, a bright check
shirt and an air of great self-importance appeared behind us.

"Ah! so this is the new girl? I hope you showed her how to mix the
milk shakes." Turning to me he said, "They are our speciality and I am
most particular that all my girls learn to make them efficiently."

He bent down and scooped two large lumps of ice cream into a metal
container.

"Now watch carefully, please," he said.

He flipped the lid off a bottle of milk, added a few drops of flavouring
and poured it into the container. Then with a professional air he stretched
up to the wall, where an electric mixer was attached. He set the container
under the lip that was supposed to hold it firm while the machine worked,
but he must have misjudged, because almost immediately there was a
terrific whirring noise. Then *crash*—the whole thing exploded and fell
to the counter below. We were all covered with chocolate ice cream and
milk, and the pompous little manager looked furious as he dabbed at his
ruined trousers and soaking shirt.

Most of that evening I spent staggering in and out of the dairy bar with
heavy containers of milk bottles, and found the work consisted mostly of
selling dairy goods and a few groceries. The soda counter was very slack
and so we made little in tips.

Jean, the other girl, was a bright little thing who kept us all laughing
with her jokes, and the new companionship and busy work made the
evening fly past. During our fifteen-minute supper break I took the plate
of free ice cream allowed us, and made sure it was covered to overflowing
with whipped cream, butterscotch sauce and nuts.

But the evening was not without its minutes of worry. The first time a
customer asked me to make a banana split, I glanced hurriedly at the
illustration on the wall above and started to look for a glass dish. When

I was finished my concoction was a frightful mess; the sauce was over-flowing and running in little rivulets over the counter, the banana had a drunken lurch to it, and the whipped cream on the top had come out in a horrible splurge down one side. The fat over-fed lady customer took one look at it and exclaimed, "This is the *worst*-looking banana split I have ever seen!"

I hurried out to the back to collect some more milk and hide my blushes.

But somehow the evening passed, and about midnight I said goodnight to Mrs. Hunter and Jean, and with just thirty cents in tips in my pocket I went to catch my bus. The welcoming thud—thud of Matelot's tail on the cabin floor was a good thing to hear after a hard evening's work. He was overjoyed when I let him out to go careering round the block in the hot night air. My feet ached so badly that I took off my shoes and followed him barefoot.

The week wore on; long hot days during which I slept almost until it was time to take Matelot for a run before work. I was just managing to buy a little food with the tips, which were very small and far between. It was hard to find even enough money to mail my letters, and I was very glad one day when Carl-Erik enclosed in his letter several international reply coupons, which I was able to cash at the post office for stamps.

After I had been working just over a week at the dairy and still had no word from England about the money, Mrs. McKaye, the Scottish cabin manager, came over to see me. She brought bad news.

"The owners were here yesterday when you were out, and when they heard about you and the dog they made a great fuss and said you would have to leave."

That, I felt, was the last straw. I was sure I would never find another place to live with Matelot in Miami, and I had no money to pay rent in advance.

But Mrs. McKaye said the owners wouldn't be back for two days and that I could stay until then.

That night, after work, I lay on top of the bed hardly breathing with the heat, and wondered if there was any solution to this horrible situation I found myself in. I just *had* to get to New York City, now that city seemed like a challenging goal for me; I couldn't give up the trip at this point. To have come so far on my own and then have to throw myself on some charitable organization—no, I just had to find a solution and finish the trip under my own steam.

The solution came next morning in the mail. Out of a bulky letter from Denmark fell five rather crumpled ten-dollar bills and a little note from Carl-Erik. For a moment I was so speechless that I didn't realize I was saved; my feelings overwhelmed me.

CHAPTER XIX *Northward Bound*

IT was so wonderful to be back on the open highway, that the sunshine and salt air went to my head almost like champagne. Miami was left behind as we tore along on the way to the Florida Keys. My conscience told me that instead of going southwards to Key West I should have been headed north. But I didn't think this four-hundred-mile detour would delay my arrival in New York by more than a couple of days. Now that I was so near to this unique hundred-mile ocean highway I didn't want to miss driving over it.

It seemed strange to be scooting across one narrow coral island to the other, with the Atlantic Ocean on one side and the Gulf of Mexico on the other. The long bridges connecting the islands were packed with people fishing; some just dangled a piece of string into the water in place of a rod. Even I, from the saddle of Oppy, could have gone deep-sea fishing quite easily.

I was just driving across the seven-mile bridge and marvelling at this great expanse of water all around me, when I saw that the horizon ahead had clouded over. The sky was rapidly turning black and the wind began to tear at the palm trees. I had meant to go right to the southern end of the Keys and have a look at the city of Key West, but I certainly didn't want to get wet just before camping time. Rather regretfully I turned

Oppy round and headed north into the sunshine, leaving the storm behind us.

When I reached the island of Islamorada again, I saw a stretch of green grass that looked inviting; I could use the Atlantic for my bathroom and then wander across the road and fish in the Gulf of Mexico. It seemed like a camper's dream. Apparently the rain clouds had decided not to come any farther north, and as it was only a couple of hours from sunset I decided to pitch the tent right here. This proved quite a struggle, as the wind was blowing fairly strongly; but at last the unruly canvas was billowing out, making the inside of the tent twice as large as usual. I went to sleep early, tired from so much strong sea air and wind. I could feel the canvas walls near my face beating against the wind; and a few yards away, on either side of me, the waves were lapping over the beaches.

I awoke with a sudden start; the tent had completely collapsed on top of me! Jumping up, I struggled desperately to right the fallen poles and uprooted tent pegs, but in vain. Matelot crawled out from under the mass of billowing canvas and sniffed the rain-scented air. The wind was blowing harder every minute, and then suddenly the air mattress slipped from under the tent, rose in the air and took off in the direction of the gulf. Then down came the rain.

Now for the moment a lost air mattress seemed relatively unimportant; I was scanning the inky darkness for a possible shelter. Earlier in the evening I had seen a launch moored to a small jetty; so pulling on my jeans, I ran through the torrential downpour as fast as my legs would carry me.

The boat had been blown several feet away from the jetty and was straining at its moorings against the gale. I was just trying to decide whether to pick up Matelot and throw him on to the deck and then jump over the gap of water myself, when the bright headlights of a car flashed into view. There I stood in the darkness and rain, clad in nothing but my pyjamas and a pair of jeans, clutching a sleeping bag in one hand and my purse in the other. I never felt so ridiculous in all my life.

The car slowed down, pulled over on to the grass opposite and turned out its bright lights. That definitely put an end to the idea of jumping on board the launch, so I turned around and walked very fast up the road.

The car started up, and with its lights still off it began to move over the grass toward me. I began to run—Matelot must be lost somewhere in the darkness. Then I saw the light from a house just ahead; I raced over the wet grass and in a second Matelot was bounding at my heels again.

Climbing the steps of a small white frame house, I peeped through the lighted window and saw a large, comfortable living room full of books and trophies hanging on the walls. Water was pouring down my back and my hair hung in long, straggling ends on my shoulders; I began to shiver under the wet garments. Fastening Matelot's chain to his collar, I banged as hard as I could on the front door.

I stood there shaking miserably on the porch, my sleeping bag trailing in a sodden mass and Matelot pressing hard against my legs. As I was just about to raise my hand to the door again, it was flung open and a fierce-looking middle-aged man peered through the screen door at me. "Well, what do you want?" he snapped suspiciously.

"I was camping until my tent blew down in the storm," I began. "I suppose you haven't a shed where I could throw down my sleeping bag?"

A large aristocratic doberman pinscher was staring at us through the screen door, and beyond him I saw a slim, boyish figure in white shorts.

"I tried to shelter on that boat moored to the jetty, but then I got scared. I feel awful bothering you," I ended up lamely.

"It's a damn good thing you *didn't* get on that boat. It belongs to me and I've had so much trespassing that I shoot now first and ask questions afterwards." Then his tone changed, and he went on kindly, "You're English, aren't you?" Now he caught sight of Matelot, who for once in his life was taking no notice of another dog. So he added, "You'd better come round to the back with your dog."

I battled my way to the rear of the house, where my newly acquired host was standing in the doorway of a lighted shed. There were several outboard engines, a work bench of tools and a pile of old canvas scattered about the place.

"This will be swell," I said gratefully. Matelot had already flung himself down thankfully on to the dry floor.

"Well, you don't think I'd let *you* sleep here, do you? The place is crawling with hermit crabs and scorpions. You'd better leave your dog here though, mine wouldn't allow him in the house." The man was getting kinder and more human by the minute. Now he said, "Before you get into dry clothes I'll drive you down to pick up your motor-cycle, so you can store it here out of the rain."

As we bumped across the grass in his car, I asked my benefactor how he knew about my motor-cycle.

"Oh, Mary, my wife, said she saw you drive past this afternoon, and thought—there goes a girl after adventure."

"Well, I certainly got it tonight!" I laughed ruefully.

Soon Oppy and the soaking luggage was spread out to dry in the shed, alongside a sleeping Matelot. Bob, my host, led the way into a small warm kitchen, saying "This is Peggy, Mary. She needs some dry clothes in a hurry."

A deeply sun-tanned woman in white shorts hustled me into the bathroom, where a robe and slippers were already laid out for me. "Hurry up and get out of those wet things," she said, closing the door.

When I had rubbed myself down and put on the cosy robe and slippers, I came through to the living room. Mary and Bob were talking together and looking very amused. Bob took a look at me.

"Well, that's better. When I first opened the door I thought you were a boy standing there with your jeans and bare feet."

"That's why he was so abrupt with you," explained Mary. "There really are a lot of queer characters hanging about the Keys."

After a bit Mary disappeared into the kitchen and presently she called for us to come and eat. I am sure that this was supper No. 2 for Mary and Bob, because it was long after ten o'clock. By the time we were enjoying the ice cream my story had got back to the tent-collapsing episode, which now appeared to be rather funny.

Next morning it was still blowing hard with an occasional gust of rain, so Mary insisted that I stay for lunch. Bob was having quite a time outside with Matelot, who had discovered the monkey housed in a cage next to the boat shed. He went completely wild at the sight of it. The monkey also took a violent dislike to Matelot, and jumped up and down on his perch, chattering madly and thrusting his little paws through the netting in a vain attempt to scratch him. Matelot, wise dog, kept his distance, but he so upset the poor monkey that I had to shut him back in the boat shed.

What had started as a night of misery and discomfort had turned into a wonderful visit with a charming couple, and it was with great reluctance that I said goodbye to Mary and Bob and set off again.

I scanned both sides of the highway for my lost air mattress, and even got off and searched the beach, but there was no sign of it. Probably by that time some Cuban-bound seagulls were using it for a half-way resting raft. It looked as if my future nights were doomed to be hard ones.

I was just leaving the outskirts of Miami Beach that evening when I passed a young man on a large scarlet motor-cycle going in the other direction. I gave him the conventional friendly wave, and a minute later he drove up beside me and asked if I would pull over to the side of the road.

Then he stretched out his hand to me and said, "I'm the chaplain to the motor-cycle riders, and I'd like to give you these." He thrust a few booklets into my hand and then introduced himself.

Alan McHardy was a Canadian in his early thirties, well built and with a handsome tanned face. What I noticed most about him was his smile— he never stopped smiling. It seems that a couple of years previously he had been leading a rather thoughtless and reckless life. Then one day he had a bad smash up on his motor-cycle. While waiting for the ambulance, and in great pain, he had plenty of time to think. As a result he had decided that he was leading the wrong sort of life.

So now he had set out to travel all over the United States and Canada, helping people in his own way, and particularly motor-cyclists. He told me he was a mechanic, and when he ran out of money, which he frequently did, he just stopped wherever he was and took a job until he had saved enough to carry him on farther.

I was just as interested in Alan's travelling outfit as he was in mine. His powerful machine was attached to an enormous long red box on wheels. He opened the top of the box and proudly showed me what was inside. It made me feel as though Oppy was carrying hardly more than a toothbrush and a comb by comparison. The red box was packed with great quantities of literature, including a large Bible. Then it also held what seemed like a staggering amount of clothes and a weighty box of tools. Alan's cooking utensils completely put my modest collection to shame. Out of the four corners of the box he pulled telescopic poles, and explained how he fitted his tent over the top, so that he actually slept on his motor-cycle outfit. It was really quite ingenious and he had made it all himself.

Over a coffee at a nearby lunch counter we talked about Canada. I was very intrigued to hear that his home town was Vancouver. I got even more of a surprise when I found that I couldn't mention a single motor-cycle friend or dealer in that city that Alan hadn't known since boyhood.

But it was getting dark now, so we decided that it was time for two tent-pitching motor-cyclists to go on their respective ways. I wished Alan good luck in his work and he said he would pray for my safe arrival in New York City.

A few miles down the road I came to Hollywood Beach; by this time I was so hungry that I stopped at the beachside park to make supper. There was a large partly enclosed shelter, with two long tables and seats, and a row of gas burners against the wall. Someone had thoughtfully left behind a tin of dripping, so I quickly tossed myself up a couple of fried-cheese sandwiches and made a pan of coffee.

Then I sat at one of the tables and wrote my diary long into the evening. The electric light above me burned brightly, illuminating the notice outside that stated, "No loitering after 10 p.m. Order of the Police Department."

At ten o'clock sharp the light went out, but I decided to disregard the warning and spend the night there. First I tried to hide Oppy's bulging figure behind one of the tables; then, spreading my ground sheet on the hard concrete floor, I climbed into my sleeping bag. Camping so long with an air mattress had definitely made me soft; my unconditioned hip bones stuck against the hard surface of the unrelenting floor.

Soon a blinding light was playing on my face and I became fully conscious in a second. But I kept my eyes tight shut hoping that whoever was spotlighting me like this would go away.

"Come on there, buddy, wake up—this is the cops," said an authoritative voice. I sat up in my sleeping bag, feigning innocence, and asking sweetly, "Good evening, officer, is there anything I can do for you?"

The spotlight was immediately turned off, and the figure of a policeman drew near. He shone a flashlight over the ground all around me, catching Matelot's eyes, which shone brightly in the darkness.

"Don't you know you're breaking the law?" he asked, not too unkindly, sitting down on the seat above me and getting out his notebook. "Now, let's have it, please, starting with your name."

I fumbled around in my purse and brought out my passport, which made a short cut of all my personal data, from birth date to the colour of my eyes.

"Green eyes, brown hair, born in England," he muttered as he scribbled away in his black notebook. The fact that I was a visiting foreigner made the case against my sleeping on city property less prosecutable. Luckily he never asked me if I had read the warning notice. Then, after all the official details had been collected, the Arm of the Law relaxed and became entirely human.

"I don't like the idea of you down here alone on the beach; there are often some mighty queer characters who have the same idea. I'll be patrolling this stretch of road until six o'clock, so I'll drop by every hour to see you're O.K." He shut his book with a bang. Then added, "You sure got a nice dog there, didn't even bark at me."

The policeman wished me good-night and strolled back to the patrol car. I snuggled down into my sleeping bag again, and just at that minute something alive and hard crawled on top of me. I raised my head and looked into two beady eyes protruding from the shell of a giant crab. I let out one mighty yell and jumped to my feet, while the horrible monster scuttled noisily away into a corner.

The cop came running over to see what was the matter.

"You see, you did need protection after all," he said, flashing his light down on the large, bluish-grey crab, who was sitting down waving two large pincers in the air. He kicked at it and sent it flying across the shelter and out on to the beach.

"I've never seen such a large crab," I said. "That pincer looks as though it could bite your whole finger off!"

"It probably could. They're land crabs and live up above the beach in ground holes."

The cop flashed his light around again. The horrible beast was scuttling back into the shelter now. After that I didn't look, but I heard a nasty, squelching noise. Then I felt something brush past my feet, I looked down and there was another, even larger crab ambling across my sleeping bag.

"Quick!" I shrieked.

"Wait, I've found another too," said the cop.

Operation Crab seemed to be well under way, so I climbed on to one of the tables. And I decided I would spend the rest of the night right there.

"Well, I think that's the last of 'em," said the cop at last, scraping his shoes clean on the floor. "See you at six o'clock," he added over his shoulder and went back to his car again.

I buried my face in the sleeping bag and hoped that there weren't any more crabs lurking down there in the darkness. My last concern before dropping off to sleep again was the answer to a question—can crabs climb?

But the next thing I knew a voice beside me was saying "Coffee's on," and I looked into the face of my friendly midnight cop. He handed me a paper cup of steaming coffee and asked if I'd slept well. It was lovely sitting up in my sleeping bag sipping coffee and watching the dawn come up over the Atlantic.

"I'm not even paying any American taxes, and look at the service I'm getting from the police force," I laughed. We both finished our coffee and then the cop got up to leave.

"Good luck, and be careful where you pitch that tent," he warned, climbing back in the car.

All that morning I drove alongside the ocean and made very slow progress, as I kept stopping to swim in the warm Atlantic. By the afternoon I promised myself that I would drive another hundred miles before camping that night, or I should never reach New York.

But I was very tired with the sun and wind, and when I pulled in at a petrol station several hours later I found it was already ten o'clock. The road north led along a road densely covered in undergrowth on either side; there didn't seem to be anywhere to camp. I seemed to be driving on endlessly, then at last I came to a small town. I passed a long green lawn dotted with garden furniture, and beyond a small white house. The garden was large and rambling and quite open to the road, so it was an easy matter to drive to the edge of the grass, where I pushed Oppy against a tree. I knew I was on private property, but it was getting so late and I was sure it wouldn't do any harm to camp there.

A dog from the house started to bark furiously, and I had to clap my hand over Matelot's nose to stop him from answering. The porch light of the house was switched on, and presently someone came across the grass swinging a flashlight. Then a dark figure lowered the flashlight as I spoke up apologetically, and a kind southern voice told me I was most welcome to camp in his garden. The ground was soft compared to the beach shelter, but I still thought wistfully of my air mattress floating away on the Gulf of Mexico.

Next morning I was just pulling at the last luggage strap when a neat little woman with a sweet smile came cross the lawn carrying a steaming jug and a plate of food. She sat them down on the wooden table, and said, "Honey, you need to start the day right, and travelling like that you can't get much home cooking." She looked at travel-worn Oppy with interest.

"Oh, how lovely! Pancakes are a terrible weakness of mine," I said.

While she poured us out two cups of coffee, she apologized for not asking us inside the house.

"Our dogs go just wild with strangers," she explained.

We sat and talked about dogs and the trip her sister had once made to England.

Later my kind hostess and her husband came to the gate to see us off, and told me to be sure to drop in again when I visited Florida.

That night I camped in the loveliest spot I'd met since leaving the Pacific Ocean. The grassy plot beside the highway was soft and springy, and a few yards away the Atlantic lapped over the long sandy beach. I was up early to swim, and afterwards I sat on the sand in my swimsuit, with a cup of cold coffee balanced on a piece of driftwood, and wrote home, "Please write to me next in New York City." Casual words, but they made me feel excited. Now I could hardly wait to arrive, as I knew a warm welcome awaited me from Mummy's cousins, whom I'd never met, but who'd been writing to me regularly since my arrival from England.

One glance at the map, however, told me I was still about twelve hundred miles away, and this was no time to sit around dreaming of soft beds in cousins' houses. So I leapt into action. Within twenty minutes the grassy patch by the side of the road was as bare as when I had found it the night before. Our wandering caravan was heading northwards as fast as two wheels would carry us.

CHAPTER XX *Last Camping Days*

THE last evening that I spent in Florida stands out as one of the nicest of the trip. Ever since leaving Miami I had noticed a disconcerting wobble in Oppy's steering, which had been growing worse every day. So when I arrived in Jacksonville I made my way at once to the motor-cycle shop. Here I was warmly welcomed by the co-owners of the shop, who said they had heard about us from Chuck Johnson of Niceville and had been expecting Oppy's arrival for at least two weeks.

Milton, a gangling young man with a crew haircut and a cheery grin, got right to work stripping down Oppy's forks, while his more serious-looking partner, Bob, introduced me to his mother.

"I'm afraid I've got to go off on a trip," he said, "but Mother will look after you, and drive you over to the house for the night."

Soon after this Mrs. King, a fashionably dressed, charming, friendly person with neatly waved grey hair, took me to lunch. She explained that she helped her son with the book-keeping in the shop and lived with him and his wife on the outskirts of the city. She pecked at a sandwich and coffee, but insisted I eat a large plate of hamburger steak, ice cream and pie followed by coffee. Then later, after the shop closed for the day, Mrs. King drove me to her son's house, where I met Dixie, Bob's wife, and Bobby and Patty-Anne, his children, and passed a most enjoyable evening with them.

As we sped northwards into Georgia, the roads became very poor and the flat landscape covered with small Negro communities seemed rather depressing. Crowds of grinning, dark-skinned children shouted and waved at us as we sped along. Once I made the mistake of stopping in one of these small coloured villages for a loaf of bread. When I opened the door of the store all the customers stared at me in stony silence, and the young Negro who came forward reluctantly to serve me was obviously eager to be rid of me as soon as possible. They must have feared I would bring them trouble.

That night I camped on what appeared to be a nice, soft stretch of meadow. But next morning I found myself on the edge of a golf course and only a few yards away from a very expensive-looking country club. Two magnificent cars were parked in the drive of the imposing white club building. And because I didn't like the idea of camping in the middle of an early morning game of golf, I hurriedly pulled up stakes and drove off.

It was a sunny Sunday morning when we reached the delightful old city of Savannah, which reminded me a bit of England. There a postal clerk listened sympathetically while I begged him to see if I had any mail. Shaking his head and saying it was against postal regulations to do this on Sunday, he hunted through various pigeon holes and finally handed me four blue envelopes. Outside in the sunlit street I perched on Oppy, and soon my thoughts were back in Europe, four thousand miles away.

Camping that night just beyond the city limits of Charleston, South Carolina, I felt the first faint chill of approaching autumn. But perhaps it was really caused by the ice cream I bought from a café across the road. Anyway, I pulled a sweater over my pyjamas and for the first time in ages enjoyed the warmth of my sleeping bag. But there was no layer of warm air between me and the hard ground now, and I began to wonder whether it might be too cold for camping by the time I got to New York.

I was also worried about my money holding out. The wisest move seemed to be to drive this last leg of the trip as fast as Oppy could go, only stopping for food and sleep when absolutely necessary. Of course, in spite of my rush I still inquired for mail at the various cities I had earlier chosen as forwarding points. For not only was I getting more and more homesick after this long trip, but there was always the chance that a small additional sum in dollars might fall out of any envelope I opened!

When I stopped at the post office in Wilmington, North Carolina, a man rushed up to me as I was waiting at the poste-restante window, and pointing to Matelot said, "You'd better put your dog on a leash, there's rabies in town. All the dogs are in quarantine and the police will pick him up if he's loose."

Naturally I hurried out of that building as fast as my two legs would carry me. Then I ordered Matelot up on the box, kicked over Oppy and made tracks northward as rapidly as the speed limit would allow us.

By the time we reached Richmond, Virginia, it was pitch dark, I couldn't find a place to camp and I had just about decided that I'd have to drive the whole way across town to open country, when we hit the most enormous hole in the road. We went in so far that I didn't think we'd ever come out right side up! Oppy lurched like a bucking bronco and leapt on across the broken-up surface of the road. But fortunately no harm seemed to be done. My little B.S.A. is a strange beast, she will go out of her way to pick up nails in her rear tyre when on a beautiful smooth highway, but given rough treatment on a bad road she will run along contentedly for mile after mile without a sign of wear or strain. However, I did stop now just to check her over for any dislodged luggage or loose nuts.

As I was doing this a car stopped and a girl peered out.

"Are you O.K.? No bones broken?" she asked anxiously.

"Thanks, I guess I'm all right," I laughed.

Then a man peered over the girl's shoulder and said, "As a matter of fact, we were curious about you and we've been tailing you for the last two miles."

"I said to Chuck," the girl interrupted, "there's a kid who looks like she could do with a hot bath and a good bed to sleep in."

"And a T-bone steak," smiled the young man, holding up a large paper bag.

Well the upshot was that I had a wonderful dinner with the two of them and a heavenly night's sleep at Phyllis's apartment afterwards.

From Richmond to Washington, D.C., it's a mere hundred-mile hop up a super four-lane highway. But I shan't soon forget the night I camped just south of the national capital.

We had left Richmond rather late after lunch, and so it was dark and getting very cold by the time Oppy had covered eighty miles or so. Now for the first time on the trip I was wearing gloves for driving, as well as a sweater and windjammer over my jeans. Matelot, too, wore his jacket, an old corduroy one of mine which I buttoned across his chest, securing the hood with an old scarf to keep the cold air out of his ears.

Pretty soon we passed a small shop and petrol station, and, attracted by a good piece of open ground alongside the building, I decided to camp there for the night. One small light burned in the back of the house, but the place was shut up in front. So, without bothering to ask permission, I just unrolled the tent and up it went in a jiffy. By this time I was a real expert in the art of tent pitching. On that first camp of the year in Washington state park it had taken me at least fifteen minutes to make the tent look at all respectable. Now I could throw it up in the space of about three minutes.

This time, however, I had picked a bad spot; the grass was very thick and an ideal trap for the morning dew. Placing my windjacket under the sleeping bag to stop some of the cold from seeping through on me, I hopped into the sleeping bag. Gradually I found myself putting back on all my clothes once again; two sweaters, wool slacks, two pairs of socks, wool gloves, and finally I wrapped my head in a scarf. But still I was simply freezing and sleep was out of the question. It was, after all, only the beginning of October, so I couldn't understand why the night should be so cold. Either this must have been the first sharp frost of autumn or my blood had got very, very thin down in Florida. Even Matelot was shivering now, so I pulled half the blanket over him, tucking it in tightly.

I was just about to jump out of the tent and do a few midnight gymnastics to warm up, when the roar of a truck and the flash of two bright headlights sent me snuggling back under the blanket. There was much shouting and hallooing, followed by a good deal of tapping and swearing. Some truck driver was evidently changing a tyre. His language was appalling, and I lay there imagining his embarrassment if he had known that I was camped just a few yards away! His buddy seemed to be having trouble with his truck too; then a few minutes later a couple of other trucks pulled up as well. This must have been a regular truck drivers' stopping-place!

Eventually the various mechanical difficulties seemed to be set right and all the trucks thundered off into the night. But before they parted the drivers shouted at one another cheerily, "See you in Hell!"

As the night wore on it grew colder and damper, until with the first light of day I crawled miserably out of the tent. There was a thick dew covering the ground and in a minute my feet were soaked, so I got out my rubbers and stamped around trying to get warm. A thin white frost gleamed on the roadway beyond. After the sweltering heat in the south this sudden drop in temperature really knocked me for a loop!

Considering that Washington is the capital of the United States, I am afraid my tour of the city was very brief. But by this time I had a one-track mind. I just wanted to get to New York City as fast as Oppy could carry me there. Matelot, however, took a much greater interest in Capitol Hill than I did. He thought that the park there provided ideal squirrel chasing. But I was in constant terror that he would follow one of them right out into the roaring city traffic!

Matelot and I ate our lunch sitting in a big green park with a noisy game on one side of us and across the street the White House, where crowds of people were walking up and down the pavement and gazing curiously through the iron railings. While Matelot wolfed his last tin of dog food, I reached to the bottom of the nearly empty food bag, and found that all I had left was half a loaf of bread, some cheese and a tin of beans! Looking up at the White House, with the Stars and Stripes fluttering on the flagstaff, and the great expanse of sweeping green lawn, I wondered with amusement what Mr. President was having for lunch, as I sat there in front of his house eating my tin of beans.

It was dark when we left Washington and just as cold as the previous night. I just couldn't face camping again—lying there shivering on the hard damp ground, and getting up in the morning sleepless and with all my bones chilled to the marrow. So I decided to keep on driving all night to Philadelphia. Driving through huge sleeping cities like Baltimore was an eerie experience; their dark skyscrapers looked like ghosts as they stretched up into the night sky. Except for an occasional cop on his lonely beat and the stands of all-night taxi cabs, the streets were almost deserted.

My companions on the highway were mostly huge long-distance trucks which roared past me in the darkness, their drivers occasionally leaning over to shout unheard remarks at me. The night air was freezing, and I was bundled up in everything warm that I possessed. My poor headlights obliged me to concentrate like mad when driving at night, so pretty soon I began to nod over the handlebars. One truck roared past me with the driver hanging out to caution me not to go to sleep and advising me to stop for coffee. Just a few yards farther on I came to an all-night café. There I did order black coffee, but long before I had finished it I fell fast asleep. When I woke up the dawn was creeping across the sky outside and Matelot was barking impatiently. The other customers looked at me curiously, as I paid for my unfinished coffee and tottered out into the early morning air.

But soon after we left Philadelphia my lack of sleep caught up with me again and once more my head was nodding over the handlebars. So I stopped by the side of the road and, propping Oppy against a tree, lay down on the grass and was soon fast asleep in the sun. After awhile Matelot nuzzled my face to remind me that it was long past his lunch hour. It was in fact about three o'clock, so I hurried with the meal because we still had over sixty miles to New York City. And as we sped through Pennsylvania I wondered whether we would get there before the post office closed. I hadn't received any mail since leaving Savannah and hoped to find some letters awaiting me in New York now.

Of course just when I was in a hurry, Oppy decided to throw a fit of temperament. Soon after we crossed into New Jersey she spluttered and choked and came to a gradual stop. Her carburettor was clogged with Matelot's hairs. This had happened before, because his long tail hangs over the edge of the box, and the hairs drop down over the oil can. So quite often the oil and petrol mixture has a few hairs swimming about in the bottom of the tank. Now I was not surprised to find long black hairs in almost any part of Oppy's mechanism.

This delay wasted over half an hour, and it was nearly dark when large signs appeared showing how to get to New York City by way of the Lincoln Tunnel. Unless I travelled up-state for about fifty miles, there was no way to cross over to New York without paying for doing so. Both tunnels under the Hudson River as well as the George Washington Bridge charge a toll, and it is no cheaper to take a ferry.

So now for a moment I stopped by the side of the road and counted the last remaining money in my purse. Five one-dollar bills and a few nickels and pennies was my total wealth! I only hoped that the money from England was waiting for me at the bank.

Now the highway divided off into many turns and cloverleaves, but soon Oppy climbed up over the Skyline Highway and we left the other roads far below us. It was then that I had my first glimpse of Manhattan by night, and what a thrilling sight it was! At the top of the hill leading down to the tunnel, I could look across the dark river and beyond to where the famous skyline of buildings was a blaze of brilliant lights.

Then I glanced back at Matelot. He was gazing down intently at the river and sniffing the salt air.

CHAPTER XXI *New York City*

AS we raced down the hill toward the Lincoln Tunnel, I remembered the warning of a young motor-cyclist I had met outside Washington. The road surface inside the tunnel, he had told me, is very slippery for braking with a motor-cycle because it is covered with tracks of thick grease dropped by the countless passing vehicles. The large trailer trucks find it equally hazardous to brake suddenly because the load on the back tends to get out of control. They prefer to go ahead and bang into the vehicle in front, rather than let this happen.

For this reason my friend had advised me to drive in the slow lane behind a truck, and added "Then if someone up ahead brakes suddenly you won't have to worry. The truck in front will do the smashing for you!" I remembered all this now as I rather timidly reached for a quarter to pay the toll fare.

"You can't drive through the tunnel with that animal loose in the back," snarled the policeman refusing to take my outstretched coin.

But I certainly had not come all these thousands of miles only to be refused entrance to New York City by a tunnel policeman!

"Can you find anything in your book of regulations to stop me?" I insisted, stubbornly, plonking the quarter down on the edge of the counter. The cop glanced first at the long line of waiting vehicles, and then back at Matelot.

"Are you sure he won't jump out?" he asked, handing me a tunnel ticket. I assured the man that if there were no cats in the tunnel, Matelot would stay exactly where he was.

"O.K. O.K. Go ahead!" said the cop finally. By this time the cars behind us were starting to blow their horns impatiently.

I followed an enormous, lumbering truck into the tunnel entrance. Turning out my headlights, as requested, I pulled well into the side of the wall avoiding a long, black line of slippery-looking grease. The traffic was flashing past me on the left, but the truck in front of me was crawling along about ten miles an hour. I crawled too, until I was forced to drop into low gear. There was another truck it seemed, just on my tail, and I could hear the roar of its engine so close behind me that I drove even nearer to the truck in front. It was an insecure feeling wobbling along on the greasy surface sandwiched in between two such mammoth vehicles.

But when I glanced over my shoulder I saw there was actually nothing behind me at all. The powerful-sounding engine roaring in my ears was old Oppy herself! She had taken on a deep-throated sound in the enclosed space of the tunnel.

Suddenly the truck in front seemed to gather speed; although the floor of the tunnel looked flat, we had really climbed a small hill and were now on the downward slope. It felt as if I were going awfully fast, but when I glanced at the speedometer it was only registering thirty miles an hour.

Down here in the Lincoln Tunnel everything seemed out of proportion—the noise, the speed and one's nerves. The policemen who patrolled at intervals along the catwalk, gave us looks of horror and amazement as we flashed by. And one of them immediately picked up his telephone the second we came into his view.

Then at last we came out into the sharp autumn night air. Buildings towered all round and lights twinkled in hundreds of windows above us. I craned my head skywards at what seemed endless towers of light stretching up to heaven. There was a huge red neon sign saying "Hotel New Yorker", which flashed on and off; and the Empire State Building looked just as gigantic and beautiful as I had remembered it from films.

I found myself in a wide, bright street, and coming to a corner the sign told me this was Fifth Avenue. Now I liked being stopped by the red lights because there were so many beautiful shops here. In one window I saw such an exquisite evening gown of palest pink chiffon that I only just avoided crashing into the back of a taxicab. Then, as I skimmed past his rolled-down window with only an inch to spare, he hooted sharply. The next thing I knew the taxi was driving alongside me and the driver was leaning over shouting to attract my attention.

"Lady, where do you think you're going?" he asked.

"Well, at the moment I'm trying to find Broadway," I said. "Could you help me?"

"Just follow me, lady," said the taxi driver, pulling ahead.

He kept looking back over his shoulder to be sure that I was still in sight. I followed him through several side streets and then, turning a corner, we were suddenly driving down Broadway—the famous Gay White Way.

The lights from the numerous neon signs were dazzling, and it was almost as bright as daylight. The pavements were packed with people milling round the theatres, and the traffic was moving at a furious pace.

"Well, how do you like it?" asked my guide, slowing down his cab so that I came alongside him.

Of course I gushed as all tourists do when they see Broadway by night for the first time.

"Yep, it's not a bad little town," he admitted airily. "There's Forty-second Street," he said, waving his arm to show me the equally famous street that runs east and west across Broadway. "And this is Times Square—I guess you've heard of Times Square? Brother, you should see it on New Year's Eve!"

The cabbie was giving me a personally conducted tour of New York City; he led me slowly along the streets pointing out things of interest. At Columbus Circle he stopped to show me Central Park. This took quite a time, since Central Park is enormous for a big city. "Guess I'll have to leave you here," he said at last.

"Thanks a million," I replied. "You've given me a lovely first impression of the city. But think of all the fares I've lost you!"

"You're very welcome, and give my love to Piccadilly," he said, driving off into the surging traffic.

After the taxicab driver had gone, a clock across the street pointed to ten o'clock. This seemed far too late to ring up my strange cousins who live on Long Island. I wondered if I should drive out and just camp in their garden, but then I wondered if they actually *had* a garden. Queens Village, Long Island, looked rather a long way on the detailed road map.

As I drove slowly down past Central Park and looked across the dark expanse of trees, I wondered if it really would be too risky to pitch my tent there. Certainly the grass would be lovely and soft and the idea of sleeping outdoors in the middle of New York City, just a stone's throw from Park Avenue, really appealed to me. But I remembered all the stories I'd heard about murders being committed in this famous park, so I decided to look for some other spot. My map of the city showed that New York certainly had plenty of parks, but which, I wondered, would be best for pitching a tent?

I decided to get some expert advice on the matter, so seeing a small lunch-bar, I pulled into the kerb opposite. Then I spread the blanket on the cold pavement and Matelot immediately jumped down and curled up on it and went to sleep. He doesn't like city driving and had found our tour of New York very boring indeed.

Inside the warm and shining lunch counter I sat down to order a coffee. A tough, ape-like man banged the cup on the counter and grabbed my dime. All the customers were staring at me and nobody in the place said a word. Undoubtedly I wasn't dressed like most New Yorkers, as I sat there in my old woollen slacks and windbreaker. My face was still fiercely sunburned and my hair was bleached and untidy from riding without a cap.

Nevertheless I spread my map on the counter and beckoned to the tough-looking counter-man. Then I asked him if he knew of the nearest bit of open country where I could pitch a tent. He looked at me for a minute as if I were crazy, and then, pointing on the map to the Hudson River, he said, "I guess your best bet would be over in Jersey, but you might have to drive out quite a way."

After giving me this piece of information his manner completely changed. He wasn't tough at all any more. But now he wanted to know all about how I was travelling, where I was going and why. My next cup of coffee was on the house, and the man behind the counter accompanied all my explanations with, "Well, you don't say," and "Say, folks, listen to this." And all the customers leaned forward intently to hear better.

When I got up to leave the ape-man came out on to the pavement with me carrying a hot dog.

"Here, boy, good dog," he said, leaning down to feed Matelot, who swallowed the hot dog at one greedy bite.

New York suddenly seemed such a warm-hearted place, yet I'd always heard it said that New Yorkers had no time to be friendly. Perhaps these critics weren't lucky enough to meet people like my cab driver and lunch-bar man.

Because I didn't feel like driving through that rather frightening Lincoln Tunnel again, I took the advice of the lunch-bar man and drove down now to the Forty-first Street ferry. It was a beautiful trip across the river to New Jersey, with all of Manhattan lying across the water to the east of us. And I could just make out the light from the Statue of Liberty when a fellow passenger told me which way to look.

Leaving the ferry I climbed a steep hill into Owen City, and took the street running along the top of the Palisades. The twinkling lights of Manhattan lay just ten minutes across the river, and the view was so beautiful that I felt I just *had* to try and find somewhere to camp where I could watch this sight from inside my tent. A long park running along the Palisades looked like a perfect place, with its smooth lawn and a large tree for Oppy to lean against. For hours after I had the tent up and had got into my sleeping bag, I sat in the entrance and looked down across the Hudson River. The tent flaps were open, so that I could watch the view as I lay down with my hands propped under my head.

When I woke up it was quite a different city that met my eyes. This one was grey and covered by an early-morning mist. The outlines of the skyscrapers were hazy and a pink light hung in the sky overhead.

I dressed carefully, getting out my last clean shirt and socks to go with my recently cleaned riding skirt. After that I polished my old brogues until they shone, and uncurled my hair. I didn't want my appearance to give my cousins too much of a shock. They knew I was going to arrive on a motor-cycle, but I was trying not to look too much the part.

A little fat elderly woman came walking across the park just as I was pulling up the tent pegs. In a very strong Dutch accent she told me that she and her husband had been watching my tent from their apartment window for the last hour. Finally her husband had become so curious that he had sent her across to invite the camper to come over for breakfast.

"My husband will never forgive me if I don't persuade you to come," she said.

Over the breakfast table in this kind Dutch couple's cheerful kitchen we all laughed about my camp in a public park just opposite their apartment.

"If we'd just known, you could have slept on the settee in the sitting room," said the big bluff Dutchman.

The ride back to Manhattan in the ferry was chilly and windy; Matelot scared me by standing much too near the open end of the boat and looking down at the cold grey waters of the river. The boat was full of early morning workers, who crowded round Matelot and begged me to show them how he rode in his box. They didn't have long to wait; we soon bounced up the uneven slipway with them all standing aside laughing and waving us good luck.

Then I rode southwards down Broadway to look for the main post office and my long awaited mail. The official handed me an impressive pile, but I couldn't find any privacy to read it sitting on Oppy. Already a large crowd had gathered round the machine, staring at Matelot curled up asleep on the pavement. I pulled out a map to look for a park, and immediately there were a dozen kind people eager to direct me.

Finally I found a small park on Broadway on the opposite side of the street from which I was driving. I slowed down, and was just wondering if I could possibly manage a U-turn when there was a lull in traffic and no policeman looking, when suddenly Matelot spied a squirrel running along the grass and up a tree. He leapt from Oppy, dived in between the heavy traffic, and was off across the park like a streak of lightning. This was quite the worst and most dangerous thing he had ever done. Hastily I parked Oppy and pursued Matelot across the park to the spot where he was leaping up at the trees and barking furiously.

Then, finding a bench in the sun, I started to read my mail. There was a letter from a bank on Wall Street informing me that a draft for sixty dollars had been sent to a bank in Miami. Well, I was certainly glad that the money from England had come through, and I only hoped it would catch up with me soon!

There was also a bulky letter from Denmark. Out of a strip of cardboard rolled a ring, which caught the bright sunlight and gleamed up at me. It was like the day in the park in San Francisco all over again. An accompanying letter said, "Please, don't throw *this* one away!" But most exciting of all was a large package containing a gramophone record. This was Carl-Erik's answer by voice to my tape-recording made on Pat's machine in Los Angeles. Now I was wild to find a music shop quickly and hear his message.

Jumping up, I called to Matelot, who was still seething mad because he had failed to catch any elusive grey squirrels. We drove slowly down the street until we came to a large music store full of record players and sheet music. There I feigned interest in buying a Grieg Piano Concerto album. Immediately a helpful young man brought out a pile of records and conducted me to a recording booth. But I didn't even bother with Grieg; Carl-Erik was so much more interesting!

His voice from thousands of miles away over the Atlantic Ocean and across the North Sea was saying, "Isn't it about time you put an end to all this wandering and set out on the final journey?"

I heartily agreed, but at that moment my only assets were a little over five dollars in my purse and sixty dollars in Miami. But perhaps I could at least do something about those Miami dollars, if only I could find Wall Street.

Locating New York's financial district proved easy, but the narrow street was overflowing with pedestrians and parking space was quite non-existent. Finally I was forced to leave Oppy under a large sign reading "No Parking—Order of the Police Department." I hoped no policeman would object to finding my little machine there, because after all it didn't take up a quarter of the space of a parked car.

The entrance to "my bank" was through a big swinging door opening into an imposing hallway of marble. As I made my way to the elevator a guard gave me a very piercing look.

In the Foreign Exchange Department a sympathetic young clerk listened patiently while I told him that I simply couldn't wait for that cheque to come back from Miami; in fact, I confessed that my motorcycle was parked illegally and that I hadn't even got money to pay the fine.

A few minutes later he ushered me into the manager's office. An elderly grey-haired man listened to my outpourings and then reached for his pen.

"All right, I'm going to trust you to send us back that other cheque when the post office readdresses your mail. And meanwhile I'll arrange for you to have the cash immediately," he said, scribbling away on a piece of paper. "I don't think I've ever issued two payments for one sum of money before," he added, as he smilingly handed me the order for the teller.

I thanked the manager warmly and warned him that it might be some time before all my mail caught up with me, since I expected to leave in a few days for Canada.

"Well, just see that you send it along as soon as you receive it," he said, getting up to show me to the door.

It was wonderful to watch the clerk count those six ten-dollar bills on to the counter in front of me. But they had to last a long time!

This seemed to be a good time of day to telephone my cousin's office. He is the head of a large religious and welfare organization. So now I rang the number that I had been carrying in my address book for more than eighteen months.

"Volunteers of America," said a pleasant woman's voice, but when I asked for my cousin, she added, "Oh dear, is that Peggy? That's too bad! General Booth and his wife are in Atlantic City until tomorrow night. We've all been expecting you for *weeks!*"

After I hung up I felt a little despondent. For Mummy's cousin had written me so many kind and welcoming letters to New York and I had so looked forward to meeting him. Gone too was that pleasant feeling of security one feels when visiting blood relatives. Well, I thought, another night camping in the park won't hurt us.

A few minutes later we were driving up the street, when I passed a theatre with a long line of people standing outside on the pavement. I glanced up to see what film was showing, but a large notice stated that this was the C.B.S. T.V. theatre for the "Strike it Rich" programme. Wasn't that the quiz show which gave away money to people badly in need of help?

Suddenly I felt that my trip was really at an end and that I had no desire to push on to Canada, where winter had already begun. Why couldn't I try my luck at winning enough for that longed-for passage to Denmark?

I had to drive several blocks from the theatre before I found anywhere to park. Then, telling Matelot I might be gone quite some time, I snapped his chain over the front wheel and walked quickly back to the theatre. I joined the end of the line just as it was moving inside. And a kind woman beside me gave me a spare ticket she had been holding for a friend who hadn't showed up. As we entered an attendant handed us each a questionnaire to fill out, which he collected a few minutes later. Then we concentrated on the stage below, where a bouncing little man, full of pep and enthusiasm, was trying to whip the audience into the proper mood. He was making a very good job of it too.

Most of the audience looked like tired women taking a morning off from their household chores. Soon everybody was laughing and clapping in just the right places. Then the master of ceremonies lifted his arms for quiet and began to read out the names of five people in the audience selected as deserving enough to tell their stories and then try to strike it rich. I almost fainted when he called out the last contestant—"Now we'd like to have Peggy Thomas from England come down on the stage."

But nevertheless I bolted from my seat and hurried downstairs, while the audience clapped for all five of us lucky people as we climbed on to the stage.

"What's all this about a motor-cycle and a dog? Could you get them both and bring them here?" asked a suave young T.V. producer, scanning my card in the wings. "We're on the air in five minutes, so you'll have to hurry," he added, as I rushed out, agreeing to fetch Oppy and Matelot.

It seemed a long way back to where they were parked and for a moment I almost forgot just where I had left them. But a large crowd guided me to where Matelot was being fed raw hamburger steak by a man in a white cap and apron. Excusing myself, I pushed through the people and started to hunt in my bag for the ignition key. It didn't seem to be there, and when I had emptied the entire contents of the bag on the pavement, I still couldn't find it. This was the only key I had and Oppy couldn't be started without it. Then a voice at my elbow interrupted my frantic searchings.

"We're from the *Herald Tribune*, and we'd like to get your story and picture."

"Oh, I've got no time for that now," I snapped peevishly. "I'm going to miss a broadcast if I don't find that darned key."

At this point my chances of winning five hundred dollars seemed mighty remote. Finally, in desperation I decided to leave Oppy right there, then, grabbing Matelot by his chain, I fled up the street.

The dog and I dashed across Seventh Avenue, dodging the taxis and fast-moving cars, and raced on up to Broadway. A policeman signalled for me to stay on the pavement until the light changed, and it was then that I noticed two breathless men hot on our heels. A tall thin young man with a crew-cut and horned-rimmed spectacles and carrying a notebook had just caught up with us, while a tubby little man trailing a large camera and flash-light was stumbling along looking as if he were about to draw his last breath. Matelot was the only one of us having a good time. He was literally prancing with joy at this unexpected canter through Manhattan.

But now we had reached the side entrance of the studio, and three minutes later a harassed young man pushed Matelot and me on to the stage in front of two T.V. cameras. I dropped on a settee and two large packages of toothpaste were thrust into my hand by a smiling man with incredibly blue eyes and a smooth radio interviewer's voice. Matelot thought the toothpaste was something to eat, so he immediately seized one between his teeth. The cameras were trained on him while he gave the toothpaste manufacturer a spontaneous plug for his product. The audience howled with delight as Matelot bit into the tube and sprayed the white paste all over the floor.

I had just begun to tell why I wanted some money, when the interviewer interupted to say that the programme had run out of time, but would I like to come back and try again tomorrow? I agreed and Matelot and I scrambled off the stage.

The same newspapermen were waiting for us in the wings, and they accompanied us down the street to Oppy. After Matelot and I had posed for the photographer, the tall young reporter asked me whether I would mind coming up to the newspaper office. There Bernard Peyton got all the details he wanted, and then proceeded to read back his short-hand notes of what I had said while searching frantically for the lost key.

"Please don't print that!" I begged laughing.

Up in the photographic department of the *Herald Tribune* Matelot and I were given a picnic lunch. Somebody sent out for coffee and ham sandwiches and added a tin of dog food to the list. Of course Matelot was busy bouncing all over the office, making friends with the reporters and nosing into every wastebasket.

Then as I ate my sandwiches Bernard asked me where I was going to spend the night. When I told him of my plan to camp out again in a park, he insisted that he and his wife had just moved into an apartment with plenty of room for me and the dog too. I was delighted of course, and arranged to meet him that evening outside the newspaper office at seven o'clock.

Well, Oppy was temporarily immovable without the ignition key, but luckily Forty-first Street was on a slight hill, so I managed to push her without much effort. Then I found an electrical supply store which furnished me with another ignition key of the proper size.

All that afternoon we drove through New York's fast-moving traffic.

I had no special destination, but just trundled around, almost letting Oppy take us where she willed. First we headed north and saw something of Harlem, the world-famous Negro district. Then we drove westward to the Hudson River, climbed a ramp and took the Riverside Drive up above the docks. There were many great Transatlantic liners in port, including the *Queen Mary* and the gleaming white *America*. They made me think about tomorrow—I wondered if in twenty-four hours I should be rushing down to the nearest shipping office with a large cheque in my hand. I took another look at the liners and crossed my fingers.

It was about six o'clock, and just beginning to get dark, when we found ourselves down on the other side of Manhattan near the East River. I thought that I had better start heading for the *Herald Tribune* building to meet Bernard Peyton, so I stopped to get my bearings on the map. At that point Matelot jumped down and disappeared in a pile of rubble on a demolished building site.

Shutting off the engine, I studied the map for a few minutes and then called Matelot. After a bit I became impatient and tooted the horn several times. Matelot always answers to Oppy's horn, but this time he did not appear. I went on tooting the horn, and then started up the engine and opened the throttle wide, so that the machine roared noisily.

The street was fairly quiet and deserted. Several yards of half-cleared ground ran the length of the block, and beyond were rows of squalid-looking old houses. More than five minutes had passed and still no sign of Matelot. I walked to the corner of the street, whistling and calling, with Oppy's engine still turning over noisily in the background.

By the time another five minutes had gone by I was beginning to feel really worried. I circled the whole block, asking at two petrol stations if they had seen an airedale dog wandering around; then I stopped three kids on bicycles and they took up the search with gusto, riding off down the street whistling and yelling for all they were worth. I inquired in a yard full of garbage-disposal trucks, but still found no trace of Matelot.

By this time I was imagining every possible ghastly thing that could have happened to Matelot, lost in a strange large city. He might have lost his head and darted across some traffic-laden street and got killed, or he might have been stolen by some petty criminal!

I thought now of all that terrible desert heat I had dragged him through, and the time I had teased him by hiding around a corner to make him think we'd left him behind. I thought of Miami, where he spent long hours alone in the cabin while I worked; and the nights when I felt him shivering slightly with the cold beside me. I thought of him huddled on the back of Oppy during those snowy days in Canada, and under the tropical rain in the south.

I thought of all this, and I stood in the gutter beside Oppy and burst into tears.

CHAPTER XXII *Next Stop Denmark*

"WELL now, what's all *this* about?" said a deep, kind voice at my side.

I blinked through my tears into the serious face of a young cop leaning out of a patrol car. Then I fished out my handkerchief, feeling an awful fool, blew my nose and poured out my fears for Matelot.

"Oh, come on, it's not as bad as all that. I guess he hasn't gone very far," the cop said. "Hop in and we'll go look for him." Then another policeman got out of the other side of the car and held the door open for me politely. I got in and sat between the two large blue uniforms, and tried to pull myself together.

"Well, we know he's a wonderful dog, but what does he look like?" asked the cop on my right.

"He's got a brown head and paws, a white star on his chest, very curly

black coat and a bushy tail that really curls over too much for an airedale,"
I said.

"O.K." he said writing in his notebook, "we'll be able to check the
A.S.C.P.A. with that description."

The patrol car was slowly circling the streets, both cops and I peering
out into the dark shadows.

"Think he might have run into the tunnel, Harry?" one policeman
asked the other, as we came to the entrance of the Queens Midtown
Tunnel. His companion said he didn't think any dog could have got past
the guard on duty, but he stopped and checked to make sure. Then we
went by a small park and the driver slowed down.

"Take a look through the park, Tom," he said, handing the other cop
a flashlight. We drove round and round the block past Oppy sitting silently
in the gutter, but still there was no sign of Matelot. Harry, the driver,
stopped on the corner of the street and telephoned the nearest dog's
home, and came back to the car looking rather discouraged.

"Well, they say they've just brought in a load of dogs, but none of
them fits your description. But cheer up. Maybe he'll turn up farther
away than we think." The husky cop was being so kind that I very nearly
turned round and bawled on his shoulder.

Now we went back to the park to pick up Tom, who reported
no sign of any dogs either. After that the cops drove me silently
back to Oppy, and I climbed out of the patrol car feeling completely
miserable.

"I think you'd better go home. We'll take your address and then when
he turns up we'll notify you right away," Harry said gently.

"But I haven't got a home, and I'm not going to leave this spot until
he comes back, even if I have to stay here all night," I said hysterically.

"Well, we'll keep circling the block," Harry promised as he drove
off.

Now I was left alone on the dark pavement once again. Oppy looked
silent and empty, but I suddenly realized that I didn't care a damn for
her or the luggage either. I would have gladly thrown bike and baggage
into the East River if that would have brought Matelot trotting back out
of the darkness.

Pretty soon a clock struck somewhere nearby, and suddenly I

remembered that I was supposed to meet Bernard at seven o'clock. So I walked two blocks to the nearest café and telephoned his paper. There was a short pause before Bernard came on the line. Then I explained quickly what had happened, and after Bernard understood just where I was, he said he'd hop in a cab and come right over.

Soon after this a taxi drew up and my long-legged reporter friend got out with a look of concern on his face.

"Now, don't worry," were his first words. "Matelot can't be lost completely; it's just a matter of getting the wheels moving before we can find him. Now, where have you looked so far?" he asked, taking command of the situation.

Just then the patrol car went by again, and Tom leaned out to tell me that they had flashed a report of Matelot's loss over their radio-car system.

Bernard and I walked the streets for another hour, but there wasn't a single sign of Matelot, and nobody we met had seen him either.

"If he's still missing tomorrow, I think the paper'll run a follow-up story about his loss," Bernard told me. Then he started to insist that I couldn't stay in this deserted part of the city alone all night, but I said flatly that nothing was going to make me move.

So, cautioning me to wait near Oppy, he said he would try looking much farther up the street. Now the clock was striking nine o'clock—it had been three hours since Matelot had jumped off Oppy and disappeared into the darkness. Three hours—but it seemed like a week.

Then, far down the street, I saw the tall figure of Bernard Peyton approaching and a familiar dark shape was jumping and trotting at his side. I don't think I ever ran so fast in my life, and I don't know who felt the more relieved, Matelot or me. He practically knocked me down on the pavement, but I was much too happy to care a damn.

Bernard explained that the poor dog must have wandered off and got lost, because when Matelot passed a block of luxury apartments about four blocks away he had been noticed by the doorman. This good man, thinking that Matelot was one of the tenants' dogs on the loose, had grabbed him and shut him up in an empty room. Fortunately Bernard had happened by there and asked the doorman if he had seen anything of a missing airedale.

Now Bernard hailed a cab and suggested that he'd better take Matelot in it, because the dog was far too upset to sit on Oppy. Oppy and I trailed the cab, with Matelot's worried face hanging out of the taxi window to keep me in sight, and Bernard grinning and patting him encouragingly.

After about ten minutes the taxi drew up in front of an apartment in Lexington Avenue. A few minutes later Oppy was parked for the night in a nearby garage, and Bernard was fumbling with his keys to open his apartment door.

"Oh, Peggy, what a simply ghastly time you've been through!" said Bernard's wife almost before I was inside the door. She was a charming and beautiful hostess; tall and dark and completely unconcerned when shaggy Matelot trotted all over her new apartment. Then she bundled me off to the bathroom and lent me a very glamorous silk housecoat and a pair of slippers to wear. It was nearly ten thirty when we finally sat down to supper, and I felt very apologetic about the Peytons' upset evening, but Joan only laughed and said, "Bernard always keeps atrocious hours on the newspaper anyway."

That night I slept in a wonderfully comfortable bed with Matelot very close beside me on the floor. He wouldn't go to sleep at first; he kept getting up to lay his chin on my bedclothes and stare at me as if he were afraid he was about to lose me again.

Next morning after breakfast, as I was saying goodbye to the Peytons, Joan made me promise to drive slowly up the street, so that she could see us from the window. We started off with Matelot snuggling his head on my shoulder, and I set Oppy in the direction of the T.V. studio.

There I was warned that I would have to drain every drop of petrol out of Oppy's tank before she could go on stage. A large bucket was produced to catch the overflow, and under the eyes of three blasé T.V. men I took off Oppy's carburettor and let all the petrol out of the tank. The three men pushed from behind and I steered Oppy inside the theatre. Everyone was worried about where I should leave her; she was so bulky and awkward and they were terrified she might fall down in the middle of the broadcast and make a noise.

Luckily we were first on the programme, so there wasn't much time to wait. I swung Matelot on board, hopped into the saddle, and then with a slight push from the men behind I sailed between the curtains on to the stage. The audience screamed at the unexpected sight of Matelot, who was sitting bolt upright behind me, looking the picture of dignity.

Then, after a little preliminary chit-chat with the interviewer about the trip, I started to answer the questions on which my future destiny hung. The first three were fairly easy, and I found I had already earned one hundred and twenty-five dollars in the space of about two minutes. Then the audience began to roar with laughter, and I glanced across to the T.V. screen in a corner of the stage.

There I saw myself sitting on Oppy as large as life, but Matelot was slowly sinking out of sight! He had become more and more bored with sitting in front of a T.V. camera, and he showed his disgust by turning his back on the audience and gradually curling up in the bottom of his box. So that all the thousands of T.V. watchers in the New York area could see of Matelot now was the top of his round furry head.

Presently I answered question four, and then, with two hundred and fifty dollars practically in my pocket, I waited for question five that would bring me five hundred dollars—or nothing. The audience was deathly still.

"Can you give me the name of the author who wrote *Kon Tiki?*" beamed the interviewer, thinking I was bound to know this because of my sentimental interest in Scandinavia.

"Oh golly! He's got a frightful unpronounceable name," I said, cursing myself because I had read the book through twice. I ought to have made a horrible noise and muttered into the mike, and then I might have been cheered for giving the right answer! As it was, a loud gong of failure was sounded and we three left the stage as poor as we had been when the programme started.

Early that evening I rang my cousin's home in Queens Village. A kind voice welcomed me to New York and told me how to find the house. Three-quarters of an hour later I drew up outside an attractive brick house on a corner, which was surrounded by a large lawn and tall trees. The door flew open and out bounded a tall good-looking man in his early sixties. Behind him a pretty little woman, with the kindest expression on her face, stretched out her hands and drew me inside the house.

It was lovely to belong to a family again, and during the next few days I met a host of new cousins of all ages, and had a wonderful time getting to know them all. But, even in my new-found luxury, every day my thoughts were turning more toward Europe. Perhaps it was because I had a solid roof over my head again, or perhaps I was weary with this eighteen months of travelling—anyway I wished something would happen to spirit me home again. And I didn't feel like facing a cold winter in Canada working hard to scrape every cent together for an early boat passage.

Then one wonderful day I heard from Carl-Erik that he had got permission to pay for our passages in Danish currency, and I knew that this twenty-five-thousand-mile journey was nearly ended. Well, not quite ended; the next and final stop was to be Denmark.

Only for Matelot was the immediate future not so happy. From the minute he sets his first paw on Copenhagen docks he will be seized, chained and marched off to the quarantine station for six months, a virtual prisoner under Danish law. But Oppy and I have promised to visit him often, and when next summer comes we three will once more be bowling down the road. Although this time I think it will be just to fetch the groceries from the store at the end of the street!

Even Oppy hasn't been forgotten in these preparations for departure. The B.S.A. dealer in Nutley, New Jersey, had given me a great welcome when I went over there one day to buy spares for Oppy. Mr. Child had insisted that I leave my machine for a complete overhaul, and Bill, the mechanic, was asked to make her as near new as possible. So now there is no likelihood that she will shame me with any further breakdowns in Denmark this summer.

Well, I only had to be patient a little longer, although now I was even more anxious to get back and see Carl-Erik and my family. But I know when I sail out of New York harbour, and look back at Manhattan's skyline, I shall feel a little nostalgic. Although really the store of memories from this trip aren't so much the grandeur of the Rockies, the blue Pacific, the vast sweeping desert, or even New York City by night, but of the people we met and the warm friendship and hospitality that was showered on us from all corners of the North American continent.

And now when I look at a map of the United States and Canada it becomes alive with people's faces and remembrances of fleeting friendships.

But I am not the only one with memories; I am sure Matelot is going to have something to say about his motor-cycling adventures when he gets among those Danish dogs. And Oppy can look superior among those European machines with the label on her tank saying—Mexico City.

Page 222. The trio arrive in New York. Oppy is covered in stickers collected along their route. The label on her petrol tank is from Mexico City.

Page 223. Reunited with Matelot in Copenhagen after he spent 6 months in quarantine.

Page 224. A BSA advertisement from 1951 celebrating Peggy's first journey on Oppy, a 4000 mile trip around Scandinavia in the autumn of 1950.

*M*iss Peggy Thomas and Miss Prudence Beggs (with luggage), who recently completed a 4,500 miles Continental tour on a B.S.A. Bantam

The photo was taken outside the B.S.A. London Showrooms in Tottenham Court Road, on their return to London.

USE YOUR SHARE OF THE ROAD —WITH— **CARE**

L E A V E   I T   T O   Y O U R   **BSA**